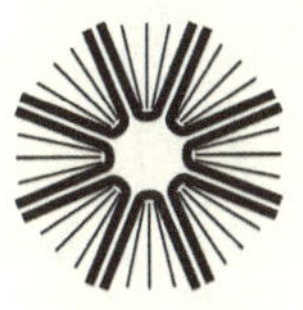

I0835974

Don't Ask the Trees for Their Names

Don't Ask the Trees for Their Names

Stories of Leaving and Becoming

Edited by
Oula Ghannoum and Loubna Haikal

GAZEBO BOOKS SUMMER HILL 2025

Gazebo Books
PO Box 375
Summer Hill
New South Wales 2130
Australia
gazebobooks.com.au

First published 2025

National Library of Australia
Cataloguing-in-Publication Entry
Authors: Mariam Maatooq, Loubna Haikal, Mary Hanoun-Khilla, Sivine Tabbouch, Hend Saab, Kilda Eid, Camilia Naim, Oula Ghannoum, and Nouha El-Khoury Francis.
Don't Ask the Trees for Their Names: Stories of Leaving and Becoming
First edition
ISBN 9781763600966

Cover and interior design by Mountains Brown Press.
Cover image: *Arbre*, Etel Adnan, ink on paper, 20 x 14.5cm
Courtesy of Kalim Bechara collection
Photograph by Artscoops, Beirut, Lebanon

To our children and to every woman who dared to start again.

Introduction

As I put the final touches on this introduction, the stories we – nine Arab women – have written have taken on an unforeseen significance in the aftermath of October 7.

Our journeys from Palestine, Syria, Sudan and Lebanon are deeply entwined with Palestine's ongoing Nakba and all it has come to symbolise: colonialism, occupation and displacement. Each one of our journeys bears Palestine's lingering wounds, offering both a historical context and a glimpse into the intimate lives of women in the region. In my own story *Pillar of Salt*, set in 1960s Lebanon, Palestine is everywhere – discussed, cherished, fought for and against. It lived in our living rooms, schools, cafés, theatres, and later, in the rubble of Beirut and the villages beyond.

When Oula and Nouha planted the seeds of this writing project in 2020, my focus lay elsewhere – writing to politicians alongside a group of like-minded grandmothers, urging action to save the planet from climate catastrophe.

As fires, floods and climate-related diseases escalated, Indigenous knowledge – long buried under more than two centuries of colonisation – emerged as a vital key to survival. Tyson Yunkaporta's *Sand Talk*, written with deep reverence for Country and the life-preserving wisdom of ancestral stories, illuminated the power of storytelling in healing both Mother Earth and her children. It gave me solace and a renewed sense of hope.

Then came 2021, and it seemed that COVID-19 had accomplished what we, as concerned elders, could not. It forced the world to pause, granting Mother Earth a brief reprieve and giving humanity a rare opportunity to recalibrate – to rethink its excesses and ask: *Where do we go from here?*

The war against the virus, waged by unprepared governments, challenged our sense of entitlement – to normalcy, to freedom of movement, to travel beyond five kilometres. We were forced to accept heightened police surveillance and restrictions in the name of safety. It seemed like a kind of occupation.

In that period of isolation, when the main event of the day was the 11 o'clock update on the number of deaths and ICU admissions, I questioned whether I had been right to leave my medical career. Literature would never save a patient in an ICU. My ambition to publish another piece of writing quietly faded away.

For a time, I felt at peace – relieved of the pressure to write. Then, one morning in July 2021, my phone rang. It was Nouha Francis, an old friend and co-founder of *Kheir Jalees* (Best Companion), an Arab women's cultural group. Her voice carried the raw, tender huskiness of women from the Lebanese mountains.

'We're starting an Arab women's writing group,' she said. 'We'd love you to join us. You can still write in Arabic, right?'

'Of course,' I replied. Writing in Arabic was too exciting to refuse. 'I can read and write in Arabic,' I added, as much to reassure her as myself. The thought of moving my pen from right to left again – reclaiming the language I had left more than half a century ago – was exciting.

'Because of COVID, we'll meet on Zoom,' she continued. 'You'll meet the other women. Some have written and published in Arabic.'

That phone call pulled me out of my existential inertia. I was eager to meet these women. Though I had lived away from the Arab community, I had always sought fleeting connections at social events – at concerts, weddings, funerals. Now in my sixties, with my children grown and gone, my longing for the intimacy of my mother tongue had deepened. Was this yearning an attempt to fill the space my children had taken with them when they left?

'You're becoming more Lebanese as you get older,' my Celtic-Australian husband observed one night, catching me listening to Arabic music and poetry.

'I am,' I admitted, envying immigrants who spent half the year in Australia and the other half in Lebanon. 'Writing in Arabic, with Arab women writers, will be such a treat. Maybe it will ease my nostalgia.'

This writing project began with Oula and Nouha in 2020, after an evening talk on photosynthesis by Oula, a plant biology professor at a dinner organised by *Kheir Jalees*. A closet writer estranged from the Arabic community, Oula was deeply moved by the migration stories she heard that night. She and Nouha envisioned a women's writing collective – one that would document migration stories, challenging the increasing dehumanisation of Arabs and reclaiming our narratives as women and as part of Australia's history.

With the help of Sivine, a key member of *Kheir Jalees*, they reached out to Arab women writers and storytellers. And so, from Sudan, Syria, Palestine, and Lebanon – both North and South – nine of us came together, bound by language, displacement, and the need to write.

At our first Zoom meeting, I met eight women – Muslim, Christian, atheist; career women, mothers, grandmothers; matriarchs, feminists, poets and singers. Women who shattered every stereotype of the oppressed Arab or Muslim woman. I was home. Their strength and humour inspired me. How hungry I was to be in Arabic, amongst the women of my community!

We agreed that our stories would follow a triptych structure: the day of departure from our homeland, the day of arrival in Australia, and the first return journey. Just one page per turning point – enough for a short story. The idea resonated deeply. We felt we were creating something meaningful, not only for ourselves but for our children.

Week after week, for more than a year, Zoom became our meeting place and our longed-for social interaction. Masks and hijabs were left behind as we read our stories aloud, connecting through words and memories. Writing became a priority and a commitment for us all.

It didn't take long for us to realise that one page per turning point wasn't enough. Our stories demanded more. The past, long buried, resurfaced with force. Every word was weighted, every memory charged. At each session, at least one of us would break down in tears, reliving what had once seemed a casual recollection.

Hend, the author of *Deep Roots*, a psychologist, nearly left the group, saying she wasn't ready to write about her private life. Mariam, *Child of Palestine*, choked up as she read about her childhood in the refugee camps and the father she had waited for but never met. Mary's *Farewell Sudan* tale of the captain and his new suit in her beloved Sudan moved us all. In *The Fragrance of Two Homes*, Camilia, a romantic poet, turned to nostalgia to avoid confronting why she had left her village. Oula, *The Urban Dervish*, clung to the photographs she had taken in her final days before departure, unwilling to relive the pain of leaving. Kilda, *Come with Me from Lebanon*, feared her past would weigh too heavily on her children. Sivine, in *Glasshouse*, had closed the door on her painful adolescence.

Discomfort and tension grew as we realised our stories needed to go deeper. We had to give more of ourselves.

In *The People's Magnet*, Nouha, the ever-positive force, soothed the group with her singing, while Sivine lightened the mood with humour, reminding us of the richness of our growing sisterhood. Oula, the mediator of our writing project, kept it on track as we took our time, attending to our families and work, and delaying the urgency of her deadlines.

I helped the women confront their fears of exposure by writing about my own vulnerable fourteen-year-old self and the compromises I made to fit into 1960s Australia. If writing in English had freed me from Arabic literary conventions, returning to my mother tongue now brought a new kind of authenticity.

For the first time, I wrote 'Palestine' freely, without fear of intimidation or offense, without self-censoring. It was no longer an unwelcome intruder, complicating the narrative with its politics. We were all on the same page. We were immigrant women from recolonised lands – serially occupied, in one form or another, to this day.

When COVID-19 restrictions eased, we were able to meet face-to-face. Sivine organised a writing retreat to recreate the space where stories happened naturally – while cooking, singing and dancing together. We spent a weekend by the sea talking about our mothers and fathers, cities and villages, our children, about war and peace, and Australia. We were able to grieve together for our shattered homelands.

Mary's sense of humour and stories of Sudan lightened the atmosphere. We were curious to know more about this rich and fertile North African Arab country, full of gold and oil, with its own history of colonisation and its recent partition into North and South. 'My beloved Sudan,' Mary would say in her beautiful Sudanese Arabic accent. We had only ever heard about its famine, its violent conflicts and nothing about its music, dance and songs. 'Sing us a Sudanese song,' we asked. The Arabic and African hybrid rhythm was enchanting. We danced to it and celebrated Mary's Sudan.

Kilda had one of the most intriguing stories. We bombarded her with questions about why she left Lebanon and her loving family at eighteen years of age. Oula, who never paid too much attention to fashion, hadn't been to the hairdresser for a while. Kilda volunteered to give Oula a new hairstyle. How we laughed at Oula's compliance under Kilda's hair dryer, which did very little to improve Oula's rebellious hair.

We sang and danced to the music of Warda and Umm Kulthum in the middle of the day, and in the evenings, we danced the *dabke* of Palestine and Lebanon.

Mariam went walking at every opportunity. She wanted to connect to the land, touch the native eucalypts, walk barefoot, close to the earth. She told us how exotic eucalyptus trees from Australia were planted on deforested land in Palestine. 'Native trees,' she added, 'such as olives and figs, are guardians of the land there, awaiting the return of its custodians.' We recited the poem *Passport* by the Palestinian poet Mahmoud Darwish, which includes the line 'Don't Ask the Trees for Their Names'. Later on, we felt this to be an appropriate title for our anthology, as trees were an important landmark in each of the stories. Etel Adnan, an artist and poet, painted a series of artworks called *Les Arbres* in which she depicts her deep spiritual connection to the earth through her portrayal of trees. Kindly an art gallery in Beirut gave us permission to use one of her drawings for our cover.

In the autumn of our lives, away from our partners, children, grandchildren, work, we were free and happy. We were working on something important and mind-changing. We meandered in and out of our past lives, speaking freely, rearranging the pieces of our past, discussing how we arrived, innocent, full of dreams or sadness, and how we found our way home. A complicity developed between us.

Suddenly our get-away ended. My suburban life seemed lifeless, impoverished by being away from my Arab women friends, their humour, their *joie de vivre,* despite all the hardships. I wanted to live in language, near these women. They had become my community. Now my story was their story. One story started by one of us was taken over by another, filling in details from her own life only for another to continue with her own, until the stories merged into one.

As our stories took shape, Oula insisted that they be translated into English. 'They must be part of the larger Australian story,' she argued.

We protested – some of us had never written in English. I, too, resisted. I had been revelling in Arabic, reconnecting with the language I had left behind. Would switching to English distance me from that adolescent girl who had been uprooted from her language and friends?

But in our hearts, we knew our stories could not remain confined to the Arabic-speaking community. We were in Australia. We are part of its story.

Translation was no simple task. Some turned to a son or daughter, others to a friend, or even to Google Translate. It took much longer than expected. It required patience from writers as well as from Oula and myself. We were translators, interpreters of feelings and cultures. Moving between languages meant more than just substituting words. Arabic's poetic, ornate and contemplative style distracted from what was too painful for the writer to expose. English stripped away the covers and the masks, forcing us to confront cultural taboos and articulate what had been left unsaid. The challenge in the translation was maintaining the appropriate cultural presence while safeguarding the individual voice of each of the writers. Kilda admitted, 'Having to explain my culture to an unfamiliar reader made me understand myself better. I feel liberated.'

The work on the English texts continued for more than a year with sustained intensity. Oula and I helped each writer individually. In return for our efforts, we asked for a favourite dish. And so, banquets of *fatteh*, fried chicory, okra, falafel and *makloubeh*, a Palestinian traditional dish, were offered.

To help free our creativity and ease the stress of writing and editing in English, I invited my sister Bouthaina, a dance teacher and therapist, to come from Melbourne and give us a workshop: 'The Body Knows the Story'. What at first seemed like a strange idea, was later enthusiastically embraced as Bouthaina guided us to trust our bodies. This workshop allowed us to liberate our creativity and access memories we had long suppressed.

Four years passed. We wrote our stories in Arabic, our mother tongue, and afterwards in English, the tongue of our second home. We watched each other grow older, become grandmothers and great-aunts, lose loved ones to the pandemic, and then to wars in Palestine, Lebanon and Syria. But we remained steadfast – committed to our writing, to each other. Free of shame, fearless, we stood by our journeys.

Nine women, from different corners of the Arab world, had come together to tell the story of the Arab woman. With every session, trust and love deepened, as did our understanding of ourselves.

We don't know what the future holds for Palestine, Lebanon, Syria and Sudan. But our stories – started before 7 October 2023 – will continue to bear witness to the histories of these lands and of Australia.

We have written for our children and their children. And for anyone who might want to understand Australia a little better.

We have told our stories as one does at dusk, alone, when the past reveals itself unedited in the fading light.

Loubna Haikal
July 2025

CHILD OF PALESTINE

by Mariam Maatooq

Through the wood-framed window of my house in Sydney, I gazed at the young jasmine tree in my backyard. Its Damascene fragrance transported me to a time buried deep beneath the rubble of my consciousness.

§

I was taken back to the day when a six-year-old girl packed her homeland into a bundle, hung its map around her neck, and set off on the road with thousands of others. In the wake of the Nakba of 1948 – the catastrophe that led to the displacement of the Palestinian people and the establishment of the state of Israel – my people were scattered to the four corners of the earth, carried by the wind.

The little girl, my mother, arrived in the Golan Heights in southern Syria. Seventeen years later, I was born on that majestic plateau. The home of our first migration was simple: a remote camp in the Golan, a small house of four walls built with red clay bricks, set amidst an orchard surrounded by poplar and eucalypt trees. There, my three sisters and I lived with our mother and father. The orchard provided us with fruits and vegetables, irrigated by the Afritiyyah Canal, which also yielded some fish. Two cows, a few sheep, and some chickens gave us milk and eggs.

§

Two years after the world heard my first cries, we were displaced again following the Naksa of June 1967, the Six-Day Arab-Israeli war, which ended with Israel capturing West Jerusalem, the West Bank, Sinai, and the Golan. My memories of that first migration were the ones relayed to me by my mother, grandmother, and the neighbours. *We fled the Golan in fear for our lives, joining thousands of Palestinians and Syrians who left behind their homes, land, and all that was precious to them.*

My father, with whom my mother had lived only eight short years, disappeared during the 1967 war. We didn't know if he was alive or dead. My mother assumed both maternal and paternal responsibilities for four daughters – the eldest only eight years old and the youngest just four months. She had already faced enormous difficulties, and this second displacement forced her to rebuild our lives alone. She worked tirelessly on neighbouring farms to provide for us. She nursed us during illness and delighted in us as we grew. Together we shared our life, our love and our sorrows. Like thousands of other women in the camps, she bore the weight of displacement, hardship, and the many injustices inflicted upon the Palestinian people with forbearance, clinging to hope that her husband would one day return.

I have no real memory of my father, with whom I lived for only two years. Even now, I tremble whenever he drifts through my mind. I would draw his face with a soft feather on the surface of the water, afraid to touch the image lest it dissolve before my eyes. The days passed as we waited for his return, huddling around the neighbour's transistor radio.

I would press my ear to the radio, my heart pounding, fear and hope intertwining as I listened for his name amongst the lists of prisoners held by the occupying army. That cruel anticipation stretched on for years. The restlessness of waiting gradually eroded my mother's hope that he would return. Yet I dreamt of him coming back, bringing gifts for us all, lifting me onto his lap, telling me heroic tales of the resistance. Over time, I crafted an image of him in my imagination – a portrait that grew alongside me and remains vivid in my mind even now.

§

Palestinians fleeing the war were scattered across refugee camps in the countryside around Damascus and other Syrian provinces. They carried nothing to sustain them but the keys to their homes and the deeds to their land. The United Nations Relief and Works Agency – UNRWA – helped erect tents, one of which became our home in the Sayyida Zeinab camp, about twelve kilometres south of Damascus. The landscape was beautiful, surrounded by water and lush groves of apricot trees. The ripe, golden fruit glistened in the sun, calling out to the young refugees. We heeded their call, defying the guards who shouted and chased us but never managed to stop us from stealing the sweet, forbidden apricots. To this day, the taste of apricots takes me back to my childhood in the camp, when we were as free as birds, stretching our wings as if about to soar into the sky.

At first, life in the camp was harsh, and then it became familiar, like an extended family. Still, I refused to accept it. Some rejoiced when UNRWA set up a school or a clinic, but an inner voice warned me: *Oh Mariam, this is not good news.* I feared my mother and my sisters would begin to settle, to complain about the cramped tent and request a better one. Even as a child, I recognised the danger – we were adapting to life as refugees, and in doing so, we were betraying Palestine. We made the tents our homes, and that was our sin.

Our tent stood in the middle of the camp, made of fabric that neither shielded us from the summer heat nor protected us from the winter cold. We stitched together sheets with weary hands and stuffed our pillows with rags recycled from old clothes – so hard they felt like stones beneath our heads. The tent floor was covered with plastic mats or fabric scraps woven on hand looms.

Our kitchen was equally rudimentary: simple plastic and aluminium utensils, a kerosene burner for cooking and heating, and small kerosene lamps for dim evening light. The tent was everything – bedroom, kitchen, sitting room, bathroom, and for making love. Our tents shook with the wind and swayed with our sadness, as if the heavens themselves wept for our tragedy. When we, the forsaken children, played in the campgrounds, the mud covered us from head to toe, which we then tracked into our tents.

Yet, we refused to surrender to the tyranny of poverty. A flame of joy burned within us. Sticks, reeds, stones, and anemones became raw materials for our handmade toys. The dolls we crafted with our own hands were the most beautiful, filling us with pure happiness. We made dolls from anemone flowers, flipping the petals and painting eyes and lips until they resembled brides on their wedding days.

I grew up in the camp, and with me, my anger grew. Our tents lacked the basic comfort of a dignified life. There was no privacy; everything was interconnected, every soul in the camp privy to the lives of others. And yet, amidst the despair, we stole moments of joy from the depths of suffering – especially during Ramadan. The air filled with the scent of cakes, breads spiced with sesame seeds and black cumin, and traditional Palestinian dishes. The tantalising aromas teased our fasting bellies. I longed for *hummus fatteh*, the savoury dish that crowned every Ramadan feast.

The children were assigned various tasks, and I bore my share of responsibilities. At nine years old, I carried water-filled buckets on my head for over two kilometres. Yet, in that task, I found a stolen pleasure: the scent of linden blossoms that erased my fatigue.

Life in the camp measured time not by years, but by suffering and burdens. Each hard day gave way to another. Destitution weighed upon us, forcing my mother, my sisters, and me to walk with heavy feet and empty stomachs, scouring the land for edible herbs to create simple meals in place of meat and poultry. Nature sustained us; so too did the produce my mother brought home from the farms where she toiled.

Despite the overwhelming despair, life within the confines of the camp offered fleeting moments of happiness – my sisters' smiles, the comforting aroma of my mother's cooking. Yellow chamomile flowers lined the canal banks and the grove, glowing under the golden sun, beckoning us to gather them. We would boil them in water and sip the fragrant tea during our evening gatherings before retreating to our tents for the night.

In the camp yard, young boys and girls sang their love for Palestine, their hearts dancing with joy for a land they had never seen.

Our absence stretched – first two nights, then a month, then two. Soon, a year passed. Then two. Then many. Palestine did not return to us, and we did not return to Palestine. Instead, the word *refugee* became etched on our faces, following us everywhere: in the UNRWA-run school, clinic, and restaurant and in the long queues where we waited to collect our food rations.

§

My innocent childhood bore the scars of a world bound by outdated customs and the unjust dominion of men over women, all in the name of tradition. At the age of ten, I lived through an experience that shook me deeply, one I wrestled with in silence for years. I held my breath, my voice locked in my throat, as I witnessed my sixteen-year-old sister being forced into marriage with our cousin, her will crushed beneath the weight of expectation.

How can I describe what I saw? My sister burned from within, a silent storm raging behind her eyes, a haze of tears dulling their once-bright light. As she emerged from the tent, heartbroken, defeated, her pain echoed in the tremor of my mother's voice, in the sorrow that clouded her gaze as she bid farewell to her eldest daughter on her wedding day.

Until then, our family had been inseparable, as the fingers of one hand. But when my sister was taken to her husband's tent, it was as if the thumb had been cut off. My other two sisters and I remained with my mother, who fought tirelessly to shield us from the same fate. 'We can eat mud as long as you get an education,' she'd insist.

My mother was only twenty-four when she lost my father, yet she turned away every offer of marriage, choosing instead to sacrifice herself for us. The salt of her tears clung to our skin as she held us close, saying, 'Work is more honourable for me than extending my hand.'

Then came the day when tragedy descended upon the camp with the force of a storm. A beautiful young woman was brutally murdered by her own father. She had dared to flee with the man she loved, refusing to abide by the laws of a conservative society. She paid for her freedom to choose with her life.

The news struck like lightning, searing through me. I couldn't sleep; it felt as if my heart were being crushed inside my chest. The cries of the unjustly murdered girl echoed in my head.

The release of the murderer after six months was a turning point in my life and transformed me into a warrior. During my youth in the camp, I helped organise literacy and homework classes as well as handcraft workshops, where women embroidered and wove tapestries to sell in the market for additional income.

This incident filled me with determination, stubbornness, and defiance – qualities that would help me overcome the difficulties I encountered at various stages of my life. I developed a deep revulsion for traditions that denied women their due respect, reducing them to wives and childbearers under the custody of their husbands.

Yes, at times, I capitulated to the male authority in my own life. I adapted too much to the harsh reality, but like 'the grass that grows between the rocks', I bent with the wind and did not break. The flame of hope kept burning inside me. I became like the olive trees of Palestine: my roots firm, deep in the ground, my trunk steadfast and resistant. I became like the Phoenix – whenever a part of me died, I was resurrected from my ashes.

§

My mother endured the cruelty of my uncles, whose interference intensified after the murder of the young woman in the camp. They pressured us to leave school, believing that girls needed no more than basic literacy. They saw my mother as a weak, ineffective woman incapable of raising her daughters alone, yet they offered her little support.

My mother's suffering distanced me from my uncles. 'Forgiveness is an act of generosity. Your uncle is a second father,' she would tell me. She urged me to forgive, to act with compassion, and to remember that they were cousins and sons of cousins, that 'blood is thicker than water'. Back then, I saw my mother as a passive woman. I failed to recognise the quiet strength and innate social intelligence that enabled her to endure life's injustices on her own terms.

She did not allow my uncles to meddle in our family affairs. She defied them when she sent us away to the Children of Martyrs Boarding School in the Mezzeh district of Damascus. She bore the heartache of separation to secure us a better education and future.

§

We took the bus with our mother to the boarding school in the Syrian capital. I was captivated by the road lined with pine and poplar trees. The autumnal weather and the multi-coloured foliage filled me with awe and admiration, but gradually, sadness crept in. I couldn't enjoy that wonderful scenery of harmonious autumnal hues because my heart ached, dreading the separation from my mother and the transition into an unfamiliar world.

When we arrived at the school, my mother gave us a final, lingering embrace. We felt her eyelashes brush against our cheeks as she hugged us tightly, as if afraid we might slip away. She inhaled our scent deeply, as if trying to imprint it in the folds of her soul. Having my sisters with me soothed my fears as our mother left us in the care of the teachers. I will never forget the sight of her saying goodbye, tears frozen in her eyes like pearls too afraid to fall.

The new school was daunting, like all new beginnings, but my enjoyment of music, dance and singing lessons eased the pain of separation and helped me adjust. When I heard the dance music of the Andalusian *muwashahat* – dating back to the Arab rule of Spain – my soul soared. My body swayed like the branch of a mallow tree as I watched the dancers' hands move left and right, up and down. The Oriental lace costumes shimmered with vibrant colours, and as I danced on stage, I felt like the great Queen Zenobia of Palmyra.

During my school years, I learnt to respect time, organisation, and the discipline of working within a structured framework. I learnt how to manage the chaos that had once characterised my unstructured life in the camps, where spontaneity often ruled my actions. The school provided opportunities that were unavailable to the girls in the camp, allowing me to channel my impulses into sports and artistic activities.

To this day, I still enjoy playing table tennis, a skill I picked up at school. Life became immeasurably richer, and I embraced new habits and values. Some old habits remained, but overall, my mind became more open. I was a lily blooming without restrictions.

§

During the next few years, I finished high school and pursued a degree in Psychology at Damascus University. While studying, I worked as a teacher, securing an additional income that enabled my mother to stop working on the farm. By then, she was living in a small brick house built on the site of the tent. After finishing my teaching for the day, I would rush to university to catch up with my lectures and immerse myself in student life. We engaged in heated political debates in the university cafeteria, played music, sang revolutionary songs at night and marched in demonstrations following UN decisions on Palestine. That phase of my life was one of the most beautiful – I met a group of friends with whom I still maintain close ties.

After completing my university degree, I participated in a forty-day camp with a group of Palestinian youths from the diaspora in Damascus. There, I met a handsome, intelligent young man who shared my values and love for the same music and poetry. We discovered the poems of Mahmoud Darwish together and were elated. '*All roads lead to you, even those I took to forget you.*' Darwish's words unleashed the wings of our imaginations, and I knew that this Palestinian refugee, who lived in Kuwait, had conquered my heart. He was emotionally expressive, spontaneous, and blessed with a sharp wit and insightful outlook. It felt as if God had singled him out for me. We crowned our love with the sacred bond of marriage.

My wedding was a prelude to my second emigration – to Kuwait. I was the first in my family to marry from outside the country and leave Syria. Though I had thought constantly about the impending day of departure, it arrived suddenly. My mother and sisters stood in the middle of the living room, struggling to find words. Who had the courage to utter the last words? Who could sum up all the feelings and memories in a single sentence? There was a long silence; no one dared to speak. They were our last moments together, and then, it was over.

At Damascus Airport, I was overwhelmed by mixed emotions – sadness at leaving my mother, sisters, friends, and the place where I had grown up, yet joy in knowing that I was embarking on a journey with the man I loved, ready to build a family and seek a better future.

§

When I arrived in Kuwait, my life changed drastically. The sun felt different, even though it was the same sun that had shone over the camp. Had I turned my back on my former life? As the days passed, I felt more alienated. I felt like a grain of sand removed from the desert; a drop of water separated from the ocean. Alone. No family, no sisters, no friends. I was consumed by an intense longing. I moved around the rooms of my house, smelling my clothes, which still carried the scent of my mother, and saying to myself, 'Oh Mum, how nice you smell!' I sipped coffee from a cup I had carried with me from Syria – the same cup my mother had used for her morning coffee. She remained an absent presence, living in the space between her home and mine.

I missed my friends, and the evenings spent singing along to Marcel Khalife, Sheikh Imam, Fairuz and Abdel Halim Hafez. I missed the fragrance of my past – the scent of jasmine.

From its very beginning, Damascus had been a refuge for the oppressed, the poor and the exiled.

When I first arrived there, displaced from the Golan and lost amongst hundreds of other refugees, I was carried in a donkey saddle led by my uncle. This time, I arrived from Kuwait by airplane. As I flew over Damascus International Airport, I smiled, my heart fluttering like butterfly wings in the dewy air. I spent one month with my mother, sisters, extended family, and university friends. I visited the public baths, enjoyed my mother's cooking, and walked through the old streets, quenching my longing for my beloved Damascus. Every time I visited one friend, others would congregate, each bringing a plate of delicious Syrian food. We feasted, sang, debated politics and reminisced about the past.

Sadly, when I recently visited Damascus, I found hardly any of my old friends. The Syrian war scattered them across the world. I learnt of the young Palestinian schoolteacher, my mother's neighbour in Damascus – from the Sayyida Zaynab refugee camp – the same camp where I grew up in. She took her last steps onto a boat with her three children. Neither she nor her children made it to safe shores.

§

When I returned to Kuwait, I started working at a Palestinian welfare office, and my salary covered my personal expenses and the cost of my cigarettes. I set aside part of my earnings to send to my mother in Syria.

I was pregnant when the first Gulf War broke out. Three weeks after the occupation of Kuwait, I gave birth to my first daughter, Haneen, who lit my world with her angelic face and joyful demeanor. Looking after a newborn on my own, with little experience, was overwhelming. I longed for my mother's support, and the absence of my husband's family in Kuwait deepened my sense of isolation. But my daughter's cheerful face eased my loneliness. I had never imagined that I could love so intensely.

Events in Kuwait filled my mother with fear. I frequently called to reassure her. Having a phone in the camp in Syria was a luxury – her home had no luxuries and no phone. I would call her neighbour's house and patiently await my mother's voice. To ease her anxiety, I'd begin with a common Kuwaiti reassurance: '*Nahnu bi khayr huna fi al Kuwait, wakayfu halukum,*' 'We are well here in Kuwait, how about you?'

Soon after Haneen's birth, I became pregnant again. While visiting a friend in my third trimester, I suffered a serious haemorrhage. The war tearing through the streets of Kuwait made communication almost impossible. Terrified, and in tears, I thought my life was coming to an end. But this time fate was on my side – my husband unexpectedly stopped by, not anticipating the crisis. She was five weeks early. I'd lost blood, drained – my face was ashen. He carried me in his arms to a nearby hospital, where I underwent an emergency Caesarean section. We named her Nour.

§

After the war, Kuwait was no longer home for Palestinians. Yet, we wanted to stay in the Arab world. Perhaps Amman in Jordan could be a safer place for us. My husband agreed with my proposal to return to Damascus with our children until he finished his work in Kuwait. I wondered if I was destined to repeat my mother's history – were we going to experience the same tragedy of perpetual displacement?

I stayed with my family in Syria for a few months until I obtained a visa to travel to Jordan. My third emigration was about to begin. We went to my husband's family home, far from the Jordanian capital, where some Palestinian friends had settled. Later, my husband returned from Kuwait, and we moved to Amman, where we lived for three years. There, we built a warm and loving community with extended family, friends and neighbours.

During our time in Amman, I became pregnant with my third daughter, Farah, who brought more joy to our hearts and lit our evenings with a thousand stars. I felt blessed every time I looked at her, overwhelmed with happiness whenever I caressed her cheeks.

My husband's dreams were more ambitious than mine. He wanted better opportunities elsewhere. He decided to take us to Australia. Though I did not want to leave, I could not object – economic, political, and social conditions were deteriorating fast. We applied for emigration to Australia but while we waited, my husband accepted a job offer in Qatar.

This was my fourth migration. In Qatar, I did not put down roots. I felt like a tree unanchored to soil. Though we made friends with neighbours from Sudan and Egypt, Qatar was a place of transition for us. Finally, our visas were ready. My fifth and final destination would be Australia.

§

When we arrived in Sydney, we knew no one. A friend of a friend greeted us at the airport and arranged for us to stay temporarily in a house owned by a Palestinian family who were away in Jordan. The sun lit up the walls as I entered, but I felt sad and disoriented, wondering where we would put our belongings. We lived out of suitcases for a couple of weeks, hesitant to touch anything not ours. Yet, I was grateful to our community for the way they extended hospitality to fellow Palestinians, even if strangers. That evening, the wife of the man from the airport came by. Though she had never met us, she prepared *maqloobeh* and a fresh green salad. I did not realise how exhausted I was, and words of thanks were simply not enough; I was truly overwhelmed and could no longer contain my composure. Before she left, she handed me her phone number, telling me to call if we needed help. These acts of generosity amongst Palestinians of the diaspora embodied what we always said in the camp to lift our weary hearts in hope: 'The world is still good.'

Yet in the weeks following our arrival, I began to be riddled with anxiety. I didn't realise what toll uprooting again would take on me. Being a mother, one tends to put her own needs aside, and I had three angels to think of. I knew nothing of this faraway place. I could not speak the language and felt so vulnerable. The anxiety was debilitating. I was folding into myself with dread, paralysed by a fear of all strangers, even

Arabic speakers. I could not even make a simple exchange of money to buy a loaf of bread. After three weeks, the owners of the house returned from their trip, and we had to leave. We finally found a little home to rent and with time my anxiety subsided. At first our new home was bare. We had no furniture. It looked like a newborn – naked and fragile! Our furniture was being shipped from Qatar, and when it finally arrived, we welcomed the fifth member of our family. My furniture brought me solace. It was a relief from my estrangement and loneliness.

As we unpacked, I found a card inside one of the couches. It was from the sister of a Jordanian friend, and through her, we were able to connect with another friend residing in Sydney. She had emigrated to Australia after the Gulf War, which had scattered Palestinians from Kuwait all over the world. Finding that friend opened doors to new friendships, and for that, I am forever grateful to my furniture.

Eventually my husband found a job, and the girls began adjusting to a new school. I took my first steps toward settling by enrolling in English classes.

Across the street from our little house lived an Australian family whose daughters attended the same school as my girls did. The girls quickly became friends, and their English began to improve. One day, I walked into our garage and found my two older daughters playing the role of teachers, teaching their Australian neighbours Arabic. Following our tradition of hospitality, my daughters had placed plates of my homemade spinach and za'atar pastries on a side table for their friends to enjoy while learning the names of different foods in Arabic. The children were happily playing, eating and learning from each other. It amazes me how language is never a barrier for children. That memory still makes me smile.

Despite my limited English, I was able to build relationships with my daughters' teachers. Their music teacher once asked me to teach the children an Arabic song for Harmony Day. I chose a well-known Arabic children's song and sang it for them. The following week, I invited the teacher to our home for a meal. We had a wonderful time together. Food and music are universal languages and being socially proactive helps integration. Looking back, I realise how unusual it must have been for a teacher to be invited to a student's home. Yet, I did it many times, and I like to think that, in some small way, I helped change the attitudes just a little.

§

Over time, I began looking for ways to interact with others and get involved in my new community. The library became my refuge, and I frequently visited it with my daughters. We discovered shelves with simplified English books that helped us learn the new language.

One day, while listening to the SBS Arabic radio station, I heard a Palestinian social activist speaking about the services and activities provided by her association for new Arab immigrants to Australia, particularly those of Palestinian backgrounds.

Luck came to my rescue once again. I seized the opportunity and called her as soon as the programme ended. She warmly invited me to participate in a social event organised by her foundation. During that gathering, I met many women who later became friends, and the activist herself became one of my very closest companions.

Within a few months, I had built a strong circle of friends. Their presence eased my loneliness and offered the warm embrace I so needed. They were the pickaxes that broke down the walls of my alienation. Our arrival in Sydney coincided with the year of the Olympic Games, which helped us feel a sense of belonging in our new community. We followed the games by watching a giant screen in the park, surrounded by people we didn't know. We were overwhelmed with joy, cheering for the Australian teams, especially in the swimming events.

§

A year after our arrival, we felt more settled and decided to start a home-based business, importing the famous Al-Ameed Jordanian coffee. We also imported Damascene sweets from Semiramis, a brand renowned for its quality, along with other varieties of Syrian and Jordanian confections. Additionally, we made and sold Nabulsi *kanafeh*. My husband imported a vermicelli-making machine and a cooktop from Jordan, while I travelled to Queensland to complete a course and obtain a cheese-making licence.

We worked long hours, and it was not an easy journey. My role focused on marketing, and I worked day and night, striving to make the business viable. Despite the challenges, I found joy in the work and felt a deep sense of fulfilment. As our business expanded, so did my pride in my Palestinian heritage. I made 'Mariam's Palestinian Kanafeh' with my own hands and saw the results of many months of dedication. Our *kanafeh* became famous amongst Palestinians, as no one else was making it at the time. Even years later, some people still know me as 'Mariam Kanafeh.' Beyond providing financial stability, the business expanded my social network, introducing me to many other immigrants, primarily from Arab and Palestinian backgrounds.

Two years after my fifth migration, we were granted Australian citizenship. We were now ready and able to visit my mother. She called me back to Damascus – the homeland of my soul and my family. We packed our bags for a holiday in Jordan and Syria. I was eager to see my mother, to see my sisters, and friends, and to breathe in the scent of *Shami* jasmine once more. We stayed with my mother in the camp, where my daughters played with their cousins in the alleyways, dancing the *dabke*, using pots and pans as drums.

I took my daughters to the old neighbourhoods and baths of Damascus, showing them its historical landmarks, bustling markets, and exquisite handicrafts. Walking through the streets, I saw Damascus through new eyes. I appreciated it more after leaving, often finding myself unintentionally comparing it to Sydney.

Each city had its own character, and both occupied a distinct place in my heart.

Although my time with family in Syria and Jordan was unforgettable, I missed Australia. I longed to return to the life I had built, one that had become rewarding and stable. I looked forward to resuming work on our small business and embracing the future that awaited us.

§

As demand grew, we took a bold step and opened a café in Yagoona, offering coffee and *kanafeh* in a setting that reflected our rich Palestinian heritage. Shelves adorned with antiques, embroideries, and a collection of Arabic books and novels gave the space a deep sense of cultural identity.

Our homeland was the most important part of our lives, overshadowing everything else. Determined to support our people in Palestine, we began importing Palestinian products – oil, olives, thyme, and *maftool*, a Palestinian grain dish. We participated in exhibitions and set up stalls at local markets in Sydney and Canberra, selling these products without profit to bolster the economy back home. I took immense pride in introducing the taste of Palestine to the Australian palate. The olive oil came from ancient Roman and Nabali trees, offering an opportunity to educate Australians about Palestinian olives and their significance as symbols of peace and life. Participating in these exhibitions gave me a profound sense of purpose. I felt as though I had raised the name 'Palestine' as high as the Australian sun.

Those years were amongst the most demanding of my life. With my husband now working in Saudi Arabia, I had to manage the house, care for our daughters and run the café with the occasional help of a friend. Despite the challenges, these experiences taught me valuable lessons and motivated me to keep learning. I wanted to set an example for my daughters – to teach the importance of education, hard work and self-reliance. I encouraged them to read, took them to the library when I could and challenged them with academic tasks during school holidays. Without close family or friends nearby, we built our own world of knowledge and resilience.

At one stage, the business required long hours, and I began to feel I was neglecting my daughters. Eventually, I faced a difficult decision: continue working tirelessly to maintain the business's success or prioritise the family. In the end, I chose to close the café and focus on my daughters while continuing to work from home. Though it was a painful choice, it was one that reaffirmed my belief in balancing ambition with family.

§

One day, I saw an advertisement in the local newspaper, *The Torch*. They wanted a community worker who could speak Arabic. Without hesitation, I called the number and applied, my English still hesitant and broken. I emphasised my fluency in Arabic, a vital skill in an area where many residents spoke Arabic and very little English. The person on the other end of the line recognised my determination and suggested an organisation where Arabic-speaking staff were in high demand. To my surprise, I was offered a job. But that initial shock quickly turned into a deeper realisation: When you find the courage to explore new pathways, doors begin to open.

My work in social services strengthened my language and organisational skills. Through reading and self-study, I filled the gaps in my knowledge, for there had been no formal child welfare system in the Arab countries where I had previously worked. Exposure to new ways of life broadened my understanding of the human condition. I poured my heart into assisting those in need, drawn to their pain by the echoes of my own struggles. Yet, some cases lingered in my soul like shadows. When children were forcibly removed from their mothers, I saw the same anguish that had once filled my mother's eyes as she left us at the Children of Martyrs boarding school. Some memories never truly fade; they resurface, entwining past and present.

I recall such a moment in Sydney. It seems my existence is an affront to the Israeli occupation there and here. At a function someone asked me where I was from. I replied, 'Palestine.' The attendee from Israel objected, 'No, *not* Palestine – Israel.' I met her gaze, 'It is the same land. It is Palestine for me.' That ended the conversation. We are under erasure. That's what the occupation means. Our history is being purposefully rewritten and the names of our hometowns and villages have been altered.

Years later, at a gathering, I met the attendee's daughter, who worked with a refugee and human rights organisation. She asked me where I was from, and when I answered 'Palestine,' she held my hand and said, 'I am so sorry for what is happening there.' We embraced, shedding quiet tears on each other's shoulders. She told me she had not returned to Israel for twenty years, unable to accept the injustices inflicted upon Palestinians. She introduced me to her migrant and Indigenous colleagues. The Indigenous woman nodded and said, 'I truly understand your people's suffering.' 'I understand yours as well,' I told her. 'We share the same history – ethnic cleansing, dispossession, and devastation of our people. We share the same anger at the absence of justice.' As a Palestinian who has known the cruelty of occupation, I feel a deep kinship with Indigenous people. I knew that, like my people, they carried the burden of dispossession and intergenerational trauma.

During team-building exercises for my community work, we visited native forests with an Indigenous guide who spoke of their spiritual significance – forests are considered 'Country' and are deeply connected to identity for the Indigenous people of Australia. I could deeply relate to our guide. Our olive trees back home have so much meaning. They are the most powerful symbol of our attachment to our land. Since 1967, when I was two, at least 800,000 trees have been uprooted, burnt or destroyed by Israeli authorities or *settlers*. I see each one of our olive trees as a person. How many of us have been uprooted?

To this day, I am in awe of the invisible forces that link my world to theirs. The forests of Australia became my refuge, wrapping my heart in their towering bark. Whenever sadness or anxiety weighs on me, I find solace amongst the trees. Inspired, I helped form a walking group with colleagues from different backgrounds, where we share stories of our homelands, our memories and our struggles.

§

I am Mariam. I left Palestine one day, not yet formed in my mother's womb. I grew, and with me the dream of returning from an imaginary Palestine to the real Palestine. For most of my life, Palestine was a magical box full of stories until I was finally allowed to step on its soil. As a Palestinian refugee whose parents were expelled from their homeland, I had no right to return or even visit. It was only in 2006, with an Australian passport, that I could finally set foot in Palestine. It was the greatest gift Australia had given me.

On my first visit with my family, we stayed for a few days with one of my husband's cousins in his home village of Silet-Aldaher, between Jenin and Nablus. Our first attempt to cross into the West Bank was met with rejection at the checkpoint. While we waited, we saw a woman from Umm al-Fahm pleading with Israeli soldiers to allow her to attend her sister's funeral in Jenin. She was denied entry. My daughters watched in silent distress. Young Palestinian men rushed to us, asking, '*Khalto*, how can we help you?' *Khalto* is a polite term and means aunt. I was a stranger, and they were living under torment every day. They arranged for a taxi to take us to another checkpoint. Along the way, the driver, seeing our exhaustion, offered to host us for the night. It was late, and the air had turned cold, but we were eager to reach my husband's village. We pressed on and finally arrived. We stayed for three days, enough time to show our daughters the village mosque and cemetery, built on land donated by my husband's family. It gave them a sense of pride and connection, a tangible piece of their history.

Later, we took a bus to Jerusalem. The main road was closed to Palestinians, forcing our bus onto winding backroads between houses and olive groves, stopping at countless checkpoints. A young Israeli soldier climbed aboard, his rifle aimed at terrified passengers. He aggressively asked for identification. I avoided looking into his eyes, not out of fear, but because I did not want him to see the anger in mine; the pain was scorched into my soul. Amongst the joy of that first trip, my family and I saw first-hand the daily humiliations of life under occupation.

On my first trip, I was overwhelmed with mixed emotions – I felt euphoria mixed with a searing anger at those who had stolen and destroyed our homes and tormented my people. As I walked the ancient streets, the voice of the Lebanese diva Fairuz echoed. The song was: '*Al Quds al Atika,*' 'Ancient Jerusalem'. She sang, *Let my voice reach like a whirlwind inside the conscience of people to tell them what's happening in Old Jerusalem and make the tormenters stop. Tell them what is happening and make them stop.* This song was released in 1967 when I was two years old. My father never returned from that war, and we fled from the Golan to the camps in Damascus. Fairuz's pleas fell deaf on the world. No consciences were awakened in *1948*, in *1967* or in the *present time.* I wondered what happened to his body. How was my father killed? Did he think about me as he died? I arrived at the Al-Aqsa Mosque in old Jerusalem to witness Israeli soldiers stamping aggressively through its sacred grounds. My euphoria after arrival gave way to grief. I performed ablutions and prayed fervently, reclaiming, just for a moment, a piece of what had been stolen from me, from us.

Since that first visit, once I was freed from the constant responsibilities of raising young children, I returned to Palestine year after year. My journey back is like a sacred pilgrimage – I go whenever I can, as often as I can, to be physically present on the land. I go because it is an act of resistance. And I go because, despite everything, I find joy in being on my ancestral land.

Each visit deepened my understanding, revealing layers of the land and its people through the eyes of those who remained. My friends took me to the high peaks where I could see the golden dome of Al-Aqsa, the many Orthodox churches, the Via Dolorosa where Christ walked. They showed me houses and villages where Palestinians once lived, now erased or occupied by others. In Sheikh Jarrah, families continued their long legal battle to remain in their homes. In the streets, I found one of the last remaining manhole covers bearing the words 'Made in Palestine' – a relic of a city being reshaped, piece by piece, to erase our history.

My friends in Palestine amaze me with their quiet forms of resistance. I watched as they collected seeds from local stone fruits, drying them on their rooftops and windowsills. During hikes through neighbouring villages, they would stop, dig a small hole, plant each seed, water it, and move on. They pray for the trees to grow, to take root and reclaim the land in their absence. I also learnt about how Palestinian men incarcerated for tens of years without trial circumvent the occupation by smuggling their sperm out of prison for their women to ensure the survival of the Palestinian people. Others travelled between

Palestinian villages, urging farmers not to capitulate to torment and abandon their land. They buy produce from struggling farmers and sell it in the markets, ensuring that they have an income.

§

Every time I return to Palestine, my first stop is Bayt Sahur, where my closest friend lives. When I got married in Syria, it was her husband who gave me away. After spending a few days with her, we travelled together to visit other friends. I move between familiar places and discover new ones each visit. On my second trip back, I visited Nazareth with a couple of friends. We booked a hotel run by a Palestinian family – a charming place, more than 120 years old. Its stone walls seemed to whisper stories of the past. In the morning, we were served a Palestinian breakfast of local cheese and watermelon, and for a moment, it felt as though we were home. After breakfast, we wandered through the streets and the bustling markets, where people still preserved their Palestinian customs and traditions. Inside a church, we saw many depictions of Jesus, each imagined differently – some with golden hair, others with dark skin. The contrast stood as a testament to the diversity of belief, of history, of people.

From Nazareth, we travelled to Haifa, where we met a Palestinian Jew who led us on a three-hour walking tour of the city. Haifa's history stood alongside its modernity – historic sites nestled amongst contemporary buildings, remnants of a past both cherished and erased. Our guide spoke of 1948, when Zionist forces advanced on the city. The Palestinian residents, desperate for protection, turned to the British rulers. They were ordered to evacuate *temporarily*, until the fighting ended. And so, thousands were forced onto ships and taken to Beirut, their exile framed as a short-term solution for their own safety. They were never allowed to return. Their homes, their shops, their livelihoods were taken, resettled by Zionists. Haifa was no longer theirs.

On the outskirts of the city, in a place called Ein Hod, Palestinian houses had been confiscated and turned into residences for Jewish artists. The original occupants were expelled. But the Palestinians of Ein Hod, refusing to sever their ties to the land, built an encampment just across from the village they lost. Every day, they watched strangers take over their old homes. They stood, shattered, watching as *settlers* occupied their houses. As I walked through Ein Hod, I came across a pomegranate tree, its ripe fruit split open, spilling its ruby-red seeds. I reached out, plucked one, and ate it. As I did, I said to myself, 'This is part of my rightful share of Palestine, and I reclaim it.'

In Hebron, I prayed in the Ibrahimi Mosque, walked through the narrow streets, and witnessed the way Palestinians supported one another so that no one would go to bed hungry. I visited the city's oldest olive press and its oldest stained-glass factory. I bought a traditional Palestinian dress, knowing that each stitch carried a history, that by wearing it, I was prolonging both the garment's life and the story it told. From Hebron, I travelled to Safed and its surrounding areas – the birthplace of my family before they were displaced. Though the physical traces of Palestinian life have been erased, every wall, every door, every street conspired against silence, telling the stories of those who once called this place home.

With a friend from Jerusalem, I visited Lake Tiberias. It's a freshwater lake of Galilee. It is where Jesus walked on water, where he calmed the storm and performed the miracle of catching a multitude of fish. Tiberias is resplendent with sacred, precious and powerful events. My family had lived here and had often described its warming sweet waters to me, painting images of its gentle waves in my childhood mind. When we arrived, the lake was crowded with Israeli hikers. As I swam, a wave of emotion washed over me – despair, sorrow and grief. Our history is in these waters. I captured my precious visit to Lake Tiberias in a short video and sent it to my mother in Syria. I wanted her to see the waters she and her family had once swam in. I wanted her to see where her people had swum and fished and where they'd felt awe and sacredness.

§

On a later trip to Palestine, I visited the villages between Safad and Tabaria, where my father and mother were born. I went to Bisan, Khalsa and Jaouna, the villages where the camp children were from too. They would never know their parents' village. I recalled how we waited to hear our father's names on the radio. From here, I collected sumac, sage, and thyme to take back with me to Australia.

On another visit, I returned to the occupied Golan Heights in search of my birthplace, the land I was forced to leave at the age of two in the 1967 war. I sought the Bteha of my mother and grandmother's stories – a village full of houses and farms, with the Afritiyya Canal winding through it. But the Bteha of memory no longer existed. In its place, I found only an orchard of mango trees. The canal had been transformed into a rowing park. As I walked through the park, I saw remnants of demolished homes – stones buried beneath the grass, telling stories of life before the Israeli occupation.

I wandered along the paths of the Golan Heights, looking around, speaking to my daughter Nour, who had accompanied me on my journey: 'Here, I was born. Here was our camp. Somewhere here, my father was martyred. Here, … here – everywhere.' I sobbed and my heart trembled. Nour embraced me and said, 'We will never forget Palestine. It will always be our homeland, and it will live forever in our hearts and minds.' I was comforted to know that the diaspora children would hold this place as precious in their memories and acknowledge the suffering of our people.

For my children, Palestine is a source of pride and cultural identity. They don't live with the stamp of *refugee* on their foreheads as we did in the camps. Nour, Haneen and Farah and all future generations will always be the children of Palestine, because it will remain beautiful and glorious in their hearts, and its memory will stay alive in their souls. My children have a different relationship with Palestine. For me, it is a legacy of personal struggle and suffering. For them, it's a matter of identity and a question of justice, which they will uphold and defend.

I've raised my daughters to embrace transformation in their own lives and foster progress in the lives of others. Each chose a different path of service: the eldest in humanitarian work, the middle in law and justice, the youngest in media and advertising – a reflection of the culturally rich and progressive upbringing they received. I find joy in seeing how my own exploration of adapting and paving a renewed life has reverberated in theirs. It's as if they've followed in my footsteps, becoming beacons of light and taking a stand for change. They create loving, conscious communities wherever they go.

We live in Australia, but I continue to be an ambassador for our motherland. I sing its songs in a choir so that people can hear its beautiful melodies. I participate in the yearly Tales of Homeland, a live performance celebrating Palestinian culture, costumes, wedding rituals, food, dance, music and songs. Every year we focus on a particular issue, such as the ongoing plight of the Palestinian prisoners and their families.

§

Through the wood-framed window of my house in Sydney, I gaze at the jasmine tree and contemplate the current tragedies of our people, trapped in genocide in Gaza. All this while the world watches in silence. Is there no escape from the circle of fire? The tragedy of our displacement continues.

PILLAR OF SALT
by Loubna Haikal

Leaving Lebanon was easy. My parents' plan was simple: complete the education of their five children, make enough money – preferably a fortune – and return after a few years. There would never be a need for a permanent home in another country, let alone in a faraway, barely heard-of continent called Australia. We already had a home. We had a beautiful home. A lounge room with enough couches to seat all of us and visitors, as well as two bedrooms with large windows to look at the moon from our beds at night. A blue-eyed Virgin Mary holding a blond baby Jesus hung in each bedroom. She protected us and helped us pass our exams but was capable of throttling us at night if we ever told a lie. We had two toilets: an Arabic one and a French one. How I boasted to my friends at school about our French toilet, the bidet, and the bathtub used only for washing our feet before bed. We had a study full of French and Arabic books, a German piano, and an aunt who loved literature and snubbed family members, who knew nothing about symphonies and the classical composers, when they came with seasonal produce from the village. She called them 'vulgar' and refused to sit with them.

I listened to the banter and sarcasm of these rugged men around the dining table, their mouths full of food cooked by Teyta, my grandma, laughing and splattering particles of irony about my aunt's advanced age of thirty-something and still not married. I watched her scrub the table, giving Teyta dirty looks for feeding them, snatching the plates from beneath their chins as they wiped up sauce with bread.

My aunt waited in the study for us after school to check our homework, our music practice, the cleanliness of our nails, and to find out whether I had divulged any family secrets during accidental street encounters with relatives. I had, as a five-year-old, caused a family feud that lasted years. I had mentioned the head lice in a distant aunt's daughter's hair when she invited me over to play.

'Who told you?' the distant aunt asked.

'Mum and my aunt,' I replied. They said I was never to visit.

From that early age, I earned the title of family gossip. The guilt I felt kept me awake at night and drove me to be overly obliging during the day – helping with housework, making coffee for my aunt in the afternoons when she needed it most.

We were my aunt's five children, for she had none of her own. She lived with us, setting the criteria for which friends and family members we were allowed to love. To side with those she disliked was a betrayal of her love.

Teyta, my maternal grandmother – illiterate, tolerant of my aunt's moods – lived mostly in the kitchen. The smell of coffee and cardamom, along with the rhythmic clink of the spoon stirring the kettle, drew me to join her on the terrace at dawn. We watched the mountains rise into the morning light. At the age of six, she taught me to roll her Bafra cigarette, a relic from the Ottoman occupation. She showed me how to light it, take the first puff and follow it with a sip of coffee. She smiled, watching me, her morning companion, cough as I tried to exhale the smoke through my nostrils.

'Don't tell your mother,' she'd say.

She told me stories of her little brother, who died at twenty by the bakery while begging for a loaf of bread.

'Why didn't the baker give him a loaf?' I asked.

'I don't know. *Il Atrak*, the Turks, they were in our country.'

She told me stories of her husband, my grandfather, who worked as an interpreter for the Vichys when they were in Lebanon. My grandfather died following an injection a doctor gave him when a nail pierced his foot. He left Teyta with seven children and no money.

'Why didn't the doctor marry you?' I asked.

'He had to flee the country.'

In that kitchen, I learnt to core zucchinis and stuff them, and cook using fresh cinnamon, nutmeg, aniseed and the seven spices. The fragrance from Teyta's kitchen flowed through the house and onto the street at lunchtime. I knew exactly what awaited me as soon as I reached the front of our apartment building after school. That aroma filtered to the neighbours through their balconies, drawing them to our dining table by pretending they were dropping by to check on how we were. The number of guests was never a problem. Since quantities were not measured, there was always plenty in the pots to go around. The tasty sauces on the plate, mopped up with bread, were the best substitute for seconds.

My mother mostly lived in the dining room, which she converted to a sewing workshop after breakfast. The radio was on all day with Fairuz singing Lebanon in the background. My mother was silent. She pedalled her Singer sewing machine, giving instructions every now and then to the two women helping her. She seemed permanently stressed by a deadline for a client's wedding, a night out at the *Cave des Rois*, or a show at the *Casino du Liban*. How beyond our reach, how foreign, was the world of leisure – and how I longed to be beautiful like my mother's clients, with their chignons, their jewellery, speaking Arabic with a French accent.

Visiting the Beirut districts of my mother's clientele with my aunt felt like travelling to France. She took me to the Capitol, the Rivoli, and the Élysées cinemas. We sat in burgundy and maroon-coloured velvet chairs watching Jane Fonda in *Klute*, Anouk Aimée in *Un Homme et Une Femme*, Jean Gabin in *Les Misérables*, and my aunt's favourite, John Wayne in *How the West Was Won*. That film was also one of my father's favourites. He hailed the superiority of the West and the importance of being part of the West if we wanted to get anywhere in the modern world. However, his pride in our independence from the French created in me a feeling of confusion, an ambivalence towards my country Lebanon as well as the West.

After the movie, I was treated to *chocolat mou* and éclair at the classy French Automatique restaurant, served with a spoon with a long handle to dip into the melted chocolate and a fancy glass of water. Women in miniskirts and platform shoes sat with men in black roll-neck jumpers, holding hands across the table, smoking Gitanes and fancy coloured cigarettes. Waiters in black suits and white shirts stepped around the tables to the music of Yves Montand, Dalida, Charles Aznavour and Patricia Carli.

On Sundays, when my parents could afford it, we travelled to Hamra, Beirut's central district. Though only four kilometres away, Hamra felt like another country. Avenue Verdun and Avenue Charles de Gaulle, with their famous brand shops and *cafés trottoirs* where young Lebanese and Arab intellectuals gathered, drinking, smoking, discussing Sartre and de Beauvoir, George Habash and Che Guevara while writing about the Arab Cause, fashionable at the time. We went to that Beirut for special treats: a chicken-and-garlic sandwich at Marrouch, followed by a walk along the Corniche, with pistachio ice cream from Wared. We stopped by Raoucheh, staring at the giant rock in the middle of the sea, as my father told us stories of desperate young men throwing themselves off the top of it to end their obsession with love. How fit and determined they must've been to climb that enormous structure.

We strolled along the Corniche with other families, honeymooners, men walking hand in hand or eyeing young women, and tourists admiring our city. We bought roasted peanuts, scooped into rolled newspapers from the Sudanese man, and corn cobs from the young southerner turning them on the embers with his bare fingers. We walked the city to witness and to be witnessed, claiming it for a few moments as ours. We returned home refreshed, our senses invigorated, proud to belong to our beautiful capital, Beirut.

§

My home was the suburb of Achrafieh in Beirut, where many residents refused to speak Arabic, insisting instead on French. We, on the other hand, spoke Arabic with loud southern accents. Our father was proud of us. Once the French colonialists left, in 1943, he insisted on reclaiming his Arab heritage, naming his children after poets and figures from classical Arabic literature. My name was that of Juliette from the famous love story of *Qais wa Loubna*. How I loved my name then, hearing it repeated with a welcome surprise and even joy whenever I introduced myself: 'Oh, Qais's lover', or 'Loubna Abdel Aziz, the great Egyptian actress!'

Home was Ghazalieh Street, around the corner from my school, the Jesuits' Holy Hearts Convent, near

Hôpital Prince, where a crippled child sat against the wall. Over the years, I watched him grow into a young man. He would sit, begging, cross-legged on the ground, one arm limp, palm open resting on his thigh, the other hand trembling and outstretched as I passed him on my way to school. However, early one morning, my mother caught him out standing tall and urinating on the school wall.

'Oh, you're not crippled. Liar! You should be working.'

She made him confess with his Kurdish accent to his journey from Turkey to Syria to Lebanon, his inability to find work anywhere, crippled not by his arm but by his place of birth. She then called him a mischievous boy and they laughed.

'May God guard your children,' he said, sitting back down to beg with his fake disability, thanking her for the quarter lira she gave him.

'Poor thing,' she muttered as she dropped us off at school.

Mum understood the young beggar, for she had grown up in poverty, without a father and one of seven children.

Our home on Ghazalieh Street was tough, full of harsh judgements, but also tolerance for the lies told out of necessity. Home was full of paradoxes, normal only to those who grew up understanding the need for complicity, understanding the necessity of the young beggar to deceive and save face.

Home was the lower ground floor of a seven-storey building, opposite the deli owned by Abou Adel, to whom we owed a large debt that spilled over from one month to the next. My father catered for a family of five children and an extended family that dropped by daily, knowing there would be a warm welcome and a hot meal from Teyta's capable hands.

Home was full of friends, laughter, love – and also envy and mistrust. When a teacher living in the neighbourhood learnt about our monthly expenditure on food and the number of visitors we fed, she relayed the information to the school principal, who had been giving my father a discount on school fees. The discount was promptly cancelled. 'I'll take my daughters out and enrol them in government schools.' My father knew our academic excellence was an asset to the school, and the principal wouldn't want to lose us.

The teacher who exposed our lavish diet to the principal was Egyptian. Each time she visited, she would recount how Abdel Nasser had confiscated her family's wealth. 'He gave our hard-earned assets to the primitive, lazy *fellaheen*. We had to smuggle out guineas in my daughters' underwear.' How uncomfortable her daughters would have been sitting on a bunch of coins and jewellery all the way from Alexandria to Beirut, I thought. But we understood why she would betray us. She must've noticed the delight in my father's eyes as he listened to Abdel Nasser's political speeches on the radio, empowering the *fellaheen*, deriding the rich – the fat, lazy bourgeois exploiters of the poor. Even though she loved my Teyta's cooking and used bread to soak up the last drop of yogurt from the *shish barak* plate, we understood. We understood betrayal and envy as much as love and forgiveness.

§

We lived in Dr B'chara's building. He was a well-known orthopaedic surgeon who looked after my aunt's back pain when her illness spread to her bones. He prescribed exercises for her incurable condition. His French wife, also a doctor, never smiled. Her *bonjour* was stiff. How she snarled at her two children in the morning as they ran towards me from the lift. She was France; it was no longer the authority, and she needed to be consoled.

The postman often knocked on our door to deliver letters from pen friends. On the envelopes was my name and address: Mademoiselle Loubna Haikal, Dr B'chara's Building, opposite Abou Adel's deli, Rue Ghazalieh. No numbers. Everything, everyone, had a name and belonged to someone. My pen friend was from Switzerland. Her address was full of numbers beneath her name. I wrote to her in French about my country, 'the Switzerland of the Middle East', about my two brothers, two sisters, my grandma, and my aunt. She sent me photos of her brother and her parents.

I told her about my best friend at school, Josephine, and how we wanted to start a revolution, free the Palestinian refugees from the camps and liberate their land. I asked her to join my revolution. She liked me, and I felt the Western world would like me and join my revolution too. My life seemed bigger than hers – aunts arguing, reading fortunes in coffee cups, going to clairvoyants to erase curses, predict travel and foretell marriage proposals. My mother's dressmaking workshop was a station for news and gossip; an uncle threatening revenge to restore his sister's honour, Dad mediating the release of a relative from jail, or paying a brother's debt – much to my mother's chagrin. Our house was a stopover for a cousin staying a week or two until she could elope with her penniless lover. A world large enough to fill fourteen years of my life.

I was so proud of Lebanon, my Switzerland! At school, we stood tall celebrating our Independence Day, singing our national anthem, proclaiming our loyalty to Lebanon, its apples and snow-covered mountains, its pine forests and cedars. Beneath that pride, we lived a duality. We celebrated our independence while feeling abandoned by our coloniser, arguing with each other, trying to sort out our identities and allegiances. As the Palestinians lost control of Palestine, we weren't sure how long we would be able to avoid the fate of our neighbours. We were looking for a parent country to protect us.

'There's no reason why the Jews from Germany can't live in Palestine with everyone else. No need to divide the land,' my paternal grandmother said. She had a cross and the year 1954 tattooed on her wrist from when she'd gone to the Hajj in Jerusalem.

The shadow of Kissinger in the 60s, as he met with local politicians and officials, brought speculations and uncertainties into our home. My father called him 'The Fox', scheming in the dark, waiting for the right moment to strike. 'He wants to solve the Palestinian refugee problem at our expense and donate our south to Israel.'

Dad sat on a Thursday afternoon tuning the radio, trying to control interference, turning it towards the mountains or west towards the sea. He listened to the speeches of his hero, Nasser, calling for a united Arab nationalism. As Nasser spoke to the poor, the *fellaheen*, and the disenfranchised, giving them hope, he also empowered my father. He would have liked to name his eldest son Jamal or Nasser, but knowing how unstable his little Lebanon was, how power shifts could demonise any name – and at times an entire village – he chose to name his children after heroes from his beloved Arab literature. He knew that, with the fall of Palestine and the rise of Palestinian commandos in Lebanon, the country was set to become the next Vietnam.

§

For twenty years, my father worked as the accountant for an American-Lebanese tourism company. He had dealt with the Americans. His mother, my grandmother, had worked for their evangelical missionaries, teaching English in their schools. She was the editor of their newsletter, distributed all over the Arab world. She had converted from Maronite to Evangelical, securing a free education for her five boys. Once they graduated, she reclaimed her

Maronite faith. 'They thought I was giving them five evangelical men,' she'd say when she visited us, pulling out handfuls of barley sugar from her pocket, along with her latest play, novel or her translation of Shakespeare's *King Lear*.

I grew up in a house where Che Guevara, Castro, Gaddafi and the Palestinian guerrillas were heroes. We looked to Iraq as an example of an open society, with a rich culture, a highly educated population, and low unemployment. In our living room, friends and relatives discussed the fate of Lebanon, Israel's eyes on our Litani River, our soil, and our mountains. At school, we debated the legitimacy of the Palestinian commandos launching attacks on Israel from our soil, endangering us with war. I wrote my first poem at the age of eleven about the Palestinian woman fighter defending her olive trees. That poem was published in the left-wing *Al Ahdath* newspaper.

On 6 June 1967, my father switched off the radio, walked to the dining room, and announced: 'Egypt lost the war. Nasser's generals betrayed him. They will be facing the gallows.'

'What do you expect from the Arabs? They're all traitors anyway,' my mother replied.

That year, 1967, was full of defeats. My aunt, at thirty-six, lost her battle with cancer six months after her diagnosis. Her brother, my uncle – tall, handsome, the youngest of his siblings – had been working in Qatar's oil fields for three years. He used to return for a week or two with presents: musical ashtrays and a statue of a Black woman's torso. He brought joy and a sense of plenty. He died three months after his sister, of leukaemia. A dark cloud hung over our house. Black were my mother's and grandmother's clothes, and black was my father's view of Lebanon's future.

§

Not long after Nasser's announcement, we were listening to Shahrazad's story of Sindibad the Mariner on the radio, when my father walked in from work and asked, 'Who wants to go to Australia?', all of us children answered in unison, 'Me.' So did Teyta, eager to leave Beirut – the funeral processions, the solemn bands playing funeral marches, the horses cloaked in black, the coffins swaying and waltzing on the shoulders of young men, the wailing women bidding farewell to a son who never got to be a groom.

'I'll come with you. I can't live without the children,' Teyta said, looking at me.

'You will come too,' I reassured her.

My mother remained silent. Her head down, she pedalled her Singer sewing machine.

'What do you say?' my father pressed.

'You're dreaming. Who will pay the fares of eight people?'

As Shahrazad's story was ending, Rimsky-Korsakov's music swelled, opening up vast seas in our imaginations. How proud we were of our Shahrazad, inspiring the Russian composer, enchanting the world – a world we were eager to conquer.

We listened with anticipation to Dad recounting how he'd met an Australian tourist of Lebanese origin that day, Barry Redmond. 'Apparently, they change your name to make you a proper Australian,' he said. He had left Lebanon as Bou Remmeneh and became Redmond in Australia.

'Stop fantasising. Carting five children into the unknown,' my mother interrupted.

'America says Lebanon is no longer safe for tourists.' My father spoke about America as if it were an old acquaintance. 'America is shutting down the company in a couple of weeks. I'll be out of work. How will we afford school fees? University fees? Our oldest wants to study medicine. Your dressmaking barely covers the food bill. This Redmond, Bou Remmeneh fellow tells me education in Australia is free. They are desperate for children. We have five. He promised he would be our guarantor. We have nothing here so we have nothing to lose.'

'Let's go, let's go,' we children insisted, excited at the idea of travel.

'He advised me to go first, alone, to see if I liked it. If I did, you and the children would follow – your mother too.'

'I'm ready,' Teyta said, eager to escape her own grief.

I felt safe. As long as Teyta was with us, we would remain a family. We would be strong.

My father went to his mother, asking for his inheritance – a piece of land in the southern village of Iktanit, south of Saida.

'Don't go,' his mother pleaded. 'Once you leave, you and your children will become foreigners. No one will know them. Your roots are here.'

The word in Arabic for foreigner is *ghareeb*, a word that stems from *gharb*, meaning the West, where the sun sets. My grandmother's siblings had all migrated to America at the turn of the 20th century, escaping famine under the Ottomans. They returned to Lebanon as tourists, strangers in their mother's land and to their mother's tongue.

'I have to go and I'll only come back as a millionaire. I'd rather be poor in a foreign country than in my own.'

Having lost his job, my father felt belittled by his relatives offering him work far beneath his status – a junior clerk, a salesman, a receptionist at a hotel.

'I'd rather sweep the streets in Australia than be at the mercy of relatives,' I overheard him tell my mother.

A few months later, my father, at thirty-nine, became a 20th-century Sindibad. He left his family on an adventure to the land of no return, as his mother called Australia. We were impatient to join him. His letters home contained money – fifty-dollar notes that looked like Monopoly money – along with photos of koalas and kangaroos, lush gardens, villas owned by ordinary people, and, more importantly, tales of how he impressed the local Australians.

A year later, our lounge room was stripped of furniture, sold to relatives for next-to-nothing, replaced with boxes packed with our books, clothes, photographs and, most precious of all, cassette tapes of Fairuz, Charles Aznavour, Sabah and Dalida. Our piano – my father's gift to my eldest sister – was swaddled in woollen blankets and doonas. In the years to come, its melodies would drown all feelings of loneliness.

Teyta packed the coffee grinder and roaster, the marble mortar and pestle for pounding meat to make our favourite Sunday dish, *kibbi*. I reminded her to bring the zucchini corer and her rosary beads, though she found the latter had become useless since the day she farewelled her two children.

An acquaintance who had lived in Australia before returning to Lebanon advised us to bring shoes. In her words, 'Australians have poor taste, they're backward when it comes to fashion.' We laughed as it confirmed to us that our Beirut was the capital of fashion and style. She also said that women there are more like men, they walk barefoot and fight in the street, pulling each other's hair. My mother, who had a standing appointment at Salon Elle for her *coup de peigne* every Saturday morning, asked if there were hairdressers.

'Yes, but they are mainly women, and they're not great cutters. Make sure you get a haircut here before you leave.'

We didn't want to believe her stories of Australia. We didn't want to be disappointed before we had even arrived. But we were certain of one thing – Salon Elle would still be here when we returned in a few years.

My mother could no longer wait to leave Beirut that August of 1969. Since my father's departure, our apartment had become surrounded by construction work, eclipsing the sight of any mountain or sun from our terrace. Dust filled our lungs and clung to our clothes. Teyta and I threw buckets of water on the terrace to get rid of the dust before we lit our first cigarette.

That year, 8 pm curfews were introduced in preparation for the possibility of war. We closed our shutters, turned off the lights. We children played hide-and-seek. We weren't worried. Why would anyone wage war on our apples and olives? We never took my father's predictions seriously: 'Lebanon will no longer be the Switzerland of the Middle East. With our mountains and forests, it's an ideal place for guerrilla warfare. It will become the next Vietnam.'

The imposed curfew, then, was a time for us children to re-enact *Combat!*, our favourite American TV series about the Second World War, or to play 'Cowboys and Indians'. We never imagined that, one day, we would become the Indians – fighting in vain to defend our history, our heritage, our very existence.

On our last day in Dr B'chara's building, our lounge-room flooded. The miserly landlord refused to repair the rusted water pipes, so we waded through scalding water. Buckets, mops, and blankets to protect the piano were brought out as we cursed the doctor who, for years, had wanted us to vacate in order to raise the rent. From the seventh floor, his mother gave us her own farewell – a bucket of urine dumped over our little garden. My father had paid a fortune trying to grow grass on that patch of soil. Gardeners had brought every kind of fertiliser, planted seed after seed, but nothing took root. They blamed the dry soil despite Dad's constant watering. Now the reason for his failed endeavour became evident.

We left, never looking back, fleeing the stench of the old woman's urine, the cloying perfume of funeral wreaths, fearing Beirut's dust would turn us into dust, and that the heat of August 1969 would trap us forever.

Port Beirut was crowded with relatives, and faces I barely knew, offering farewells because they owed it to my father who had helped them with employment or a family dispute. My school friends were there too, laughing, teasing: 'You'll come back speaking Arabic with an English accent!'

'Please write. Tell us what it's like. Don't forget us.' Josephine was crying.

I felt I was at a party thrown in my honour. The only thing I could think of was not so much of leaving, but how this journey, a short excursion, would transform me into a trendy Westerner and then I would belong to all of Beirut. No street would feel exclusive or foreign. I would no longer be out of place in its rich suburbs. All of Lebanon with its trendy cafés and boutiques would be mine.

§

In 1969, the way out of the Mediterranean for our ship, the *Angelina Lauro*, was through the Strait of Gibraltar. Nasser had closed the Suez Canal.

For forty days and forty nights, we ate pasta, watched the same band in the evening playing the same music. We learnt English from an Australian teacher in the morning and watched her in the afternoon being courted by the ship's captain. We stared at the two of them as they kissed and cuddled.

'Don't look,' Teyta pulled me away, fearing I'd adopt bad morals.

On the deck we had fun making friends with European passengers, most of whom had their fares subsidised by the Australian government. They were the immigrants Australia wanted. Our fares were not subsidised. Our whiteness was still questionable. We needed to prove ourselves worthy to Australia.

The five of us children and Teyta were a curious, interesting lot – the only Lebanese passengers on board.

My mother spent the trip in her cabin, dealing with severe sea sickness, unresponsive to medication. Yet she managed to sew a dress for my youngest sister, who won the national costume parade competition as the ship crossed the equator.

But the fun would not last much longer. Once in the Indian Ocean, the ship began rolling from side to side. Ropes were installed on the deck for passengers to cling to. Huge waves crashed over us. We could see only water out of our cabin's window. Then came the announcement that the ship's stabiliser was broken. The threat of capsizing became real. The Italian passengers took out their rosary beads, knelt on the deck and prayed. Teyta found use for her rosary beads again and rushed off to find my youngest sister. In her panic, she tripped and broke her wrist. The morning English classes were suspended. Neither the teacher nor the captain were to be found.

On the third day, a calm blue reappeared and the band restarted its evening music.

We landed in Fremantle, where some passengers disembarked, and the ship's stabiliser was repaired. The next morning, we headed for Melbourne. The high waves of the Bass Strait forced my mother back to her cabin. All we children could think of was our appearance on arrival, and the crowds that would be welcoming us at Port Melbourne.

My two sisters and I put on our new dresses and new shoes. My brothers wore their new suits. For the first time, since we left Beirut, I saw Teyta in a colourful dress.

I had overheard her a few weeks earlier tell my mother, 'I'm thinking of leaving behind my black clothes and wearing colourful dresses. What do you think?'

'Why not,' Mum said.

'Maybe I'll dye my hair too. No one would know me there.'

§

In her new floral dress and with her arm still in plaster, Teyta looked different, less mine.

We walked out of the ship into an icy September evening, proud, joyful, eager to meet Dad and the Australian public waiting to welcome us into their homes with bouquets, banquets and celebrations.

At Port Melbourne, a quiet sadness filled the air, with none of the commotion we experienced in Port Beirut. The customs officers greeted us with an expedient hostility. I spotted Dad smiling in the distance. His eyes shone with joy and anticipation. He pointed us out to the three men waiting with him and all of them walked towards us.

'Goodness, he's put on so much weight,' I overheard Mum say to Teyta.

'It's okay.' Teyta nudged her. 'Poor thing, he's so eager to see you – go and kiss him.'

In Beirut, Mum would've carefully monitored the portions on Dad's plate. We weren't to know that we would all gain weight in Australia. Whether it was the comfort, or the distraction from boredom we found in cooking and eating, or the abundance of meat we consumed, our bodies were the first to expand and change.

'I was missing the family. I ate to distract myself,' I overheard Dad tell Mum later when she asked him why he had put on so much weight.

At Port Melbourne that cold September night, I saw Dad and Mum kiss and hug publicly for the first time. Perhaps in his year in Australia, Dad had become a Westerner.

'Did you get a house? Furniture? Will there be enough beds?' Mum asked.

'There's everything. You'll see,' Dad replied.

I could tell from the way he turned away from her that he wanted to avoid further questions.

He introduced us to Najib, his Lebanese friend, a neighbour from his childhood in Saida. Najib's name changed to Jim in Australia. Dad's other two companions, Chris and Bob, were his bosses at

PurePak, the packaging company where he worked as a clerk. They asked us to repeat our names and spell them out. They couldn't pronounce mine. My name lost its meaning with our arrival that evening.

'Beautiful family, Ed,' Chris said, putting his arm around Dad's shoulders. Our dad, Edward, had become Ed. I looked at him and tried to recover the dad I knew, the one called Abou Hadi, customary in Lebanon to be known as the father of his first-born son. Though his increased weight made him look bigger, his status shrank with the abbreviation of his name. How quickly Edward became Ed. Would our transformation begin with our names as well? I wondered what mine would become.

Eight of us were squeezed into two cars and driven for more than an hour along flat, dark, deserted roads lined with broken-down cars and bright Coca-Cola signs.

'Where are the kangaroos? The koalas?' my brothers asked.

'And if someone gets hungry along the way? What do they eat?' Teyta asked, looking for the men roasting corncobs and chestnuts by the roadside.

The roads were desolate. Not one living soul in sight. Not one poster introducing us to a local face, a leader, a politician, or even to a singer. For a whole endless hour, no signs of humanity or human activity anywhere aside from the broken-down cars on the sides of the asphalt roads. Najib did not honk his horn once. It was unnecessary. The road was dead-straight all the way to a suburb called Dandenong.

'Where are all the people?' Teyta asked Najib.

'Well…' he said, stretching out the word, turning his head away from the road to look at us. 'Well, people go home to sleep and get up early the next day to go to the factories.'

'Yes, but don't they want to see the face of God, or another human, after work?'

'Here, everyone waits for the weekend to go out. But the problem in this country, there are too many people killed driving on the road every weekend, at least ten or twelve, sometimes even twenty people.' He said that while turning his head towards us seated in the back. We became anxious at the possibility of becoming a road statistic.

'Strange that with so few cars on the roads there could still be so many casualties,' my mother said.

Teyta fell silent. She, who wanted to escape all reminders of death, seemed lost in thought at his comment.

Najib had lived in Melbourne for twenty years. Twenty was a big number, a lifetime away from

Lebanon, away from my friends. We would never stay away from Lebanon for that long.

He spoke about the weekend, the drinking habits of the Australians and the pubs, the Lebanese clothing manufacturers who had become millionaires, milk bar owners, business owners. Material pursuits and commerce seemed of paramount importance in the community. This mindset was foreign to us, incompatible with our academic ambitions.

'This is a free country,' he continued, interspersing English words with anglicised Arabic ones. We laughed later on at the way he spoke, about the number of road victims, the *bazeniss* (businesses), *faketir* (factories), the people going to bed early and the empty roads, but mostly at the name Bob. Bobie was the name we used for dogs in Lebanon.

§

The house was on Heatherton Road, number one thousand and something. We couldn't have imagined such a long road; it would've taken us from Beirut all the way to Damascus.

An old lady, a widow, Jamileh, opened the door. 'Take your shoes off,' she said to the eight of us appearing at her door. Her house was covered in wall-to-wall white carpet. We left our new, shiny shoes at the entrance and followed her with our suitcases to the bedrooms. She left us there and went back to her rocking chair to watch TV and to knit.

'She's Palestinian,' my mother muttered.

'Yes, but she's very nice,' my father replied. 'You'll like her.'

'Now we are the refugees. Why didn't you tell me? And you didn't buy furniture. I don't want to live with a stranger.'

'I'll explain it all later,' my father replied. 'People drink tea here. I'll make us all a cup.'

I laughed with my siblings at the idea of tea, drunk in Lebanon only as a remedy, with many spoons of sugar to relieve abdominal pain and diarrhoea.

Now in Jamileh's loungeroom for the first time in our lives, we children sat on the floor, a demeaning position in Beirut. We watched the outrage on Mum's face from the shock of having to live in someone else's home – worse still, in a Palestinian woman's home.

Jamileh, who had long swapped her morning Lebanese coffee for Nescafé, and drank tea with milk in the afternoon, lectured us on Australia.

'Here, unlike in your country, the law applies to both the rich and the poor. Workers get annual leave and sick pay. It's a British system,' she emphasised, proud of having worked with the British in Palestine.

In Dandenong, for a short period of time, Teyta and Mum made friends with Jamileh. Teyta was happy. There were no signs of death or mourning anywhere in the deserted streets. Death seemed to have no place amongst the living. Here in Australia she could stop grieving and start to live. She wanted to look like the old women in Australia, to wear bright clothes, lipstick, have purple hair, and colourful hats.

A week after our arrival, I started at Dandenong Girls High School. There, I drew crowds of girls around me – examining me, touching my curly black hair, curious about my name, where I came from, what language I spoke.

When they heard I spoke Arabic at home, they seemed confused and asked about the number of wives my father had, the desert, the camels, the tents, and how I found living in a house here in Australia. They seemed incredulous at whatever information my broken, almost non-existent English relayed to them. They asked the same questions over and over, to find out if my answers would change and the truth would finally slip out.

Initially, I enjoyed the attention. But then, once the girls found out all about me, came isolation. I was no longer of any interest to them. I, who had felt privileged to have grown up in Beirut and proud of my culture, felt diminished by their ignorance. Their assumptions were too difficult to shift with my poor English. There were no other Lebanese students, no knowledgeable ally who could support my narrative of my country.

I stood at recess for the first time on the margin, invisible, unable to understand the nuances of jokes and intimacies, missing my friends, trapped in a mistaken identity. I felt dumb, small and afraid. I was on alert, watching out for every gesture, every facial expression indicating I might be an object of derision.

I couldn't wait to return home to my siblings. There in the bedroom, away from Jamileh's gaze, my siblings and I took our frustrations out on the 'Australians'. We mimicked their drawn-out accents, their sounds and gestures, their 'G'day, mate'. We laughed – how we laughed at their names, how they shortened them to one syllable, we laughed away the sadness and loneliness we felt in the daytime, where we were called 'New Australians'.

At the end of the year, a teacher, having learnt that I had studied ballet, invited me to perform a dance from *Coppélia*. I wore my pointe shoes from Lebanon. On stage, I was visible again. Parents congratulated me. I felt respected, loved. I remembered what it was like to be Loubna.

Every Saturday Mum and Dad went to Victoria Market, returning with boxes of apples and oranges, and a whole side of lamb that they carved for *kibbi*, *kafta* and stews. Teyta complained about the smell of the meat, the tasteless apples, the enormous size of zucchinis and cucumbers. She and Mum spent the weekend cooking, filling the house with aromas of cinnamon, cardamom, allspice – trying to recreate the tastes of home.

'You're using too much water – we've just come out of a drought. I can't walk anywhere, boxes of fruit and veggies are everywhere,' Jamileh grumbled as she tripped over a box of apples.

'Drought? Have we come to Africa?' Teyta muttered as she helped Jamileh off the floor.

Jamileh scoffed. 'When I first came, I had to use the same water to bathe and wash my clothes. You're lucky you don't have to go out to the toilet at night like I had to.'

On Sunday afternoons, Jamileh sat in the corner, on her rocking chair, knitting, watching her home transform into chaos. The eight of us were sprawled across the lounge room watching World Wide Wrestling on

TV – Mario Milano, the great Italian wrestler, and Wadi Ayoub exercising his Egyptian deadlock on Ken 'Killer' Dunlop. How vindicated we felt when the 'New Australian' triumphed over the 'Real Australian'. We cheered, rolling across the carpet in delight.

Jamileh could not bear the noise. Her home was no longer her sanctuary. She had become a refugee in her own home. It had been invaded by five giggling, rowdy children and she thought we were making fun of her.

'I can't deal with you Lebanese anymore! You are rude. You think you own everything.'

She threatened to call the police if we didn't vacate within two weeks.

'This is the law,' Najib explained to my father. 'Here, the landlord owes nothing to the tenants – even if you have nowhere to go. In Lebanon, it's different. A landlord must provide alternative accommodation or key money to evict a tenant.' We learnt then that, in Australia, law overrules compassion.

No landlord would rent a house to a family of eight. Buying was the only option. Dad insisted on living away from the Lebanese community gathered around the Maronite church, in Carlton and Fitzroy. He saw these suburbs as ghettos for factory workers and milk bar owners who had come to make money and had no interest in intellectual or academic pursuits. He wanted to live amongst Real Australians, to become one of them – or better than them – and raise the name of Lebanon through his high-achieving children.

Chris and Bob, his two bosses, helped him find a house in Templestowe, near their own. They lent him the deposit for the $20,000 home – no papers signed, just trusting Ed's word.

From Jamileh's house in Dandenong, a suburb where no human was seen in the street, we moved to Templestowe, a similar suburb on the other side of Melbourne. We occupied a suburban villa, just like the ones in the postcards Dad had sent us: a big garden, a fence, four bedrooms, and a mortgage that forced Mum, once again, to turn the dining room into a sewing room. We were the only New Australians in the area.

We noticed that neighbours never invited each other into their homes but spoke across the fence for hours. 'People here want their privacy,' Dad explained. 'They don't share their personal sorrows or joys, unlike us. We are warm-blooded, emotional. They're not. But that's why the West is more advanced than we are.'

In Templestowe, we learnt that privacy was more important than hospitality and friendliness. On Saturday mornings, the sound of lawnmowers and the smell of cut grass filled the air, waking Teyta, who sneezed and wiped her burning, watering eyes.

Saturday afternoon was a highlight for my father. He lit the incinerator in the backyard, feeding it newspapers, fallen leaves, cardboard boxes. He stood there for hours, staring into the flames, trying to break the monotony of a weekend with no visitors, and the weight of an enormous debt, wondering if he had made the right decision to leave Lebanon.

One Sunday, to break the boredom of the weekend, Mum and Teyta decided to go on a family picnic. They packed *kibbi*, *shish kebab* and tabbouleh. We walked to the end of the street, where the nature strip was large enough for us to place our picnic rug and food. No sooner had we laid down the food than the neighbour appeared with his German shepherd. He ordered us off his nature strip despite my father's invitation to try our food with a drink of Pepsi in case he got indigestion. According to Dad, cracked wheat can cause severe gastric symptoms in the Real Australians.

But the man refused. We repacked our picnic and walked home, confused by the hostility of a man who had felt the need to bring a guard dog to face down a family with five children and a grandmother.

We learnt the value of the backyards and how much the Real Australians feared us as they drew their blinds closed when we walked past their houses, admiring the gardens and calming their dogs. We learnt how much they valued the company of their dogs – and what it was like to be treated as foreigners. And yet they needed us five children. Our number had granted us a visa to this country.

Soon, my parents realised that no matter how much they saved on food at Victoria Markets, they were unable to keep up with the mortgage repayments. My two older siblings had to go to work. I insisted on working too. I wanted to contribute. I was so proud when they finally agreed.

I had a string of jobs where I underperformed due to my very basic English: as a salesgirl at Myer in the men's pyjamas and dressing gowns department, dealing with older women asking for fabrics I'd never heard of; as a switchboard operator, receiving calls and connecting executives to secretaries and workers with names that sounded all the same; then as a tea lady, a girl Friday... all while attending night school for Year 11 and spending Saturdays at the Victorian Ballet School, pursuing my childhood fantasy of becoming a prima ballerina.

As the year passed, my mother's sewing business flourished. She sewed evening dresses for the exclusive salon Le Louvre on Collins Street, catering for artists and the women of high society. She earned fifty dollars per dress, as much as my father's weekly wage. This secured the mortgage repayments. I was then able to return to school full-time to finish the last term of Year 11 at Templestowe High School.

At school, teachers had no interest in dealing with this new girl who spoke little English and would most likely have to repeat the year. They sat me at the back of the classroom. I enjoyed the challenge of proving their assumptions wrong and excelled in all the science subjects. I was soon promoted to the front of the class, sharing my maths solutions with struggling students and falling in love with the Chemistry teacher who looked like Rock Hudson. Despite feeling nervous and losing concentration every time he looked at me, I managed to pass the exams.

Lonely and in love I looked for Josephine in the faces of other students, hoping to find her. I stood with my peers at recess, silent, laughing when they laughed, mimicking their Australian expressions without understanding them. I craved the intimacies of my friendships in Lebanon. I wanted to go back. I cried myself to sleep. The feeling of invisibility intensified on weekends, and I felt that had I died, no one would have cared or noticed.

During the week, with my parents out working, Teyta was left home alone. No one knocked on our door for a coffee or a meal with her. The days were endless. She waited all afternoon by the fence for me to come from school. She welcomed me with a smile and a hot meal.

No one had time to take Teyta to the hairdresser to dye her hair, nor take her shopping to buy new clothes. Church on Sunday was the only outing she could ask for, even though she had already lost her faith in a just God. My older brother, having just got his licence, was asked to drive Teyta to the Maronite church in Carlton one Sunday morning.

On their way back from church a car driven by a man without a driving licence crashed into them. I had been studying for my HSC exams that afternoon when I heard my mother crying in her bedroom. Despite all the questioning by my father, my brother couldn't remember what had happened. He was in shock. My parents didn't understand the impact of that accident on their son, which took our Teyta's life.

After the accident, my brother sat blankly, staring for hours by the fireplace, preoccupied and unable to speak. The once gregarious eighteen-year-old, studying electronic engineering at RMIT, grew withdrawn, consumed and haunted by his Teyta's death. Helplessly, we watched him transform, until he ceased to exist as we once knew him.

The psychiatrists blamed my parents for my brother's delusions, and hallucinations. We carried the loss and the stigma, trying not to look back. We were barely able to handle the present.

I wonder now, had Teyta dyed her grey hair, would the ambulance paramedics have worked harder to resuscitate this migrant woman who couldn't speak English, and who looked much older than her sixty-seven years?

§

My high marks in the HSC exam granted me entry into medical school, a career that had never featured in my dreams. But the seven of us in the Haikal family had become one. One unit trying not just to survive but, if possible, to succeed. We children wanted to make our parents happy, reward them for their hard work and, if need be, sacrifice our own dreams to fulfil theirs. The success of one was claimed by all. I owed it to my parents to shelve my dream of dance and theatre and become a successful doctor. The arts were valued as hobbies, not as reliable careers. Besides, my father wanted his daughters to be independent women who didn't need the financial support of a spouse.

How proud my parents were when I chose to do medicine. I overheard them talking about my achieving all that they had come to Australia for.

All through my university studies, however, I battled with loneliness and, in retrospect, I think isolation that led to depression. Though I was popular, surrounded by students who sought my company as they found me interesting, funny and exotic, I was unable to connect with their outings, holidays, and drinking at the pub on a Friday evening. I couldn't share with anyone the revolution I dreamt of that tied me to Josephine. In Australia, Arabs were labelled as dirty and Palestinians as terrorists. Most of all, they couldn't understand how I could be happy living at home with my parents. 'Don't you want to be independent?' they'd ask.

It seemed strange to my adolescent Lebanese immigrant self that anyone would want to live away from their parents. I learnt about the Australian family unit and the generation gap, privacy and independence, the individual, and looking after oneself. But the self I was then was lonely, and I didn't know how to look after it by myself.

At university, I remained trapped in that perceived exotic persona. All ambition for a just world, for Palestinians and refugees, was met with sarcasm and 'You're on the side of the terrorists'. In 1972, the Munich massacre left no room for any explanation of the Palestinian Nakba or of life in Palestine before the creation of Israel, as described by our Palestinian relatives in Lebanon.

In order to normalise myself, I had many parties at home, inviting students over to a night of Lebanese music, dancing and food. I think I needed to be seen in context. They loved the Arabic music and the food. However, though I was the centre of attention, the food and music reaffirmed their perception of me as the exotic girl they had imagined.

I soon became afraid to shed that persona. Loneliness frightened me. So did dying while still alive. I didn't enjoy the outings to the pub, but I forced myself to go and drink, to remain relevant.

My longing to return to Lebanon intensified with time. But it was out of the question – even for a visit – initially due to lack of money and later, in 1975, because of the war.

'It will only last a couple of weeks,' my father had said when the fighting began. But the weeks stretched into months, and the months into years. We watched in disbelief as our beautiful country was destroyed, becoming the Vietnam of the Middle East, just as my father had predicted. Lebanon finally became newsworthy. At dinner parties, I was asked, 'Why are you people so violent? You must feel lucky to be here!'

I could no longer wait to get out of Melbourne. I chose to do my final-year medical elective in the next-best destination to Beirut: a hospital in Paris.

There, I wandered along Avenue Charles de Gaulle, Rue Verdun, Rue de Rivoli, the Champs-Élysées. I was at home in Beirut's street names, surrounded by a history I had studied at school and the names of writers whose books I had read and loved. I felt alive again. There, I wanted to reclaim lost time.

I met Lebanese students who had fled the civil war. I too had fled a different kind of war. Though my homesickness faded, Lebanon was still where I wanted to be and to renew my life. However, with Beirut's airport closed and the war intensifying, I had no choice but to return to Melbourne and finish my final year.

§

My first trip back to Lebanon was in 1984, fifteen years after I had left. By then, I was a fully qualified doctor working in a hospital but still aching to return home. My relationship with Australia was a purely functional one. I lived in a comfortable house, owned a car, earned a good wage, and could afford nice holidays. Yet my spirit was elsewhere.

By the time I arrived in Lebanon, it had endured

nine years of war and had lost any sense of itself. Beirut was divided between East and West. Hamra was unrecognisable. Wared and Marrouch, the souks, the cinemas had disappeared. Bullet holes ravaged the buildings. In Achrafieh, I felt disoriented. Salon Elle had disappeared. I had to ask a passer-by for Ghazalieh Street. I searched for Dr B'chara's building, where we used to live, and for the Egyptian teacher's apartment. My school looked out of place, as if translocated into another suburb. The local shop where we bought roasted peanuts after school, the few trees where we sheltered from the rain, even the footpaths, had disappeared. No matter how hard I looked at the faces in the streets, hoping to recognise a school friend, they remained foreign.

I insisted that a relative take me to our old apartment in Dr B'chara's building. A middle-aged woman there welcomed me. She had a warm smile and kind eyes. A photo of her son, who had been killed in a bomb blast while driving from the mountains to East Beirut, hung on the wall where our piano had once stood. Sadness filled this house the same way it had the year my aunt and uncle died. The woman, dressed in black, led me to her late son's bedroom – the room where I had once slept beside my Teyta. There was no trace of me or of my past.

My relatives questioned why I had come back. They told me stories of sleeping in bomb shelters, of sharing their beds with rats. I had no right to feel lonely, exiled in the safety of Australia. I became a burden as they tried to protect me from bombs and drive me to safety.

Having left Melbourne with the intention of living in Lebanon despite the war, I packed my bags two weeks later, and flew back, feeling more like a foreigner there than in Australia.

Back in Melbourne, my older sister and I – both doctors now – set up a general practice. The clinic reconnected me to the Lebanese community. New immigrants, refugees who had no English came to our surgery seeking treatment for their ill-health as well as help with their relatives' illnesses back home, in war-ravaged Lebanon.

While in general practice, I sought an alternative connection to Lebanon through the art world: theatre, acting and directing, and eventually producing a community play, a folkloric ballet, *Near Saida*, for the Melbourne Spoleto Arts Festival. Musicians, composers, set and costume designers, poets and dancers from the Arab community brought their creativity to the production. We were all eager to connect to our artistic and cultural heritage. *Near Saida* was a re-enactment of the Lebanon we couldn't go back to – a love story set against the backdrop of the war that was ravaging our country at that time. On a personal level, the play was my way of feeling alive and surviving in Melbourne.

For my parents, a new opportunity arose – the chance to open a restaurant. My father, a clerk trapped in meaningless paperwork with nothing left to look forward to in life, was revived. He woke up at four every morning, eager to embrace the day – and Australia. He named the restaurant Almazett, after the traditional Lebanese *mezze* dishes. There, he spoke to customers about his beloved Lebanon, his country before the war, the one we were all proud of. He was an intuitive marketing expert, and people loved the food before it arrived at the table.

My mother, like her mother before her, was a wonderful cook. She gave up dressmaking. With the help of her sister, who had fled the war with her three children, they ran the kitchen. The waiting time for a booking stretched to six weeks – unless the customer wanted a table in the kitchen, which soon became prime seating. Dad's 'insurance against hunger' menu offered more than just quality – it embodied the generosity and warmth of a true Lebanese home. His general knowledge, eloquence and wisdom attracted politicians, TV and radio personalities, writers and local as well as international actors. They came to converse with Edward. Alan Alda from *M*A*S*H* sent a basket of flowers after dinner with a card: 'Thank you for making my taste buds smile.'

Almazett became a landmark in Melbourne. My father had finally succeeded. Now, he was ready to return to Lebanon.

'I'm going back to die. You are all educated and independent,' he said on his way to the airport. 'There's nothing left for me to do. My mission is accomplished.'

I knew then that Dad had accomplished only a part of his mission. The car accident that had taken our Teyta's life never stopped haunting my brother. My father could not bring his son back. Guilt chased him out of Australia, away from his son, back to Lebanon. Dad left as a successful immigrant, but a defeated father, vowing never to return to Australia.

He phoned the day before he was due to return: 'I've visited every corner of Lebanon, Syria, Jordan and Palestine. Palestine truly is a bride,' he said. He was quoting the Polish Jew who, upon first seeing Palestine, had remarked, 'The bride is beautiful, but she has a bridegroom already.'

I couldn't wait to hear more about Dad's journey.

I wanted to know if Lebanon had recovered enough from the war for me to return. The following day, early in the morning, as we were getting ready to pick him up from the airport, the phone rang. The message was short, my uncle's voice choked with grief.

The road to Iktanit, our village in the south where my father's parents were buried, was closed due to the Israeli occupation. He was laid to rest in an unmarked grave in the cemetery of the church in Beirut where he married.

I returned many times, trying to settle in Lebanon, searching for my father's grave as well as the home of the fourteen-year-old girl in Ghazalieh Street. The cemetery lay abandoned, and I was never able to find the graveyard keeper. The war had erased all traces of my father's life and of his death.

In Lebanon, I felt lost, unmoored. Back in Melbourne, the excessive material comfort highlighted the vacuousness of my life and my feeling of alienation. It wasn't until I moved to Sydney – with a partner and a child – that I found an anchor. Within the chaotic street life that resembled Beirut's, and the Pacific Ocean that beckoned me for my daily walks, I found a restful connection.

Approaching forty and now the mother of three boys, fulfilling my own dream of writing gained an unprecedented urgency. My father, a gifted writer, had kept postponing his own dream with the words, 'One day, I am going to write.' But he left too soon.

As a child, he had encouraged me, making the task of writing feel possible. 'One book,' he would say, 'that's all it takes. One book and you can change the world.' Karl Marx, Harper Lee, Francoise Sagan – they wrote one book, just the one. Having a partner willing to support my new adventure gave me the courage to take up the pen. I found the confidence to claim the language, English, which until then I had used only to write other people's medical histories and diagnoses. It had held no space for my own story.

As I wrote more in English, the language became an interesting new friend with whom I could explore stories of migration, and of all the becomings and confrontations in a new society. Travelling through this deep, wondrous, and enchanting forest of writing, I found a more authentic way to settle.

§

Fifty-four years have passed since the fourteen-year-old girl landed in Port Melbourne aboard the *Angelina Lauro*. Australia has changed and I have too. My sense of justice – whether it was protecting a classmate from a bullying teacher or advocating for the return of Palestinian refugees to their homes – remains unchanged. It has driven me to join many causes: for Aboriginal rights, and more recently, in the fight against climate change, to ensure a healthier planet for all, particularly for future generations.

The memories of the first fourteen years of my life become more vivid as time goes by – and especially now, since 2024, as I watch Beirut and the South being destroyed yet again. I cling to those memories in protest of their erasure with each bomb that falls. I hold close my memories of Achrafieh, where the aunties sipped coffee at dawn on multicoloured balconies, where arches led to quiet gardens with the ever-present statue of the Virgin Mary, and ceramic-tiled staircases with arabesques and geometric shapes alluding to the stars. Teyta, my aunt, and my uncle visit me at the slightest prompt: when I make my morning coffee, when I sit at the piano, when my eye catches a French book that travelled with us on the *Angelina Lauro* years ago, too hard to part with, even though no one will read it again.

I am now a grandmother. I raised my children with the culture and the love I grew up with, keeping the extended family close, as well as the friends who became family. My three sons have been to Lebanon many times. They love their mother's country and never hesitate to correct any prejudice or misconception wherever they are. They are proud to have been brought up in the richness of Lebanese culture. At times they worry about Lebanon and its future more than I could have ever anticipated.

My inability to find my father's grave somehow erased the boundaries of belonging; he is resting in Beirut, my mother and grandmother in Melbourne, and I, for now, am alive in Sydney. I try not to look back too much, lest I turn into a pillar of salt, but I carry Lebanon in my body and soul. Its soil, its history, its cities and people reside within me, silently and side by side with the sounds and landscape of Sydney.

FAREWELL SUDAN
by Mary Hanoun-Khilla

When I woke up on Sunday 2 April 1975, two questions weighed on my mind: Was it truly my last day in Sudan? Would I soon be emigrating to Australia? The clamour in our humble home confirmed my fears. From my bedroom, I could hear the voices of my mother, brothers, aunts, cousins, and neighbours as they discussed preparations for my farewell party that evening. My simple yet cherished life in Sudan was about to end, and the unknown lay ahead.

I remained in bed, lost in a flood of memories. I saw my two brothers competing with me to collect the most raindrops in our buckets from the leaking roof. I saw my little brother's face that I had coloured with my mother's red lipstick and deep brown mascara. I remembered her screaming when she caught us. I recalled the boy next door passing me secret notes that I swallowed as my mother sashayed past in her orange dress. We spent countless hours at our friends and neighbour's homes, jumping over fences to eat, to play and to get up to childish mischief.

At the age of seven, my parents sent me to the Catholic Sisters' Boarding School in Khartoum, the same school where my mother had studied. Unlike her, however, I was required to learn classical Arabic, which had become a prerequisite for university education in Sudan following independence. The school, run by Italian nuns from the Sisters of Verona, was a three- to four-hour drive on the unsealed road from my hometown, Wad Medani. It was among the most esteemed schools in Sudan at the time, where students either sat for the Sudanese High School Certificate or undertook an additional six months of study to qualify for the Oxford or Cambridge High School Certificate. My classmates included the daughters of ambassadors and elite officials, among them Ismail al-Azhari, Sudan's first prime minister after independence from the British.

Despite the immense financial sacrifices my parents had made to send me to the best school in Sudan, I hated it. Life there was regimented, filled with commands and strict discipline, as if we were in the army. At that tender age, I was too young to grasp the depth of separation from home. Now, at twenty-one, I fully understood the pain of leaving behind the warmth of family and the familiarity of home. Today I was leaving for Australia. Yet, I trusted my mother's decision to plant new roots in a foreign land. It was her way of securing a better future for her children.

The countdown to my departure had begun. In a few hours, I would leave my beloved homeland permanently. A suffocating lump grew in my throat, and I felt as if my very essence was being drained, leaving behind a hollow shell.

As I stayed in my room, meticulously packing my suitcase and double-checking my passport and airline ticket, our home bustled like a beehive. Outside my bedroom, the air vibrated with lively chatter, the scraping of chairs being rearranged and the selection songs for that night's celebration. Among them were the popular hits of the three sister singers Amal, Hadia and Hayat Talsam. They were known as Al Balabil, meaning The Nightingales. The three sisters began their singing career in Khartoum in 1971 and one of our favourites was '*Al besaal ma betouh*' – 'Those Who Ask Don't Get Lost'.

Memories continued to surge through me – my school and university friends, my church and its moral teachings, particularly the message of forgiveness that had become my compass in life. The voice of Reverend Father Toumazo echoed in my mind as he preached the Sermon on the Mount, from Matthew Chapters 5, 6, and 7, which he described as the constitution for a life of dignity and grace in forgiveness and love. He told us that Jesus's disciples were asked to do good works and we all must be 'the salt of the earth and light of the world'. I smiled as I recalled the times we teased and asked him whether the Gospel's message of universal love included our boyfriends. He would shake and stutter, unsure how to answer in our conservative society, where such things were unspoken yet tacitly understood. Many of us had boyfriends, but doing good in the world was for me a core value since childhood.

I thought of my volunteering at the Legion of Mary and my weekly visits to Almygoma Orphanage, where unwanted children, mostly born out of wedlock, were left in the dead of night. I pictured baby Ali, his face lighting up whenever he saw me, the way he would bury his tiny head against my chest. What would happen to him once I was gone?

I remembered my elation when our Catholic club netball team won, the thrill of swimming at the Syrian club until midnight on Thursdays, since Fridays were the start of the weekend in Sudan. The festive seasons of Christmas and New Year and Saint Barbara's

Feast, and the indulgence in *karabeej* with *natif*, made from *halva* (soapwort root). As teenagers, we flitted from one club to another – the Armenian, Italian, and Greek community clubs – dancing until dawn, observing who danced with whom and wore what.

Most girls wore a new dress for each festivity, often purchased from England or Lebanon during school holidays. My father, a textile merchant, imported the *toub* from England. The *toub*, made from the finest Sudanese cotton, nine metres in length, was wrapped gracefully over a dress. My father allowed me to use some of his finest *toub* material to design an original dress, much to my mother's disapproval – after all, the remaining fabric was not enough to sell. But my father was indulgent when it came to his only daughter, and my mother would chide him for spoiling me. Perhaps, in his heart, he had known he would not live long.

§

I was sixteen when my father died. My mother worked tirelessly to provide for her three children. She made immense sacrifices, overcame the challenges of a patriarchal society, and was known as the woman who was equal to one hundred men. In return, we were expected to study diligently, with only two choices:

the book or the stick. My neighbour, Balsam, often marvelled at how my mother encouraged me to express myself, while she herself was expected to obey her parents without questions. Balsam would often say, 'Your mum is ahead of her time'. These recollections played in my mind like a slow-motion film; each frame was steeped in sadness.

My mother possessed both foresight and an uncanny ability to read people. She spoke four languages – Arabic, English, Italian and French. She worked as a supervisor in two five-star hotels, the Oasis and the Excelsior, and also as a bridal dressmaker. Her interactions with foreign tourists inspired her to be more ambitious than most women in our community, who were primarily housewives.

The idea of leaving Sudan was unpalatable, but whenever I objected to emigrating, my mother would firmly say, 'Mimi, I have explained that we must all leave for the family's safety. Have you forgotten the fear, the chaos we endured during the coup?'

In 1971, Major Hashem al-Atta's coup d'état against President Jaafar al-Nimeiry failed within three days, leading to executions of the mutineers. Among those executed was a young officer whose wedding we had attended – my mother had even made his wife's bridal dress. Panic gripped us when university students who had supported the coup were arrested, and the government began nationalising Sudanese companies, particularly those owned by Sudanese of Italian, Greek, Armenian, and Syrian descent. Many upper- and middle-class white Christian businessmen, who had long enjoyed privileges from British colonial rule, were arrested. We watched with sadness as families departed for what was supposed to be a holiday, only to learn later that they had permanently resettled in countries like Australia.

§

My youngest brother opened my bedroom door, and the irresistible aroma of food from our kitchen pulled me out of my daydream, awakening my senses. He hugged me and said, 'I will miss you.' A wave of sadness swept over me. I would miss my mother, my brothers, and my father's grave. A chasm of emptiness gripped me, along with a fear of losing my Sudan.

I stepped out of my room and headed to the kitchen, where my mother and two aunts were chatting while cooking the traditional Sudanese dish, *'aseeda-wa-mullah*, a savoury pudding made with yoghurt and cornflour, served with minced meat, onions, and tomato sauce. My mother avoided my gaze. Beneath her feigned cheerfulness, I saw the unmistakable veil of sadness. She was trying valiantly to hold back her tears. One of my aunts began to sing to lighten the sombre mood, but the reality of my departure hung thick in the air, and soon, we were all crying.

My friend Gandoura came to the rescue with her exuberant voice. 'Hurry up, I'm taking you to the hairdresser!' I declined – guests were expected – but she would hear none of it. '*Kalam sheno alawaleq dah*? Nonsense, let's go,' she insisted.

As we drove through the streets, I sat in silence, taking in the buildings, all the places that had been part of my youth. After the hairdresser, Gandoura took me on a tour: past my school, university, church, the Catholic club, Syrian club, and to Kalandar Park. I waved goodbye to the baobab tree at the park's edge, where so many teenagers had engraved hearts and arrows bearing their initials.

Gandoura asked whimsically, 'Do you remember the story about that creative electricity officer who conveniently turned the lights off in the park to give his brother ample time to meet his girlfriend in the dark?' We both laughed.

She parked in front of the house of the handsome news broadcaster who was admired by many young girls. We looked at each other and burst into hysterical laughter. One day, a few minutes prior to reading the news bulletin, my friend contacted the television station pretending to be a nurse from the hospital, informing them that the broadcaster's father had been in a traffic accident and requesting that his son come immediately. We then watched the news read by another broadcaster, wearing the jacket of the previous broadcaster who must've left the studio in a hurry.

That drive allowed me to bid farewell to the cherished places of my youth, offering me a quiet sense of closure. By the time we returned, our home was filled with family and friends who had come to say their goodbyes. '*Ya helelik ya* Mimi.' You will be missed, Mimi.

My friends showered me with parting gifts – ivory ornaments and items made from crocodile and snakeskin. Music played, dancing followed, laughter erupted and stories were told. Some friends imitated our teachers and lecturers, prompting peals of laughter. Surrounded by such love and warmth, I felt euphoric, forgetting – if only for a moment – that these were my final hours in Sudan.

Yet amidst the joyful chaos, I caught the wistful gaze of my university friend, a young man fond of me. He studied political science at the University of Khartoum, while I read English Literature in the Faculty of Arts. I had often accompanied him to seminars and political debates, impressed by his eloquence though I barely grasped the politics. He would laugh at my naive comments but encouraged me to pursue higher education. He promised to help me apply for a master's scholarship in England after my degree – an opportunity that could one day lead to work in a Sudanese embassy.

He motioned for me to come closer and, in his charming Sudanese slang, said, '*Enti samha shadid ya Mariam betjebe alhawajes*' – You are so beautiful, you cause distractions. Then, turning to a mutual friend nearby, he added, 'Mary is someone who might be proud, but she would never disown Sudan.' I was both embarrassed and flattered.

With his natural leadership, he urged the guests to form a circle. 'It's two a.m. – time to leave,' he announced. He began singing the farewell song that we traditionally sang at graduations and New Year's Eve. The words, written by Ahmed Mohamed Saad, were about friendship and faithfulness, and were sung to the tune of the Scottish song 'Auld Lang Syne'. We all had tears in our eyes as we sang and held hands. I spoke spontaneously, from my heart: 'I love you all. I will not forget you. And we will meet again, God willing!' But that reunion never came. As the situation in Sudan deteriorated, most of my friends scattered across the globe.

§

When I returned to Sudan in 2009 to show my daughter where I was born, only two of my close friends from that farewell party remained. The visit made a profound impact on her. 'Mum,' she said, 'I wish you'd raised us in Sudan until we turned eighteen, then taken us to Australia.' When I asked her why, she replied, 'Because generosity and friendship is so profound here. We've received endless invitations from people I don't even know – just because they want to honour us as visitors. Now I understand what you meant about the cohesion of Sudanese society.'

She was especially moved by an encounter in a souvenir shop in Shukri Park, in Wad-Medani, my hometown. The shopkeeper, a stranger to me, refused to take payment once he heard I was the daughter of John Hanoun – a man remembered for his generosity. He filled our bags with goods, insisting it was his way of paying tribute to my father.

§

After the last guests had left my farewell party, reality struck. My mother came into my room and reminded me that it had taken her sweat and tears to raise me, and that if I ever betrayed our values, it would cost our family's dignity. Her words have guided me since.

My two brothers carried my bags to the car waiting to take us to Khartoum International Airport. I walked slowly, weighed down by a storm of emotions, forcing a brave face for the sake of my mother, whom I knew was also hurting beneath her strength.

My first destination was Lebanon, where I was to obtain an entry visa from the Australian Embassy. When the final boarding announcement for Beirut was made, I broke down, sobbing like a child, clinging to my mother. But there was no turning back. My body ascended the aircraft steps – while my heart and soul remained in Sudan.

§

It was my first time on a plane. I had often dreamt of travelling by air for a holiday, like many of my friends. But such luxuries were beyond our means – my mother could only afford to meet our educational and basic needs. The dream of flight had become a nightmare. As the aircraft ascended, I resumed sobbing, overwhelmed by the pain of uprooting. Fatigue gradually consumed me, before drowsiness dulled the ache. I eventually fell into a deep sleep. The wild waves of my inner turmoil settled – if only temporarily.

The flight attendant gently woke me to announce our descent. I looked out the window and was mesmerised by the view: cedar-covered mountains and a shimmering oasis in the distance. A sense of serenity washed over me. I felt renewed and thought it was no wonder such landscapes had inspired poets I was fond of, like Khalil Gibran.

At Beirut Airport, I was quietly amused by the Lebanese Arabic accent, though I understood it easily. At customs, some of my ivory ornaments were confiscated – considered commercial goods. I tried to explain they were heartfelt gifts from childhood friends, handcrafted by skilled Sudanese artisans. They were priceless to me. But the officer insisted on their monetary value and demanded a fee in Lebanese Lira, which I did not have. It broke my heart to part with them; they were tangible links to my friends and to Sudan.

At the arrivals hall, a young man called my name. With a warm smile, he introduced himself as Karim and took charge of my luggage. He reminded me of my brothers and cousins, bearing the unmistakable Hanoun family trait – he was short! My mother had arranged for this family connection to collect me and take me to the Mar Elias Convent in Antelias, Beirut, where I would spend the night. Sister Therese, a distant relative, greeted me kindly. She shared stories of how, when her mother in Sudan was in need, my mother, Janette Hanoun, had offered compassion and help. Karim told me he would take me to the Australian Embassy in Beirut and then on to Syria, where I would meet my father's relatives who had remained there. That night, I called my mother to assure her I was safe and being well cared for.

The next morning, we went to the embassy, heavily guarded by armed police. Karim explained that Beirut was facing increasing unrest. The embassy official requested that I return in two days to have my passport stamped with the Australian visa. This delay postponed our trip to Syria, but it gave me a chance to explore Lebanon. I visited the breathtaking Jeita Grotto caves, marvelled at Beirut's charm, and wandered through the vibrant Hamra shopping district. I saw my first electric escalator.

Once I received my visa, Karim and I took a taxi to Aleppo. Along the way, the driver asked how someone with fair skin could be Sudanese. I surprised myself by replying, 'My roots are Syrian, I was born and raised in Sudan, and now I'm migrating to Australia.'

At the Lebanon-Syria border, my anxiety surged as an officer inspected my Sudanese passport and questioned me about my relatives in Syria. I remembered my mother's advice: Never argue with authorities, stay calm, and rely, when necessary, on luck rather than rights. Soon we were on our way again, arriving in the Aleppo suburb of Al-Selemanyah, where I received a rapturous welcome from my father's family. Neighbours waved from their balconies, and someone exclaimed, 'She looks like her aunty!' – a woman I had never met, who had passed away before I was born.

I learnt that when my eldest aunt married in Syria, my grandfather and father had travelled from Sudan to attend the wedding and ended up staying a full year before returning. I also discovered my father had been a talented footballer and learnt carpentry during his time in Syria. My great-grandfather had been a farmer named Hanna (John), and my father was named after him. I would later name my own son John.

To my astonishment, I discovered our family's original surname was Hanounian. It had been shortened to Hanoun to conceal our Armenian heritage and avoid persecution under the Ottoman Empire. This revelation felt like finding a lost treasure, and I vowed to uncover as much of my family's hidden history as I could.

Visiting the cemetery where my aunt was buried, I noticed that many tombstones bore names familiar in Sudan – with the final letters erased. Like my family, these Armenians had disguised their ethnicity to survive. I was outraged by the historical silence. None of my school textbooks had mentioned the Armenian genocide or the flight from Ottoman persecution.

I recalled a moment in Geography class at age thirteen. We were studying the 'African man'. Our teacher read a line describing African facial features, followed by the outrageous claim: 'They are trying their best to be like European man.' To our shock, he slowly tore the page of the textbook and declared it nonsense. The same book had remained silent on the Armenian tragedy – something I had only learnt about as an adult.

My own family had never spoken of it. My grandparents were too traumatised. Perhaps they didn't want to disrupt the life they had worked so hard to rebuild.

I later discovered that many of their generation had chosen silence. A young scholar researching Syrian migration to Sudan once interviewed me, puzzled by how little information had been passed down. Why hadn't families preserved their stories of migration? Even basic questions – why and when they had left Syria – remained unanswered.

Standing in that Aleppo cemetery, my mind was flooded with questions. Why had no one ever spoken of these atrocities? Was the pain too great? Had trauma sculpted a new identity for Armenians in Sudan? Why had my family chosen Sudan over Latin America, where other relatives had resettled? Perhaps it was because Sudan was seen as a welcoming refuge, a sanctuary.

Karim managed to arrange a meeting with the record keeper of the Catholic Armenian Church in Aleppo. We were to examine the registers of marriages, births, and deaths of those who had fled to Sudan. I was elated by this rare chance to unearth the buried threads of our history.

But a day before the meeting, my relatives urged me to leave Syria immediately. The Lebanese Syrian border was at risk of closing, as civil war loomed. I was devastated, but I could not afford to be stranded. To this day, I associate the start of Lebanon's civil war with the premature end of my quest to understand my Armenian roots. War tore me away from newly found relatives. Yet, a bond had been formed, and I returned to Syria three more times to attend weddings of family members, some of whom later migrated to Canada and Australia.

Heartbroken, I had no time for proper farewells. In the taxi back to Lebanon, I sat numb, shocked. The experience felt hauntingly similar to what my Armenian ancestors had endured a century earlier. Displacement, it seemed, was our shared fate – then and now.

Back in Lebanon, I hastily packed my luggage while Karim confirmed my Pan Am ticket. As we drove to Beirut Airport, the city felt like a bomb waiting to explode. Fear descended like a heavy cloud, eclipsing the joyful moments and inner peace I'd experienced in Syria. My heart pounded like a drum. I wondered if this panic resembled the terror that had once led my ancestors to flee.

As the plane began to ascend, I turned into a prayer machine, fervently thanking God that I had not been stranded. Gradually, a sense of calm returned. I reflected on the whirlwind journey: the warm embrace of relatives in Syria, the hospitality of the nuns in Beirut, and Karim's unwavering support and grace. Instead of lamenting the war that had cut short my search for my ancestors' history, I began to wonder what new adventures awaited me in Australia.

Our first stop was in Hong Kong. A strange feeling overtook me – the unfamiliar language, the sea of new faces. I was overcome by stress and the fear of missing my connecting flight. I looked inward, searching for the courageous, confident Mary. But she was gone. I was a different Mary now – vulnerable, uprooted, uncertain of what lay ahead. I was no longer the Mary I used to be, and not yet the Mary I was meant to become.

I didn't miss my flight. Soon we were flying to Sydney – my final destination. Would I find peace in Australia? Would people ever stop fleeing their homelands in search of safety?

After twenty hours of flying, the plane landed at Kingsford Smith Airport. I felt neither excitement nor apathy – just a strange deathlike neutrality. I was startled to see two crew members spraying a chemical throughout the cabin while we were still seated; it reminded me of spraying flies during the scorching Sudanese summers.

Thanks to my reasonable command of English, I was able to follow the signs, collect my luggage, and make my way to customs. There, the officers confiscated the last of my ivory and animal skin gifts – irreplaceable mementos of my friends in Sudan. I was stultified. I felt numb. Would this be the shape of things to come in Australia? My mother's voice echoed inside me: *With patience, we overcome all challenges.*

As I saw familiar faces in the arrival hall my joy returned. Among them were my dear friend Amira and several of my father's relatives who had migrated three years earlier and offered to host me until my mother arrived. My spirits lifted – I felt safe, even, dare I say, a little special. I was welcomed and embraced warmly. They offered lifts and accommodation and were eager to hear the news from our community in Sudan. Soon, I joined the ritual of welcoming other Sudanese families arriving in Australia. Only then did I understand how heartening it was to hear first-hand news from home.

As we drove from the airport, I noticed the neat traffic system, the absence of honking, and the clearly marked street signs. The roads were flanked by beautiful trees. One thing struck me: the absence of dark-skinned people, particularly Africans.

As we turned into Mascot Drive, Eastlakes, the driver informed us that thirty-seven Sudanese families lived here. The street was lined with uniform three-storey apartment blocks – as if designed by a single architect. I naively assumed Australia was a classless society. After all, some of these families had lived in grand homes back in Sudan. The driver told me that locals had nicknamed the area 'Hay Al-Masalma' after the Sudanese suburb known for peaceful coexistence. Wealthier Sudanese had the means to live elsewhere but chose to stay close to their community – where support and company were assured. Inside these homes, remnants of former wealth were evident. Lounges were crammed with oversized furniture – plush couches in modest living rooms, king-size beds barely fitting in these tiny Australian bedrooms.

That day, my hosts' small apartment was bustling with visitors offering advice, warnings, stories about life in Australia. I was overwhelmed and very fatigued. After the emotional toll of leaving Sudan and the long journey, all I craved was solitude – to process my feelings and reconnect with myself. As I closed the door behind me that night, I was transported to summer nights in Sudan – sleeping in the backyard under the stars, listening to Umm Kulthum and reading Nizar Qabbani beneath the full moon. But now I lay awake, jetlagged and disoriented.

At dawn, I awoke to the familiar aroma of Sudanese coffee. I hoped to savour it with my hosts, but they gulped it quickly before rushing off to catch buses or trains to work.

Amira, who had taken the day off to help me settle in, arrived and urged me to hurry. She would show me how to navigate public transport, open a bank account, and register for social security and employment.

On our way to the bus stop, I noticed how hurried everyone seemed. On the bus, I greeted people with 'good morning', but no one reciprocated. Most passengers were engrossed in books or newspapers, a few women were knitting and hardly anyone spoke.

With Amira's help, we completed the essential tasks. At the employment office, I did a typing test, and the officer acknowledged the speed and accuracy of my typing. 'It was an outstanding result,' she chimed. I was proud of what I had achieved in less than twenty-four hours in Australia.

On the return journey, I sat beside a young Turkish woman who had been in Australia for a year. I was eager to learn about life here. She explained that getting foreign qualifications recognised was complicated. Many skilled migrants ended up in low-status jobs – taxi drivers, cleaners or factory workers – because local experience was a prerequisite for employment in their fields. One needed experience to get licensed but couldn't gain experience without a job. Yet, she said, weekend work paid double. I listened, sceptical, thinking she was exaggerating.

Walking home from the bus stop, I asked Amira about weekend work. She revealed that she and her sister cleaned hotel rooms. I was stunned – how could a university graduate do cleaning work? Amira clarified that it had taken her time to secure a job in her field. In the meantime, cleaning paid the bills and helped her save some money. She continued to work as a cleaner even after being employed as an accountant.

She went on to explain that the only way to navigate a system that rarely recognised overseas qualifications was to adopt a new mindset. Her combined income had enabled her to obtain a loan from the bank and buy her own unit within two years of arriving in Australia.

Sensing my disbelief, Amira clarified: 'The mindset we grew up with suited the context of our lifestyle in Sudan. In Australia, we need a new mindset.' She added that in Australia, even cleaners have full worker's rights and decent award wages, whereas in Sudan, they rely on luck and the temperament of their employer. 'Perhaps we have things to learn from Australia Amira.' I realised I had never appreciated the role of domestic workers back home.

My hosts were generous and attentive. The mother asked daily what I wanted to eat, reminded me to take my umbrella, and urged me to dress warmly before going out. She even gave up her bed for me, sleeping on a sofa in the living room.

A week after my arrival, the employment office informed me of a receptionist position at a car dealership. At the job interview, the manager said he was extremely impressed by my Gregg shorthand skills, describing my work as 'outstanding'. I returned home in high spirits, expecting to be offered the job. However, the manager sheepishly told me that my appearance did not suit the position. I was disgusted – they were prioritising looks over competency.

That same day, I received a letter from my mother. Due to the civil war in Lebanon, her immigration application had been rerouted to the Australian Embassy in Egypt, delaying the family's arrival. I was devastated. In an emotional reply, I urged her to reconsider migration, warning that most available jobs were cleaning roles. She never received that letter – and I'm grateful she didn't.

Exhausted from crying, I called Amira. She listened and helped me find a weekend cleaning job. 'Try it with an open mind,' she encouraged me. 'You can always quit'. So, I accepted a hotel cleaning position.

We entered through the back entrance reserved for cleaners and delivery staff. I felt humiliated. It seemed that inequality did exist in Australia. My soul zig-zagged between hope and despair, optimism and doubt. I longed to return to Sudan.

Not long after, a relative working at the University of New South Wales (UNSW) gave me a copy of the staff newsletter, *Uniken*. In it, I saw a typist position advertised. I applied and was hired within a week of starting my weekend cleaning job. My mother must have been praying for me. While working two jobs, I began saving money to rent and furnish a unit in preparation for my family's arrival.

And so began my work at the university. I typed lecture notes – that material nourished my knowledge of human rights, equality, media bias and urban development. One lecture about the Stolen Generation shook me. I struggled to believe that children were legally taken from their biological Aboriginal families by the government and missionaries. Where was the compassion that Christianity taught those missionaries? I remembered baby Ali from the Almygoma Orphanage back home, and picturing his face, I ached for the children ripped away from their mothers in Australia. Learning about the Stolen Generation made me question my schooling in Sudan. Our history books only reflected the narratives of the powerful. They omitted the Armenian genocide, just as they ignored Indigenous suffering in Australia. I remembered Ali snuggling against my chest, and realised he would be six or seven now. Though I wasn't his mother, I still missed him. I longed to help ease the suffering in the world. Typing those lecture notes sharpened my critical thinking skills, deepened my spirituality, and led to a profound commitment to social justice and equity. I felt my mother would have been proud of me. I was inspired to resume my studies. I was soon noticed for my insights and was frequently invited to express my thoughts on humanitarian issues, especially in relation to Sudan and the Arab world. It was a perspective not often heard about.

Soon after, a lecturer at the university asked me to type his book. I was proud that within three months of arriving, I was now entrusted with academic work. Yet, I was naive about employment contractual obligations in the workplace. I poured many extra hours into that project and was not compensated properly. I was too timid and polite to clarify things with him, but I soon learnt that it was important to communicate effectively regardless of the hierarchy in the workplace. My critical thinking skills were growing. Australia was different. I realised that our education in Sudan had no place for questioning or debate – we memorised and recited like parrots. I was reminded of the famous and controversial Al Balabil sister's song from Sudan. They were The Nightingales, and their powerful lyrics whirled around in my head, whispering: 'Those Who Ask Don't Get Lost' – '*Al beesaal ma betouh*'. They were making sense to me while I was so far away from them. They were encouraging people to think in Sudan – an encouragement no less needed here. In Australia, I began to ask questions.

While I was working at the university, a Sudanese student named Garas Khilla came to our office to collect those lecture notes. We exchanged a few words, and later again in the student cafeteria. Speaking with him stirred my nostalgia for Sudan, and I found myself looking forward to our conversations. He helped ease the pain of adjusting to a new country. I admired him deeply, as did my mother and brothers when they arrived a few months later. He stood out with his genuine Sudanese magnanimity, his commanding presence, generosity and intelligence. He supported my entire family in settling into life in Australia. He was the kind of man for whom the word 'impossible' simply didn't exist.

My mother's priority upon arriving was to find a job. Garas helped her secure a job as a tea lady, but her employer soon expressed dissatisfaction with her performance. She struggled to understand the Australian accent and terms like 'white tea', 'black tea', or 'no sugar'. In Sudan, tea was always served with sugar. The following day, my mother spoke with our Italian butcher, who found her a weekday job at his cousin's factory as a process worker, and a weekend job washing dishes at a club. My youngest brother, who was attending high school in Australia, quickly noticed the challenges our mother faced with the English language. He helped us distinguish between slang and formal English. He was amused to hear her begin using words like 'bloody', 'love', 'mate' and even the occasional expletive! Around the dinner table, we would share our daily adventures in this new country and laugh at ourselves. In no time, my mother was driving, had purchased a unit, and was handling real estate agents, bank staff, and solicitors on her own. We were immensely proud of her. Even Garas was impressed by her courage and her impressive bargaining skills.

Before long, my relationship with Garas blossomed into love, and then into marriage. After our wedding, we bought a unit together, and I accepted a new role as a private secretary in a different section of the university, with a better salary.

While working at UNSW, I received a phone call from a lecturer named Frances Lovejoy. She was preparing a paper on female genital mutilation (FGM) and asked whether I knew anything about the practice in Sudan. We met, and I shared what I knew while she took notes. I explained that female circumcision was widespread in Sudan and often perceived as a religious obligation and a vital part of Sudanese culture. Uncircumcised girls were generally not favoured for marriage due to the misconception that they might be promiscuous. Anyone who opposed the practice was often seen by conservatives and reactionaries as lacking religious commitment or being influenced by colonial ideas aimed at weakening the cohesion of Sudanese society.

Frances asked whether I could assist in distributing a questionnaire on FGM to women's organisations in Sudan. My friend Gandoura, who was actively advocating against the practice, shared it through her wide network of Sudanese women. Frances was deeply disturbed by the responses and comments. Although FGM had been outlawed in Sudan since 1948 by colonial authorities due to its violation of children's human rights, tradition continued to defy legislation. In societies burdened by illiteracy and political and economic instability, women's suffering is rarely a priority. Frances insisted that I co-present the resulting paper, titled 'Female Circumcision in the Sudan: Traditional Practices and Government Policies'.

One day, my office administrator, a friendly young Australian woman, invited me to lunch. At the cafeteria, she paid for her food. I assumed she had paid for mine too. She looked at me and asked, 'What about your lunch?' Embarrassed, I said I wasn't hungry. I recalled a Sudanese proverb, '*Nacheel al deyn wa nasawi alzeen*' – Borrow money to honour a guest. Later, I shared the story with Amira. She told me about a neighbour who once invited her family for dinner and said, 'Bring a plate.' Amira's mother brought six empty ones, thinking the host lacked crockery. In Sudan, if someone invites you for a meal and you bring food, it's seen as disrespectful. Hospitality is sacred – a way to honour both guest and host. Even now, I feel uneasy asking guests to bring a dish, though practicality sometimes wins out.

§

The work I had done with Frances Lovejoy was profound and it was she who drew my attention to the mature-aged student scheme to gain entrance to university. I was very interested in feminism and sociology. Frances, my mother and husband supported my dreams. I sat the mature-age entry exam and gained admission to UNSW. Around the same time, I discovered I was pregnant. I was torn between the need to keep working to help pay our mortgage, to care for the child that was on his way to us and committing to university studies. I chose to postpone my studies for just one year. I eventually went on to complete a Bachelor of Arts, majoring in Sociology, and later I earned a Master of Arts, specialising in Women's Interdisciplinary Studies.

The birth of my first son, John, was a transformative experience. He became the rhythm of my heart and the breath in my lungs. He was my new purpose, and I was overwhelmed with gratitude to God for blessing us with a healthy, beautiful baby. After a year of maternity leave, I returned to full-time work and began part-time university studies. It was incredibly difficult, but I managed, thanks to my mother, who took full-time care of her grandson and a manager who could see my potential.

This manager knew I was struggling with working, with paying a mortgage, with motherhood and with trying to study. So, he offered me the opportunity to attend lectures during work hours. I was doing too much, and he knew it. His gesture revealed a depth of humanity I hadn't expected from this quiet and rather serious man. He was allowing me to take time off work and go to my lectures. However, my absence from work was beginning to draw resentment from other colleagues. I wore a mask pretending I was not hurt, but after I was openly insulted, I needed to address this indignation. My decision to speak up meant I was jeopardising my job, but it was important. The next day I confided in my manager my hurt over the rude words I'd received from a colleague. He knew he needed to establish a strong boundary about workplace harassment, so he stood up, walked into his assistant's office and, in front of everyone, demanded an apology to me and a commitment that such rudeness would not happen again. I learnt that truth will always prevail and speaking up was the only way to make change for oneself and in the wider world. The next day, I gave him a card expressing a lengthy and heartfelt thank you, which he read silently and without comment. My studies continued unimpeded, and I knew my voice was growing.

Years later, I received a call from the wife of this former university manager. I was surprised; I knew he had passed away, and I hadn't heard from her since then. She told me he had left behind a box labelled 'Letters' for his grandchildren. Among these precious mementos was the thank you card I had written, on which he had inscribed: 'Mary is an asset.' He was not an effusive or talkative man, but when he spoke people listened. 'Mary is an asset'. That news was a trophy that, dare I say, made me feel so special. I will always be grateful to him.

§

After I graduated with my master's degree, I left my secretarial job and took on various roles in the welfare sector. My bicultural and bilingual background helped bridge understanding between the Arabic community and the broader Australian society. While working as a family support worker at the Australian Arabic Council – dealing with domestic violence, youth delinquency, and intergenerational conflict – I was temporarily seconded two days a week to the Migrant Resource Centre. There, I supported the resettlement of Iraqi refugees, many of whom had come from Rafha Camp in Saudi Arabia. Their plight was documented in an Amnesty International report titled *Unwelcome 'Guests': The Plight of Iraqi Refugees.*

The needs of the Iraqi refugees were complex and often beyond what existing services could provide. To offer more meaningful support, I resigned from my family support position and began working full-time with them. Due to sanctions imposed on Iraq after the Gulf War, refugees needed assistance to support loved ones back home – particularly those in urgent need of medication. News of relatives' deaths in Iraq arrived frequently, inducing waves of grief. Iraqi refugee men crowded into a single unit, surviving on bags of potatoes from the Flemington markets so they could send money from their social security benefits to those in need. Enrolling them in English classes before they had processed their trauma was ineffective. My work with the Iraqi refugees from Rafha Camp was revelatory. The oral histories they shared – stories of torture and imprisonment – were incomprehensible. I remain deeply grateful for their trust.

Among the most rewarding moments in that role was accompanying a client to the airport to reunite him with his wife and children after years of separation. The Red Cross tracing service, with support from the Department of Immigration and our office, had located his family. It was a heart-wrenching scene – especially when the younger children didn't recognise their father. I remembered little Ali from the orphanage in Sudan who would be a young man by now. I returned home, looked at my own children, and felt immense gratitude that I had never known such painful separation.

Another opportunity to walk the extra mile came when a friend recommended me to the NSW Ecumenical Council, who were seeking an experienced refugee field worker. I applied and was offered the role. The council supported both authorised refugees arriving through the Integrated Humanitarian Settlement Scheme and unauthorised refugees held in the Villawood Immigration Detention Centre until their identities were verified. I coordinated volunteer church groups to assist with the settlement and rehabilitation of refugees from Rwanda, Sierra Leone, South Sudan, Kosovo, Bosnia, and ethnic Hazaras from Afghanistan. It saddened me that I was unable to empower women on temporary protection visas because they were reluctant to report incidents of domestic violence to the police, fearing this may affect their visa status.

The church groups established the House of Welcome to support asylum seekers. They provided telephone cards so detainees could contact relatives, secured pro-bono legal assistance and reported substandard conditions – such as poor food quality, harsh treatment, health concerns and lack of structured education for children – to immigration authorities. They also held information sessions in congregations, inviting refugees to speak and challenge misconceptions. Sometimes, the news was devastating. I learnt of a refugee deported back to the country that he fled only to be executed upon his arrival. I encouraged church groups to write to Members of Parliament to prevent decisions that could lead to such tragic outcomes. Detainees at Villawood often reported serious issues, but fear prevented them from lodging formal complaints. Their silence was heavy, and I felt deeply burdened by their pain.

§

One Iraqi refugee summed up the sentiment many shared about my work: 'You are our voice to the outside world. You may not be able to do the impossible, but you lead with humanity first and professional knowledge second.' I often quote his words to young people in my circle, urging them to let their humanity guide their professional paths and use their voices.

I've been using my voice in other ways these days too. As a member of the Andalus Arabic Choir, I have sung in Arabic at various venues, including the Sydney Opera House. I also support the wonderful Mirath in Mind Project, which puts on performances once a year. Here young people get to connect with their Arabic culture by dramatic performances with singing and dancing. I am proud to be part of *Kheir Jalees*, the Best Companion organisation, which inspired me to write my story. Through the Sudanese Syrian Christian Social Club, I remain involved in raising awareness and support for Sudanese refugees.

I am intentional about making retirement a rewarding time. I've been translating excerpts from my personal journals into English for my children and grandchildren. They include a wealth of joyful anecdotes – for example, I recall their birthday gifts, like the toy car with a remote control that my husband and I played with because *we* had never owned such toys in our childhoods. We laughed as our two-year-old son snatched it back, shouting to us, 'It's my car, not yours!' I recount Kathryn-Janet, our daughter, beautiful, articulate and opinionated, appointing herself my fashion consultant at the age of ten. Once, she startled me by declaring that knowing ABC and 123 was enough to start her own fashion business. Even at ten she was quite a powerhouse, and I was so proud. My youngest son, Christian, asked in Year

1, 'Mum, what comes after Year Twelve?' I replied, 'Years Thirteen, Fourteen and Fifteen.' He understood eventually that both Garas and I valued higher education for them more than anything. I encouraged them to be confident and curious about the world. 'Those who ask don't get lost' – '*Al beesaal ma betouh.*' It was a valuable life lesson for them too. I am proud of all my children's achievements. They entered the fields of education, law and music. My son John became a DJ and carved his own path creating the DJ persona MK-One – Master Khilla-One.

I wish my boys had been able to visit Sudan before the war broke out on 15 April 2023. My son John had planned a trip for June; everything was arranged, and people were preparing to welcome him. But the war erupted before he could arrive. Many Sudanese see this conflict as a proxy war – a fight over resources, gold and minerals, waged by global powers on Sudanese soil.

I thanked God that John didn't make it to Wad-Medani, my hometown, which has since been taken over by mercenaries. Once the most settled, ethnically and religiously diverse, fertile, and prosperous city in Sudan – known for growing fine cotton, wheat, and other crops – Wad-Medani has been devastated.

Unspeakable atrocities have been committed there, including systematic rape and the looting of Sudanese heritage to erase our history.

I do not recognise the cruelty that is now unfolding. How could anyone do this to their own country? It is a total betrayal of Sudanese ethics and morality. My hope is that my children and grandchildren will do good in the world. That they will stand against injustice – in Sudan or anywhere – and contribute to making Australia a leading nation for human rights and social justice everywhere.

GLASSHOUSE

by Sivine Tabbouch

I was ten years old when the Lebanese civil war erupted. A year later, our lives changed forever.

I recall dancing in our house in Tripoli. The soulful voice of Farid Al-Atrash drifted in from my brother's bedroom, while Umm Kulthum's music wafted out from the room of my sister. Blaring songs about love from their windows was my siblings' way of communicating with their sweethearts next door. I sang along with Umm Kulthum, my body swaying, mesmerised by the rhythm, when an explosion rocked the walls and shattered the glass in our windows. It shook me out of my enchantment. It was May of 1976 when my brother ran home, his face covered in dust, shaking and stuttering the name, 'Fadi, Fadi'.

'What's happened to Fadi?' My mother tried to extract a reply fearing the worst.

'My God! He's dead… Fadi… is dead,' my brother stammered. Breathless, he continued, 'We were at Abu Ahmad's shop. Shrapnel sprayed straight into his chest, and he melted into the ground.' Heaving and inconsolable, my brother collapsed in grief, rocking back and forth. My mother knelt beside him and held him in her arms, saying, 'Poor Um Fadi. May God protect all our children!'

The following day screams emanated from Fadi's house. From my mother's bedroom window, I had a full view of the procession below. Men in black suits led by two priests lowered Fadi down the stairs in an open wooden coffin. I could see into the coffin. Fadi, attired in a black suit, had a frozen grin on his ashen face. The men took great care to keep the shiny brown coffin steady as they descended. His mother and sisters wailed and ululated the *lililililesh zalghouta* performed at weddings, insisting he was a groom rising to heaven, as is the custom when a young person dies. I shuddered with fright at the sight of Fadi's lifeless body. I slunk under the bed trying to hide from the commotion. It was loud and terrifying. I was petrified.

My devastated brother wanted to avenge the death of his best and dearest friend. This gravely concerned my mother, as militias were aggressively recruiting young men to carry weapons and fight.

She took her concerns to my father.

'I want to rescue our children,' my mother argued. 'Heaven forbid!' I don't want them murdered over religion nor to lose them to bombs or militias. I don't want our hearts broken the way Fadi broke his mother's heart. She's completely lost her mind. I hear her through our walls. She screams out to God questioning why her only son was taken and not one of our *nine* sons.'

My mother's voice sounded different this time. It was shaking with fear. 'This is a civil war, Ibrahim, and it may not end soon. Their education will suffer. There is no future for them here.' She pleaded with my father to approve her decision to leave Lebanon and go to Australia.

The sound of machine guns and bombs ripped through the air, interrupting and validating my mother's pleas.

My father was stern, 'I *forbid* you to take our children away; we've already lost five to that faraway foreign land.'

My mother knew she needed to act quickly as the airport and embassies were shutting down in Beirut. She ignored my father's threats and packed a few belongings in her handbag. It was uncommon for a woman to embark on a journey such as this without a husband's approval. She was desperate to get us to safety, so she made the journey by ferry on her own to the Australian Embassy in Cyprus.

My mother, Amineh 'the trustworthy', was a remarkable woman. In the late 1940s, she started our family business, making bite-sized toffees for my father to sell on the streets of Tripoli, with the donkey she had received as a dowry. She shrewdly left gaps in the tray to create the illusion that the toffees were selling fast, enticing customers to buy before they were gone. Over the years, she learnt the art of distillation. She learnt how to distil rose water and orange blossom from flowers sourced in Damascus. Both these elixirs were expensive ingredients and used in all Levantine sweets. She ingeniously built a makeshift distillery on our rooftop. We often helped her pick through the flowers to obtain the perfect mix. Occasionally, I would roll in the rose petals spread across the floor of our rooftop sunroom, dreaming of swimming in a pond or dancing in a beautiful garden filled with flowers and white horses, inspired by the illustrations in my French school books. After years of toil and experimentation, my mother and father established themselves amongst the foremost sweet makers of Tripoli, a city renowned for its cuisine and sweets in particular. By 1975, they had a thriving business and were starting to reap the benefits just as civil war broke out.

Fifteen days after her solo journey to Cyprus, my mother returned with new clothes and visas for six of her fifteen children. It took her weeks to persuade my father to let us leave. She tried to convince him to travel with us, but deep down, she knew it would be impossible for him to abandon his newly flourishing business. With the war intensifying, we had only a few weeks to pack the essentials and prepare for the journey to Australia.

The first item I packed was the beautiful new dress my mother had bought for me in Cyprus. It had been meant for Eid al-Adha, but my mother could see no reason to celebrate during this horrifying war. It was a long red dress with a delicate satin ribbon at the waist. I tried it on with my black patent leather shoes, twirling like a ballerina on the light green tiles of our salon, reserved for visitors only. It was furnished with my mother's precious hand-carved lounges adorned with ochre-coloured flowers on velveteen fabric, where she hosted her female visitors for *sobheyeh* morning gatherings. Here she served cardamon-scented freshly ground coffee along with rose- and orange-blossomed delicacies from our sweet shop.

'You're not wearing it here, put it away for Australia,' she said, her stern demand cutting short my excitement. I carefully folded the red dress and placed the shiny black shoes next to the dress, tucking them lovingly into the bag they came in. But for now, I insisted on keeping them close, carrying them with me in a satchel wherever I went. I knew the next time the red dress appeared would be in Australia.

'Should I take my school bag?' I asked my mother as I followed her to the rooftop the next day.

'No. Only the essentials. We will be back before long, as soon as the war is over,' she reassured. 'Come help me, we need to cover the flasks and boilers and water the plants before we go.'

My mother kept over a hundred types of different plants and flowers in thirty-litre recycled ghee and olive oil cans on the rooftop. Here she grew jasmine, rose bushes, gardenias and frangipanis. She loved picking the tiny white flowers from her jasmine tree to adorn and lace through her long jet-black curly hair.

As I followed her to her sanctuary on the roof, I noticed how beautiful and somehow sad she looked. She was wearing a navy linen dress, a silk floral scarf, which covered half her head and flowed over her long torso, but I couldn't help notice she had tears in her eyes. I was to understand later how much she would ache for that rooftop paradise.

I was keen to share my travel news with my school friends, especially Lamia. I was going to travel to Australia on an aeroplane! Lamia came from an affluent family and travelled to Europe every year, always bringing back souvenirs. We would gather around her in the playground as she unveiled each treasure – a delicate ballerina figurine from Paris, a glass snow globe with a tiny snowman inside from Switzerland. When you shook it, the swirling white flakes transported us to an imaginary winter wonderland. It was magical.

Sometimes, she let us hold the gifts, passing them around so we could admire them up close. As she described where each one came from, it was as if we were travelling with her. I couldn't wait to tell her that this time, I would be the one bringing back presents. I was finally going on a journey of my own. I would see koalas and kangaroos – just like the postcards my siblings sent from Australia.

However, I never got the chance to say goodbye. Everything happened so fast, and before I knew it, I had to leave without seeing Lamia one last time.

§

Saying goodbye to my father was even harder. I was the second youngest of fifteen children, and I had spent afternoons in his loving company. I would part his hair in the middle, tie it up on both sides, and paint his toenails bright-red or pink while he dozed on an afternoon *siesta*. Then I'd giggle and flash an audacious grin at my siblings. He never complained, always obliging.

One year, just before Palm Sunday, I asked him

to buy me a white dress and matching shoes as well as a tall Pentecostal candle – just like my Christian neighbours. He laughed and explained that Muslims don't celebrate this feast, but I insisted. Eventually he acquiesced. I was ecstatic. On the day of the service, I sat proudly at the front of the church, candle in hand, waiting for the ceremony to begin.

I took great advantage of being his favourite. I recall that on days when I was hungry and didn't fancy what my mother had cooked, I hatched a plan to get what I desired. At the end of the day, I would visit my father at the family sweet shop. He would stop whatever he was doing, lift me onto the bench, and smother me with hugs and kisses.

'What are you doing here, my little darling?' he would ask, though he certainly already knew. Before I could extract his permission, I'd wink and dash across the street to the butcher's shop. In my loudest voice, I'd announce, 'My father sends regards and requests that you make me a *kafta* sandwich and put it on his tab.' The butcher would smile and prepare the sandwich just the way I liked it – plain, wrapped in fresh bread. I made sure he left out the tomatoes and tahini sauce; I didn't want anything dripping on my clothes.

My father had a sharp sense of humour and a generous heart. He was a worldly man and very kind. He never turned away a customer, especially those who couldn't afford to pay. He made them feel welcome, offering sweets in exchange for helping in the kitchen. He carried himself with pride – after all, he was the father of fifteen children, nine of them boys.

Before we left Tripoli, I overheard my mother say to my father, 'We will only be away for a couple of years, until the war is over.' Her voice was trembling. She was worried about leaving him behind, about taking us so far away, but she assured him we would soon return. This impacted my understanding of our time in Australia; I believed we would not be gone for long. Her promise echoed in my mind for years.

The day of our departure arrived too soon. I hugged my father tightly and cupped his face in my small hands. Tears streaked his cheeks. I looked into his eyes and said, 'Ibrahim, please look after yourself. We will be back soon.'

I was inconsolable for the rest of the journey and a long time afterwards.

I travelled with my mother and only five siblings. Three brothers and one sister remained in Lebanon. Five others had gone to Australia before us – one through marriage, and the others in search of a better future.

The plane was breathtaking, like a doll's house come to life. Everything was tiny yet perfectly arranged, each passenger nestled in their seats as if placed in an immaculate little compartment. As the engines roared, preparing for take-off, I clutched my mother's hand against my chest. I was caught between exhilaration and fear.

'It's okay,' she reassured me. 'That's just the sound of the engine. We're far from the fighting now.'

The small window reflected my own image, and beyond it, the world below shrank into a meticulously detailed landscape. I couldn't stop thinking of my father – was he watching us from below waving goodbye with a broken heart?

For the rest of the flight, I clung to the plastic bag containing my red dress and shiny black shoes, determined to wear them as soon as we landed in Australia.

§

The first thing I noticed when I arrived in Australia was how low and hot the sun felt. It seemed almost within my reach, unlike the sun I left behind, which was hidden behind the hazy smoke of gunfire. I wondered if I had grown during the five days of travelling from Lebanon to Australia.

Three sisters and two brothers were waiting for us at Sydney Airport. Their faces bore a mixture of joy and relief that we had made it safely. I don't think

I ever fully recovered from the rib-cracking hugs of my older siblings. I was passed from one embrace to another, showered with kisses, holding up a line of travellers trying to move through the terminal while I still clung tightly to the red dress and shoes in my plastic bag.

We took a yellow taxi to my sister's house, where she lived with her husband and two children, who were only a few years younger than me. I clutched my plastic bag close to my chest, staring out of the taxi window. Australia felt vast compared to tiny Lebanon. In Lebanon, we lived in narrow streets, packed with tall buildings so close together that you could pass a plate of food from your kitchen window to your neighbour's balcony. The Sydney streets were wide and divided into many lanes. The houses seemed like small islands with red-tiled roofs and black doors, surrounded by green lawns forbidding entry. Australia seemed silent; there were no bustling streets with children playing, no honking horns, no neighbours conversing through windows and across balconies, only the taxi driver rambling about how wonderful Australia was.

The taxi pulled into a long driveway leading to a small apartment block. My sister's unit was on the second floor. The living area and kitchen were small. One bedroom had a double bed, and the other had a bunk bed stacked against the wall. I looked around me, taking everything in. *Too many of us here*, I thought. *How are we all going to fit?*

The commotion of greetings lasted for hours. Then, suddenly, I realised my plastic bag was missing. I looked everywhere, but there was no sign of it. Frantic, I retraced my steps. And then it hit me – *I had left it in the taxi.*

Panic set in. There was no way to track down the taxi. My siblings offered to buy me a new outfit, but I was heartbroken. I cried inconsolably. No one could bring back the dress or the image of the little girl in the mirror in Lebanon – the girl in the red dress and black shoes, tap-dancing on the green tiles of our salon in Tripoli.

§

I spent my first week in Australia writing letters to my father, telling him how much I missed him and asking him to send me a pair of black patent leather shoes and a red dress – just like the ones I left in the taxi in Sydney. I also spent hours writing down the names of my many siblings, carefully listing them all in chronological order. I asked my mother for help with some of the birthdays, but she wasn't certain about the dates. She told me one brother was born the year we bought our first television; another was born when Egypt's president, Jamal Abdul Nasser, was elected – after whom he was also named.

Two weeks after settling into Australia, my eldest sister enrolled the three youngest of us in the local primary and high schools while the older three siblings attended a special English class for migrants.

My primary school was a brown brick building with a sign that read 'Built in 1913'. It looked old and unwelcoming. Thankfully, we wouldn't be here long. I knew my dad was eagerly awaiting our return and I'd go back to school in Tripoli soon. The musty classroom in Lakemba felt suffocating, the wooden desk anchoring me in place. I compared it to Ebrin, my private school in Lebanon, where we sat at colourful desks and chairs in bright classrooms with high ceilings, large windows and beautiful paintings on the walls. The white school building resembled a castle, surrounded by jasmine trees, climbing vines and roses of every colour. When it rained, the garden gleamed a shade brighter. We would pluck the large leaves and lick the droplets of rainwater from them. It was a safe place. I excelled there: studying, singing and dancing. My teachers and the nuns liked me. While we had a solid foundation in Arabic, we were required to speak only French at school.

A few months after settling, we needed a place of our own. We found a three-bedroom unit on a busy road. I'll never forget my mother's face when she saw the tiny bedrooms. One balcony faced the relentless traffic; the other the entrance to the building's driveway. She glanced at my brother and said, 'Let's sign the lease. We'll manage.' She had two children under twelve and four over sixteen. My sister, nearly seventeen, negotiated endlessly for her own room – a cramped two-by-three-metre space that barely fit a single bed. Every Friday afternoon at 3:30 pm, the agent knocked on our door to collect rent. It was very strange for my mother, who used to be the landlord back home, collecting rent from our tenants.

She furnished the unit with bunk beds and lounge chairs. The rest was a mix of hand-me-downs from friends eager to offload their old furniture. Our home looked like a salad bowl – everything thrown together, nothing matched. But it didn't matter. After all, we were only staying for a couple of years, until the war ended. The plan was for all of us to continue our education. But the money Mum brought with her from Lebanon was depleting, and soon some of us had to sacrifice school and help with living expenses.

Every second Saturday, my mother found her way to Flemington markets, where she bought boxes of fruit and vegetables to share with my older siblings. It wasn't until late 1982, when Lebanese butcher shops opened, that she could buy meat suited to our cooking style. She frowned at the butcher's window display and insisted on stepping into the cool-room to choose the freshest cuts herself.

During my first year in Australia, I attended a special English class and made friends with other Lebanese students who had also fled the civil war. I picked up basic English quickly, helped by my fluency in French. Some words were spelled the same but pronounced differently, which made learning easier. My first English teacher had pinky-violet hair, a colour I had never seen on an older woman – it reminded me of fairy floss. Back home, elderly women either covered their hair with a headscarf or pulled it into a neat bun. She spoke loudly and slowly, using stern facial expressions.

'This is David. David is a boy. He is a boy. And this is Susan. Susan is a girl. She is a girl.'

She repeated the phrases again and again to make sure we understood. The monotony bored me. I felt like I had been thrown back into Year 1 when I was already reading classical Arabic literature and studying history and geography in French. Eventually, I started mixing up the sentences: 'This is David – she is a boy. And this is Susan – he is a girl.'

It sent my classmates into fits of laughter.

The school band had a hypnotic effect on me. I loved music and dreamt of joining the choir and learning the violin. But we were still adjusting to life in Australia, and my family knew little about the school system. Watching without participating was frustrating, yet I never missed a rehearsal. I was mesmerised by the conductor, the harmony of voices, and the variety of instruments the students were playing.

I spent a year and three months in primary school but never took it seriously. In my mind, we weren't staying in Australia for long. My mother had assured my father we would return to Lebanon soon – to my special friend Lamia, and to Ebrin, my *real* school.

§

However, eventually, I found myself in an all-girls high school in Wiley Park, surrounded by familiar faces from my primary school. The atmosphere was relaxed, with little emphasis on learning. Some students in my class were openly disrespectful – talking back to teachers, sitting on desks, chewing gum, and even singing Pink Floyd's lyrics: 'Hey teacher, leave them kids alone.' I giggled at the thought of what Mother Bernadette at Ebrin would have done with a class like this.

Navigating Year 7 was challenging from the start. Seeking a sense of belonging, I gravitated toward the Lebanese girls who gathered in the schoolyard. We were fascinated by the white Australian girls – their silky blonde hair, blue eyes and flawless white skin. We watched them with admiration, but they interpreted our stares as provocation, a challenge to fight – something unfamiliar to me.

One day, on my way to class, I accidently bumped into a blonde girl from Year 8 in the corridor. She didn't take it lightly. Before I knew it, she shoved me so hard I hit the ground. Then she kicked me in the stomach. I scrambled to my feet, stunned and enraged, screaming in shock. I used every colourful Arabic word, mixing them with my broken English. I managed to say, 'I'm going to tell my mother about you.' Back home, this would have been a threat – any mother had the authority to discipline another family's child. But here, my mother's authority extended only to our home. In fact, she often reminded us to behave because we were *guests* in this country, and our actions reflected on her parenting. My threat only made things worse. The girls laughed at me.

The incident happened in front of the deputy principal, who took me to his office. I was crying, desperate to go home. He was gentle, calming me down with a glass of water. But I lacked the ability to explain what had happened. The blonde girl, however, wasn't finished with me. She gathered her friends to provoke me further. Whenever she saw me, she muttered under her breath, 'Here comes the wog.' I didn't know what *wog* meant, but the way she spat it out cut deep. I was scared. I didn't know what to do.

Two weeks after the corridor incident, I said goodbye to my friends at the school gate and started walking home. As I looked up, I saw the same girl waiting with a few of her friends just outside the school. My heart started racing. I was shaking. They were older, and there were three of them.

'Hey, you little wog, this is *our* country and *our* school,' one of them sneered.

Then came the famous words: 'Go back to where you came from.'

At first, I thought if I kept my head down and walked past them, then ran, I might escape. But before I could run, they pushed and shoved me, trying to provoke a fight. To this day, I don't know where my strength came from. I still can't believe how I managed to defend myself against the three girls before running home – shaken, confused, blood dripping from my right hand. I had split my pinkie finger. The scar remains, a proud reminder of that fight.

I didn't know what the consequences would be. But soon, rumours spread around the school that I had *won* the fight. Suddenly, I found myself in a leadership role in the playground. I had gained respect, and before long, I was protecting my Lebanese friends. Even the deputy principal consulted me about incidents involving the so-called 'wog' girls. But this new reputation came at the cost of my education. The bullying never stopped. We were always on edge, with no real guidance at school or at home. We didn't understand the school system, and our parents – struggling to adjust to a foreign country – left us to navigate our education alone.

Despite the challenges, I loved sports and excelled at roller-skating and swimming. I wanted to be like the white girls who represented the school. The coach at the Roll Arena skate rink saw my potential and offered to train me in figure-skating. But the intense training required a dedicated family member for drop-offs and pick-ups – something beyond my family's reach. I begged every older sibling to buy me a pair of proper roller skates. In the meantime, I spent my afternoons skating up and down our street while my family sat in the front yard, sipping coffee and Coca-Cola. I taught myself how to skate backwards, jump high in the air and land on both feet. Sometimes the neighbours would applaud. My mother, however, would call out, 'You will break your legs jumping like that.' Luckily, I never did.

My mother, who had travelled alone under the threat of bombs to Cyprus to secure our visas and brought *us* to safety in Australia, was now struggling. The language barrier left her humiliated, powerless and dependent on her children. Yet we were too busy. I could see the frustration on her face whenever she asked about our availability. She even delayed visiting a doctor. To alleviate her frustration, I offered to go with her.

At the clinic, she was surprised at the condescension of the doctor.

'*You* need to learn English!' she derided him. She understood enough to know she had been insulted. 'Is this the doctor? Does *he* speak French and Arabic?'

'No Mum, he only speaks English.'

'Then how is he going to understand my health issues?'

'It's okay, Mum, I'll translate for you.'

She turned to me and said, 'Do you know what Australia has done to me? It has muted me. It has paralysed me. It has silenced me. I'm not in control of my life anymore.'

As I sat beside her in the doctor's office, a wave of emotion washed over me. Watching her struggle to understand his questions and noting his rudeness made me angry. When we left, the doctor made another offhand remark about her lack of English. He didn't see her intelligence and her bravery, or appreciate her sharp wit and sense of humour. He didn't see the incredible woman who began a culinary empire and built a distillery on a rooftop in Tripoli.

After that day, I paid more attention to mother. I spent many hours cooking with her, laughing with her and listening to her stories. I learnt about her dreams and wishes for all of us, I learnt about her childhood, her neighbours and her family. I heard about her experiments with floral distillation and how she travelled the Levant for the best ingredients. She taught me how to cook. She had once stood tall in her homeland, confident and capable. Now, she felt incompetent and infantilised. It was hard to reconcile the woman she had been with the woman burdened by loneliness and this tiresome lack of belonging. Returning to Lebanon after only a few years did not eventuate for her or for me. How I longed to go home, back to my father, to my friends, my neighbours and my school. But for now, we had each other. And I knew, no matter what, I would always be there for her.

§

Adapting to Western culture was a difficult process for us all. We did our best. My youngest brother and I were especially eager to make new friends. He even suggested we adopt the Australian diet of 'meat and three veg'. One look from my mother was enough for him to abandon the idea. He didn't argue – he knew a flying shoe would be next. I decided it was best not to mention the hundreds-and-thousands sandwich I secretly wished I could take to school. She had already deemed Vegemite 'shoe-polish cream with no nutrition'. In our attempt to fit in, some of us changed our names to more easily pronounceable English versions such as Jimmy and Sue. My mother wasn't thrilled. She often made fun of the new names, shaking her head at how quickly things were changing. It was hard for her to keep up, especially as some of us abandoned further education to take on jobs she didn't approve of. 'I haven't uprooted my life for you to become factory workers or labourers,' she would repeat.

She worried as she watched us forge our own paths – some of us losing focus, making choices that went against her wishes. Yet, no matter how things changed, she remained a steady force in our lives, always reminding us of where we came from and the importance of holding onto our heritage.

§

It took my father five years to accept that the war in Lebanon wasn't ending anytime soon. In 1981, he left his hometown of Tripoli – his business, the chaos, the destruction – to join us in Australia. I was sixteen when I saw my father again. I looked at him and said, 'I am older now. I cannot play with you anymore.'

His arrival was a major turning point for our family. Unaccustomed to paying weekly rent, he used the hard-earned money from the sweets business to buy our first home, amongst the Lebanese community in Western Sydney, for $52,000. But he had left most of his money in Lebanon, believing the Lebanese Lira would hold its value. It didn't. The spiralling inflation wiped out what he had left behind, forcing us to confront a new reality – we would have to rebuild our lives in Australia from scratch.

§

For most of us, high school was just a pastime. Our parents assumed we were passing, but we were advancing from one year-level to the next based on age rather than performance. By Year 10, the school encouraged us to leave, steering us toward TAFE courses like homemaking, dressmaking or hairdressing. Our career adviser had all the forms ready.

At the same time, many of my school friends were receiving marriage proposals. Their parents welcomed the idea, encouraged by older Lebanese settlers who saw early marriage as a means of safeguarding their daughters from forming relationships with Australian men and engaging in behaviour outside their culture and religion. My mother was livid at the thought of girls as young as fifteen getting married. She had always believed that education was a girl's greatest asset. As far back as the 1960s, she had supported my older sisters in pursuing university studies, both in Lebanon and abroad.

I will never forget the disappointment on my mother's face when I told her I wanted to leave school. She glared at me and said, '*Enti majnouneh*, you are crazy if you think I am going to let you!'

I argued endlessly, telling her how unhappy I was at school. I laid out all the reasons why the last four years had been a waste of time. My year had been filled with engagement parties – I needed something more serious to help me grow. We came to an agreement: I had six weeks over the Christmas holidays to find a job. If I failed, I had to return to school.

At sixteen, through my sister's connections, I started volunteering with a Lebanese organisation, filling out forms to help clients secure sponsorship for family members affected by the civil war in Lebanon. I worked hard and soon my efforts were recognised, and I was offered a paid position. This opportunity launched my career in community work, supporting Arabic-speaking families as they navigated life in Australia.

That same year, I got my driver's licence. A year later, my father surprised me with my first car – a vibrant yellow Mitsubishi Sigma. I was ecstatic. I seized every opportunity to drive my friends around, attending lively Lebanese parties where we danced into the night. I felt strong, free, finally a real young adult, working, earning my own money, driving my own car. Those were some of the happiest days of my life.

Despite my personal joy, Lebanon was still in the grips of the war. Inflation was spiralling out of control, triggering a new wave of migration. I devoted myself to assisting the newly arrived families in our community, determined to make a real difference in their lives.

At eighteen, I secured my first full-time job, working directly with the Arab community. My proficiency in both English and Arabic allowed me to help newly arrived migrants navigate the system, understand their rights, and access essential resources. I had barely overcome my own struggles with settlement when I began assisting other Arab women fleeing war-torn countries. They faced enormous challenges – language barriers, unemployment, social isolation, mental health struggles, the loss of loved ones, and domestic violence.

Some situations required unconventional thinking and quick decision-making. Seeing families emerge from their hardship made me proud. I discovered that my greatest skills were empathy, respect, and the ability to truly listen.

§

Growing up in the Lebanese community in Western Sydney, my family and I were deeply immersed in the close-knit social scene. Weekends were spent visiting each other's homes – beautifully decorated double-storey houses with pristine, plastic-wrapped furniture designed to last a lifetime. The highlight of these gatherings was always the backyard, where the men fired up their homemade coal barbecues. The women marinated juicy chicken in the kitchen while children played on freshly mowed lawns. These visits weren't just about food and company; they were also opportunities to catch up on the latest news from home, celebrate milestones and even arrange marriages.

With my father's encouragement, my older brother opened a sweet shop in Marrickville. Seeing our family name displayed on the shopfront filled my father with pride. Around this time, other migrants were also establishing their own businesses – grocery stores, halal butchers, law and accounting firms, medical clinics and pharmacies. My mother was in heaven. She could communicate in her native tongue with shopkeepers and find the exact ingredients for her cooking. Food was her love language. Through cooking, she brought us together, creating moments I will always cherish.

Over time, our family became well known in the community. Our house held a prime location – right across from the park where the annual Arabic Carnivale was held. With ample parking space and a front-row view, it became the perfect place for gathering. The festival was a joyful occasion, a grand celebration of our culture, drawing the Immigration and Foreign Affairs ministers, along with other government officials, providing us with a platform to advocate for better settlement services and support. We eagerly anticipated this event every year, where we came together with dancers, singers, skilled musicians and stalls offering lovingly prepared Lebanese food.

Despite our religious and political differences, we were a united community. We raised funds and supported families back home, standing in solidarity with those affected by the war. Our commitment to helping others inspired other communities to do the same. The Carnivale was also a time for welcoming new arrivals, sharing endless stories of the Lebanon we had left behind. And, inevitably, every gathering ended with the same debate – who was the right leader and who was the most corrupt.

§

At twenty-one I had a fulfilling job and a vibrant social life, through which I met my future husband. We shared big dreams and worked tirelessly to buy our first home, sacrificing many social activities along the way. A year later, in 1988, our first daughter, Karima, was born, and everything changed. I was overwhelmed by her arrival. I couldn't but wonder how my mother managed *fifteen* children of her own. As a first-time mother, I was suddenly alone in the day-to-day care of this tiny human, while my husband worked long hours to provide for us. Then, just eight months later, I fell pregnant again. Before I knew it, Suzy was born, and we had become a family of four.

I devoted myself fully to raising my daughters, unwilling to sacrifice those precious early years. But as time passed, the daily routine of motherhood began to take a toll on my well-being. I longed for a sense of purpose and connection that came with working, and my daughters needed more interaction with other children. After spending three years at home, I returned to the workforce, while Karima and Suzy attended daycare.

From the very beginning, I knew my most important role as a mother was to connect my children to their culture – to give them a strong sense of identity. School introduced them to the Australian way of life, and I made sure they remained deeply rooted in our heritage. I took them to family gatherings, community events, Eid celebrations and Sunday Arabic school. They grew up surrounded by the love and support of our community.

Balancing two cultures wasn't always easy. There were challenges, compromises and moments of uncertainty. But as my daughters grew, they became independent, outgoing and successful young women – connected to their heritage.

§

I took my first trip back to Lebanon. I was married and had two young daughters. We spent time in Akkar, in my husband's village Hrar and in my hometown of Tripoli.

When I left my beloved Tripoli as a child, I used to think of our house as a grand castle. But when I returned, I found a tiny, worn-down home with crumbling rooms and neglected balconies. The air was heavy with silence – no Uum Kulthum, no Farid al-Atrash playing in the background. The green tiles of our beautiful visitors' salon had faded, and the walls were wounded, riddled with bullet holes and shrapnel scars. I searched for the eleven-year-old girl who had once danced in her castle – but she was gone, buried beneath the grief of what had been lost in 1976.

The war not only destroyed Lebanon's infrastructure; it fractured its people. The country was divided, and even a six-year-old child could engage in a heated political debate. Education remained a priority, yet many highly qualified Lebanese couldn't find jobs in a system plagued by bribery and nepotism.

I struggled to adjust. Every interaction, even something as simple as a trip to the shop, seemed to turn into an ordeal. Shopkeepers would look me in the eye and say, 'You live in a country that respects its citizens and provides for their welfare. Why are you being stingy? Should I beg on the streets? We survive on tourism.' I had no words.

The trip began with a visit to my husband's family in Hrar, a village of about 2,500 people in northern Lebanon. Each night, we gathered with extended family and neighbours – men and women always segregated. One evening, a woman, barely twenty-four, sat beside me. She had five children under the age of seven. Half her teeth were missing, and she spoke of chronic pain in her joints and hips, struggling to get a decent night's sleep. Then, she turned to me and said, 'You have two girls. You need to try for a boy.'

I looked at her and replied, 'You need to stop having children and take care of your health – your physical and mental well-being.'

Total silence. When I looked up, I saw disbelief on the faces of the other women.

Two weeks later, the village leader paid me a visit, accusing me of *qat'innasl* – 'terminating our lineage'. It was a phrase I had never heard before. He lectured me, saying, 'Women in this village are raised to bear children and obey their husbands. There was no place for any *falsafeh*' – 'nonsense'. Then came the word that struck me the hardest: *enti gharibeh* – a stranger. Not just an outsider but a foreigner, even in my husband's village, even in my own country.

I didn't argue. I looked him in the eyes and said, 'Women in this village have no access to adequate healthcare. They've never been checked by a doctor or a dentist in their lives. Their health is at risk. If their only purpose is to bear children, then you have a much bigger problem in this village.'

For days, his words echoed in my mind: 'You are a foreigner. A foreigner… a foreigner.'

During our stay in Akkar, we took a day trip to El Qammouaa, a vast forest with an elevation of 1,106 metres. Among the juniper trees, hairy oaks, and ancient cedars, I met an elderly man who had built himself a tin shed in the wilderness, choosing solitude when the war erupted.

I stopped and greeted him with, '*Assalamu alaykom*' – 'Peace be with you.'

He looked at me and replied, '*Wa alayki assalam*' – 'Peace be with you also'. Then, he said, '*Enti ma min hon*' – 'You are not from here.'

I asked, 'How did you know?'

He said, 'I watched you admiring the forest. You were hypnotised by it.'

He told me about the land, its history, and the geologists who had estimated that the forest was over 1,000 years old. When I asked why he chose to live there alone, his voice hardened.

'I would rather be protected and governed by this forest than by the *ekht sharmouta* (bitch) government. Did you see what they did to Tripoli? Lebanon was once generous to its people. We lived with good morals and value systems. We were closer to our Christian neighbours than to our own Muslim families. Do you know why?'

Before I could answer, he continued.

'Because Allah commanded us not just to love thy neighbour but love up to the seventh neighbour in line, meaning everyone. And look at us now: the government corrupted its own people, turned them against one another for greed. It destroyed our economy and mark my words – our banks will collapse because our leaders are sending Lebanon's wealth overseas.'

He went on, asking, 'Do you know what this will mean in thirty years? We won't survive. This country will experience famine. People will turn on each other. It won't just be the poor who suffer – it will be the middle class and even the rich.'

He had predicted it all so accurately. Lebanon's economic collapse ranks among the worst in modern history. Depositors are locked out of their own bank accounts. The Lebanese Lira, once equal to the U.S. dollar, has lost more than 98 per cent of its value. Meanwhile, Lebanon's political elite continue to evade reforms – for fear that transparency will expose their corruption.

Our original plan was to stay in Lebanon for three to six months. My husband and I wanted our children to experience our way of life, to be immersed in our culture. But as the weeks passed, the relentless chaos took its toll. The children grew restless, their behaviour shifting under the strain. Six weeks into our planned stay, I boarded a plane back to Sydney with my daughters.

In Australia, I was a *wog*. In Lebanon, I was a *foreigner*.

Returning from that trip was a reality check. A time for reflection. I found myself filled with gratitude for my mother, for the courage it took her to step into the unknown. For the stability and opportunities we found in Australia. And yet, despite the hardships, I was also grateful for the time I had spent in Lebanon – reconnecting with family, friends and my roots.

But in the end, my fondest memories of home always return to the eleven-year-old girl twirling in her red dress and tapping on the green tiles with her shiny black shoes.

She is the only one who truly belongs there.

The time she inhabited no longer exists. And neither does she. But they belong to each other.

§

In 1996, our third daughter, Amany, was born, and life could not have been happier. I continued to nurture a small but strong community of like-minded, supportive friends who enriched my social life. I joined an Arabic choir, singing the songs of my childhood – Farid al-Atrash, Umm Kulthum, Abdul Wahab, Fairuz, and many others. The choir focussed on *Tarab* (classical Arabic music), with lyrics I had memorised as a child. My fellow choristers marvelled at how I could recall the poetic verses of some of the greatest Arab lyricists. Singing and dancing lifted my spirit.

As a social worker, I dedicated myself to supporting refugees and their families. Witnessing their strength and courage only deepened my passion for helping those in need. The privilege of making a difference in their lives enriched my own and expanded my understanding of humanity. I was surrounded by colleagues – social justice advocates and humanitarian thinkers – who inspired me with their relentless optimism and commitment to change. Though I faced discrimination and prejudice along the way, both subtle and overt, I never allowed it to deter me from fostering an inclusive and welcoming environment.

Later in my career, I met Indigenous workers through training workshops. It was then that I paused to truly reflect on their history and struggles. I began educating myself about colonisation and questioned why our communities – both Indigenous and migrant – were not connecting, not sharing our stories. I actively sought Indigenous friendships and saw the deep wounds left by forced removal from their families, the loss of land and the erosion of culture. In their pain, I found echoes of our own migration experience – the sense of displacement, the fight for recognition. I asked myself, 'If this is how our First Nations people are treated, how can we, as Lebanese and Arab migrants, ever be fully accepted?'

That realisation ignited a new purpose in me – to keep communicating, protesting and sharing stories. Through the generosity of Indigenous Australians, I learnt that this land belongs to us all, but we are merely its custodians. We must protect it and ensure its future for generations to come.

A year into the COVID-19 pandemic, I made the difficult decision to leave social work. At the time, I had been co-developing a gender equality programme that required me to interview women and men separately, to address domestic violence in a culturally sensitive way. With families locked down together, my work became impossible. There was no privacy, no safe space for these conversations.

Soon after, my eldest daughter and I launched Sunday Kitchen (SK) – a small business where we teach traditional Lebanese cooking. SK was born from love – the love my mother passed on to me through food, the love I shared with my own daughters in the kitchen. Cooking with my mother had been more than just a practical skill, although her magical elixirs of roses and orange blossoms are never forgotten in our sweets. Cooking with my mother was more about sharing stories. When my daughters were growing up, the kitchen became our sacred space – where they confided in me about their lives as we chopped, mixed and stirred. Now, I pass this tradition on not only to them but to my three granddaughters, Layla, Eden and Celine. I hope they, too, will carry on the tradition with their own families.

At SK, we celebrate Lebanese cuisine with people from all backgrounds. Around the table we eat, drink and share stories – sometimes there is laughter, sometimes tears, but we always leave enriched by the experience. From my upbringing as the second-youngest in a large family, to migration, motherhood, advocacy and singing in the choir – every experience in my life has led me to this work of Sunday Kitchen.

Following SK's success, we were given the opportunity to write a cookbook, *Sofra*, sharing our recipes and our passion with the world.

Through all of this, I have come to realise that settling in a new country is about more than just housing and work. What truly makes a home are the people around us, even those who are long gone and buried. My beloveds are still part of me. While people build houses, relationships create the essence of home. Over the years, I have built a small community of like-minded people I call home. Home is where love resides.

I am a woman, a daughter, a sister, a mother, a grandmother, a friend, a social worker, a cook, a storyteller, a dancer and someone who deeply cares for others. Some mornings, when I look in the mirror, I see my mother. I smile and say, '*Sabah El Kheir,* Amineh' – 'Good morning.'

After all these years, I'm still grateful to Amineh for her brave resolve to bring her children here, to safety, away from the war that consumed our homeland. Amineh paid dearly for that safety. And now, it seems we pay again – watching, helpless, as bombs fall upon our people. Every day, I see images streaming out of Gaza. Dead, bombed, mutilated or unearthed from rubble. With every image of a mother crying, a grandmother tormented or a child shaking and hungry, I relive Lebanon's own destruction. I see Fadi in every murdered young man.

As I finish writing this story, nearly 100 weeks of rallying for a ceasefire in Gaza have passed. Governments have done nothing to stop this killing and their silence is complicit. Does Australia care? Does the world care? I choose to hope that hearts will open, and the killing will stop. I must hold onto hope as I attend the rallies. I choose love as my heart breaks with sorrow, and like Amineh, I still wait in hope for the end of a war.

DEEP ROOTS
by Hend Saab

The sun was approaching its zenith in the blue sky. A few white cloudlets, painted by a soft brush, reflected the magnificent azure. This splendid display confirmed to me that nature had detached itself from the evil deeds of destruction and misery committed on that beautiful day and inflicted upon my people. A day recorded in history with our blood and tears; it was 5 June 1967.

I sat crowded into a rickety wagon with my family and neighbours, pulled along by an old brown tractor. We were heading north in search of safety, fleeing our village in South Lebanon with other people forced to leave their homes, farms and livelihoods. Some had even mounted the back of the tractor, which was now winding its way along the tracks between the fields. As we passed the village cemetery, the mother of my friend waved at her own mother's grave and lamented, 'Will I visit you and recite the *Fatiha* for your soul ever again?'

As we progressed in our northbound journey, I became increasingly captivated by the rolling valleys and hills that stretched as far as the eye could see. At every turn, the splendour of the countryside was revealed by diverse and vast landscapes that I had not seen before, nor had I been aware of their existence. My contemplations were interrupted by the deafening sounds of the Israeli war planes buzzing above our heads, accompanied by the wailing of the women and crying of the children who overcrowded our tractor.

The petrified faces of the men conveyed a general sense of helplessness, which deeply unsettled me. I was seven years old. My fear was confirmed by what was said around me: 'Oh, my God, are we going to suffer the same fate as the Palestinians? God knows if we will see our homes and fields ever again.' This was one of my early memories of the Arab–Israeli War that ended with the 1967 Naksa or Setback.

I grew up hearing about the beauty of the Galilee and the prosperity of Haifa, Akka and Safad across the border. When I was young, I was mesmerised by the stories of our elderly neighbours, the two cousins Om Khalil and Om Kassim. They often reminisced about how they bathed in the hot springs of Tiberias with other South Lebanese women to enhance their fertility and treat their ailments. These stories made me feel so deprived because the Nakba of 1948 made it impossible for my generation to set foot into Palestine. Standing on the front terrace of my parents' house, which faced Jabal al Jarmaq in Palestine – the Israelis call it Mount Meron – I had always wondered what the world looked like beyond the barbed wire that separated us. The roads that connected my village to Palestine for thousands of years had been blocked.

Before the Nakba, Palestine was the *qibla* (destination) to which the South Lebanese were bound for trade, work, medical treatment and tourism. The people of South Lebanon and North Palestine had close commercial and social ties. There were intermarriages and similarities in dialects.

The Nakba severed these ties. South Lebanon was amputated from Palestine and continues to bleed. The subsequent 'truce' with Israel was frequently violated by kidnappings, and clawing of more Lebanese land, property, cattle and sheep.

§

The '1967 Arab-Israeli War' ended quickly, and in less than a week, we returned to our village, Yaroun, in South Lebanon. The humiliating defeat of the Arab coalition countries inflicted a profound and long-lasting wound resulting in collective trauma. New borders were drawn, triggering a new phase of fear and uncertainty.

For many years after the Naksa, the towns and villages on the southern Lebanese border were the battlegrounds for the ongoing confrontation between the Palestinians and the Israelis. The border inhabitants were helpless and lived in a constant state of dread, robbing them of their sense of security and stability.

One of the most horrifying events cemented in my memory goes back to the early 1970s, when I was twelve years old. During a night of intense Israeli shelling that targeted our village, my family had taken refuge in a corner of the house. I was fighting frightening thoughts that we were a hair's breadth away from being severely injured or dead. A missile landed a few metres from our house and shattered our back windows. My father went into the next room to check the damage. I was terrified that I might not see him alive again.

At 4 am, returned to our hiding place, my father turned on a small transistor radio to listen to the news aired on an Egyptian station in Cairo. There was no mention of what we were experiencing in the Lebanese border area. The broadcaster announced an upcoming meeting of the United Nations Security Council. I asked my father whether the Security Council was aware of what was happening to us. He responded with an ironic smile which conveyed the distrust, profound sense of hopelessness and vulnerability we were feeling. The South was abandoned not only by the world but by the rest of the country. It was the scapegoat that was left to face its fate alone.

In the morning, we ventured out of hiding with a feeling of dread, anxious to learn about the fate of the people of our village. 'No one was hurt this time,' shouted one of the neighbours. 'It is a miracle that everyone was spared.' A mixture of reassuring and congratulatory messages circulated in the neighbourhood, restoring a temporary sense of relief. The lack of casualties did not reflect the intensity of the shelling, the ferocity of the aggressor and the scale of destruction. We believed that a divine force had intervened to safeguard our people.

§

The lack of security and employment led many Southerners to migrate. It was common for people, particularly males as young as fourteen, to leave their homeland for safety and future opportunities and support their families back home.

The expatriate would return after a few years for a short period to marry a young woman from the village, with whom he had a relationship or at least an interest before he left, or a woman suggested by his friends or family. Others came back decades later, while some never returned, forgetting and being forgotten.

The story of my marriage was similar to many others in our area but with different faces and names. It began in the late summer of 1977. A cool light breeze chased away the warmth of August, softening the atmosphere and caressing the fig and vine leaves that covered the ground, forming a beautiful autumnal-coloured rug. Flocks of birds declared their readiness to depart for warmer and safer skies. They too seemed to be fed up with the agony and fear, longing for freedom and peace. Farmers were pleased by the unseasonal drop in temperature, which promised early rain to irrigate the parched grounds and quench the hearts weary with grief and injustice.

Everyone was yearning for change and on the lookout for a glimpse of hope, but there were no signs of relief from the oppressive situation and, as the Arabic proverb goes, *If it was going to rain, we would have seen the clouds*. On the contrary, our village fell into the twenty-kilometre 'security zone' controlled by the Lebanese militias overseen by the Israelis. We were completely cut off from the rest of the country.

I met the man who would become my husband by coincidence, briefly, at a relative's house. I was impressed with the elegant way he introduced himself, and his respectful, courteous manners. I left feeling this was a new beginning and perhaps an intriguing chapter in my life. It was common in our village for relationships to progress very quickly. Indeed, my feelings were soon confirmed, and we announced our engagement to be married a few weeks later. There was no apparent reason to decline the marriage proposal or delay it. He was a reputable and self-made young man who had recently returned to Lebanon after more than eleven years in Australia, where he had worked hard to secure his future. My fiancé owned a house there and had a secure job, so he wanted to return to Australia as soon as possible. Our marriage was accepted and blessed by all. People in the village often said, 'What else would a young woman be waiting for?'

In fact, there was nothing for a young woman or a young man to wait for, because of the worsening situation and the ongoing war that was affecting all aspects of our lives. For us, at the border, male or female, migration was a given, an inevitable fate. It was the only opportunity to have a safe life, achieve our dreams and secure a better future.

Our marriage could not proceed customarily because we were under occupation by the militias. There was no hairdresser or bridal shop in the village or a nearby town. We were unable to go to other cities in the area, such as Soor or Saida, due to the hazards on the roads. Our *katb-ketab* (marriage ceremony) took place nearby in Bint Jbeil, a Southern Lebanese border town once known for its myriad modern shops. Its Thursday market attracted thousands of merchants and shoppers. On that day, the town of Bint Jbeil, the largest of the border villages, was a desolate ghost town, with only a few inhabitants due to the dire circumstances.

We entered a photography shop, the only place open besides a couple of small vegetable and grocery stores. The owner was quick to apologise, as he did not have what was needed to take and develop our wedding photos. The adjacent bridal shop was closed. The photographer informed us that the owner went to visit her family in the mountain area a month ago and had not returned. 'My family has moved to Beirut, but my wife kept her wedding dress here and she is your size,' said a young man who was present, after seeing the disappointment on my face. He left at once, and very soon came back with the dress. I took it and was excited and grateful for the kind gesture of this stranger. It has stayed with me to this day.

When I got back to the village, I styled my hair and put on some makeup. I wore the white dress and looked in the mirror with admiration and coquetry, taunting the oppressive circumstances that swamped our lives as I managed to retain and celebrate part of my special day.

The rest of our wedding day was generally quiet, except for the chatter of a few family members and neighbours gathered at my in-laws' house. The groom's grandmother defied the fear that reigned in the village and sang a couple of *aweeha* (traditional ululations), justifying them with, 'It falls upon an elder to give the blessing. I have been waiting too long for this day.' She was a resilient Southern Lebanese woman in her seventies who taught timeless lessons about the true meaning of patience and graciousness. She insisted on being true to something she had promised herself and not allowing the unjust situation to steal her joy. The groom hugged her and said with teary eyes, 'Grandma, we are taking you with us to Australia.' She shook her head, 'Your country is too far.' A few weeks earlier, his grandmother had risked her life trying to block the path of a South Lebanese Army tank. My husband had naively brought boxing equipment with him from Australia to train the village youths, but the local militiamen thought otherwise and insisted on humiliating him in public to teach others a lesson.

§

In the couple of months after we got married, I often felt nervous and apprehensive; those feelings were soon replaced by elation when I learnt I was going to be a mother.

We started preparing to leave a world where opportunities were non-existent and hope had diminished. I aspired to another world that would revive my dream of completing my studies and having a career. It was a dream that had almost dissipated from my mind and my reality, but I refused to give it up. At the time, I had no idea what career I wanted, but I was inspired at a very early age by a female engineer from Beirut who came to inspect the damage in our village caused by an earth tremor. Her presence in the technical group opened a door of possibilities in my mind.

There was no library room in our house, but it was not without books, newspapers and magazines. My father was an avid reader and polyglot who always brought home political books and novels in Arabic, English and German. I was a voracious reader. I read anything and everything I could get my hands on in Arabic. I was very impressed by the famous Egyptian writers Naguib Mahfouz and Ihsan Abdel Kouddous, especially their audacity in addressing social issues and their analysis of human psychology. This instilled in me a curiosity and a love for learning about human behaviour and may have influenced my future career choice.

My school days remain my most treasured memories. I was a high-achieving student despite the responsibilities entrusted to me from a young age as the eldest daughter of a family of five girls and four boys. In reference to my father's intellectual abilities, people in the village would make remarks such as, 'You wouldn't expect anything less from the daughter of Moussa El-Haj.' While I was proud to be my father's daughter, I often felt that the hard work underpinning my achievements was not acknowledged as my own but more as a reflection of him.

Nevertheless, their praises of my father's ability were true. There's a common saying in Lebanon which acknowledges those who have influenced our development: '*The eye is never situated above the eyebrow!*' My father mastered several languages and was regularly approached by the people of the village to write persuasive letters, compelling their loved ones to reply. He volunteered to read and translate travel documentation and fill out immigration applications, among other things. He often spoke on behalf of the people of the village and even represented the border region in his interviews with foreign journalists, who sometimes landed in our part of the world to cover the Israeli attacks on the South.

§

Less than three months into our marriage, I was granted a visa for Australia. A few weeks later, in the first week of January 1978, I stood farewelling my siblings who had gathered around the fireplace in the middle of our living room. A big lump formed in my throat, and I tried hard to fight back my tears.

My gaze followed my mother, who had a kitchen apron wrapped around her waist and seemed busy as usual, in an attempt to conceal her feelings and restrain her emotions. That's how my mother always faced life's challenges: with courage and composure. How could she not? My mother was a capable and hardworking woman who also assumed the role of 'father' for her large family through the challenging circumstances of war, because my father spent most of his time abroad, working to support us. To this day, I cherish the congratulatory letter he sent me a couple of months later from New York where he was working.

I stood in that moment, saying goodbye to the home that had been my world. I felt guilty for abandoning my mother and forsaking my duty in supporting her with housework and raising my siblings. My husband and I left with her last words of blessing and as I walked away, I heard her repeating, 'May God be with you,' and 'Take care of yourself.' I could barely see through my tears.

Slowly and carefully, through my tears, I felt my way down the stairs, which I used to jump two at a time. I reached the gate at the entrance of the house which was close to the street corner. I looked to the left, throwing a disheartened look at the houses down our street, Haret Al-Bayader, which had been the abode of our childhood and the stage of our youth. It was once named 'Hamra' after one of the famous streets in Beirut and had attracted young lovers from all over the village on their evening walks known as *casdura*. The street would fill just before sunset; friends would walk arm-in-arm hoping to get a glimpse of someone they fancied and throw a glance or smile their way. On the day of my departure, the street was deserted, gloomy and cold. My husband and I stood there waiting for the taxi to make its way around the no-through road and stop in front of our house.

Fond memories of my childhood and youth flashed through my mind. I reflected on my experiences of growing up in this neighbourhood where we all lived like a big family. There were the occasional brawls between neighbours, often instigated by children's disputes. The brawls were so belligerent you would think a world war had just broken out, but the opponents would soon reconcile and in no time, everything would go back to normal.

I glanced at the nearby fields and pictured them in their elegant winter appearance on snowy days, all dressed up in dazzling white like brides. I recalled throwing snowballs at my friends and passers-by, and our futile attempts at building snowmen. Fully immersed in our snow fun, we were oblivious to the cold or the cries of our parents warning us about getting sick. In their wisdom, the elders of the village would say, 'Snowy days are only for children and dogs to celebrate.' Winter would be followed by a magnificent spring with the best display nature had to offer. Blazing colourful flowers, with distinctive red poppies, scattered on a background of lush undulating green grass and shrubs. The long spring school holidays meant that we could fully enjoy this glorious time of the year. Then summer days had an extra-special thrill. Our loud laughs resounded on the horizon, startling the older women in the neighbourhood who usually gathered from the afternoon until sunset outside their houses on concrete seats. They retaliated and swore at our parents who, they jested, had failed to raise us properly, calling our generation too self-absorbed.

A silent tear of nostalgia escaped my eye when I remembered how, when we were teenagers, the corners and alleys of the neighbourhood had witnessed our deep secrets and adventures, our sorrows and laughter and sometimes the two combined. Despite the bleak circumstances, we had the determination and willpower to enjoy ourselves. We established the Association of Magazines and Readers, which included several young people in the neighbourhood and others from the village. We saved a lira each from our weekly allowance to share the cost of purchasing weekly magazines such as *Al Shabaka* and *Al Mawed*, or the romantic illustrated and translated film magazines *Rima*, *Delilah* and *Samar*.

While standing at the bottom of my parents' stairs, a few moments prior to our departure, I remembered our gatherings every Friday at our next-door neighbour's house to watch a weekly Arabic film. Before the film was due to start at 6:30 pm and without informing the owner of the house, our shoes piled up at the entrance so we could enter. In the dark, the neighbour used to feel her way between those lying on the floor or others sitting on chairs while we were enraptured by the romantic scenes of Abdel Halim, Shadia, Faten Hamama, Farid al-Atrash, and other renowned Arab screen celebrities of the time. We were oblivious to the difficulties the neighbour was having trying to find her way between us while murmuring to herself amusedly, '*La ehhem wala dastoor*' (Unbelievable, no permission needed or asked). Apart from her minor grumblings, we never felt unwelcome, and everyone acknowledged the generosity and hospitality of this open house. We hurried back home as soon as the movie finished, mistakenly wearing each other's shoes.

As the taxi drew near, a voice stirred within me, echoing the haunting words of an elderly neighbour in the village – one who had watched two of her children depart for Venezuela decades ago, never to return. 'Dear God, our children are scattered around the world like a handful of dust.' On this day, I felt her declaration extended to me. I was deeply saddened, pain surging through me as I realised that these authentic, carefree and spontaneous days would never return.

§

We headed to Damascus International Airport, as Beirut Airport was closed. I was leaving behind a homeland in an exhausted state, moaning under the destructive years of civil war. The border area in the South was now controlled by an Israeli-backed Lebanese militia, known as the South Lebanon Army, which adopted humiliating and oppressive practices. As they say, 'What hurts the tree is that the axe's handle is made with its wood.' We arrived at the Masnaa Border Crossing after a short stop in Beirut, where we had to change to a Syrian taxi. My husband took the passenger seat next to the driver, and I retired to the back seat. As soon as the car took off, I rested my head against the window, pretending to sleep. I had neither the motivation nor the ability to engage in any form of communication with the lady sitting on the other side with her little girl between us. More importantly, I needed the space and time to comprehend and process what had happened.

Here I was, three months pregnant, overwhelmed with anxiety, walking into the unknown with a man I hardly knew, to a country I knew little about. I closed my eyes and remembered a beautiful white dress embroidered with rose buds and soft miniature green leaves. I was about six years old when my father had given it to me in the mid-1960s. It was from Australia. This cherished gift represented the possibility of goodness and beauty in a faraway place. This memory soothed my anxiety and reduced my fear of the unknown. I wanted to keep that dress for my future daughter. Though, I don't know what happened to that dress, and I didn't end up having a daughter.

Other comforting memories resurfaced: the two large tins of honey that my father brought from Australia; the resultant times we woke to a loud banging at our front door at varying hours of the night, inevitably someone from the village after some Australian honey for a woman experiencing a difficult childbirth, or perhaps a child with a bad cold or persistent cough. I hid a warm smile when I remembered how my father would coax me to take a spoonful of honey every morning, especially on winter days, in the belief that honey would strengthen my immunity and mitigate my chronic tonsillitis. My relationship with the smell and taste of honey is still tainted by apprehension.

The woollen blankets patterned with pastel-coloured squares that my father brought back from his trip to Australia, also in the mid-60s, came to my mind. We used to tuck these pure-wool Australian blankets under our quilts to keep us warm during the bitterly cold nights of our mountain climate. Several years after I arrived in Australia, I was so excited to find the same kind of blankets at a garage sale. I still have them, connecting me to the warmth and reassurance of my childhood home.

As we passed beautiful green pastures with cows, donkeys and horses, I remembered a Year 3 geography book which depicted an Australian farmer riding a horse amongst a large flock of sheep, surrounded by thick red dust. That image, fixed in my mind, fascinated me. I wondered then if it had anything to do with my future.

Feeling exhausted, I must've dozed off before I heard that we were on the outskirts of Damascus. My husband and the lady sitting next to me at the back were clearly worried about my well-being. I sat upright, assured everyone that I was fine and thanked them for their concern.

We rushed into the airport, having our travel documents checked before boarding the plane. We were greeted and taken to our designated seats by the hostesses, whose beauty and elegance impressed me. I vaguely recall the plane stopping in London and in Singapore on its way to Australia. I was exhausted, and the smell of food completely turned me off eating. I was content with just water and bread, which left me feeling fatigued. Physically weary and emotionally drained, I had no energy left in my body to resist what was unfolding. I allowed events to flow and surrendered, embracing the inevitable developments. I gave in and fell asleep.

§

We arrived early on Wednesday, 11 January 1978. It was a bright and sunny morning with a clear sky. Sydney looked nothing like New York or London, the cities portrayed in American movies I had watched back home. I was very impressed with the smooth and ordered traffic and the lack of car horns. I remember making a comment, to my husband's dismay, given his pride over paying off his home, about how humble the houses were compared to the mansions built by immigrants back in Yaroun even during the darkest stretches of the war. At the time, I did not appreciate the hard work and sacrifices required to own a home in Australia. Later a comment from a family friend explained it all to me: 'A home loan in Australia is like a life sentence.'

The morning after our arrival I woke up at 4, terrified by a loud roar, thinking it was an Israeli warplane. I calmed down once I realised it was a low-flying plane preparing to land at the nearby Sydney Airport. I got out of bed and headed to the living room, eager to discover my new world. I turned on the TV and the first thing that caught my attention was the Australian accent of the broadcaster. It was different from what I was used to hearing after Big Ben struck the hour, a deep voice announcing, 'This is the BBC World News in London,' which my father diligently listened to every morning he was home. These initial observations were the least significant of the surprises fate had in store for me.

For the first few days our home was filled with family and friends who warmly welcomed us. Visitors who had migrated to Australia from our village and its surrounding areas came to claim tapes or letters sent by their families; with the war, that was their only way of receiving news about their relatives and loved ones abroad. For the duration of the civil war and beyond, the Lebanese postal service had been rendered non-existent. Telecommunications infrastructure had been damaged. Telephones had become inefficient and enormously expensive in and out of the country. At the end of the first week, a dinner party was held in our honour. It made up for our rushed wedding and the miserable circumstances that surrounded it.

§

A week after our arrival, at the end of the Christmas and New Year holidays, everyone went back to work. I spent six days of the week at home alone, my main company the regular chirping of the birds. The overwhelming stillness was interrupted every half an hour by the sound of the bus stopping in front of our house.

In the first few months, loneliness crept into my life in the form of a heavy hollow silence and an uneasy calm. I longed for the carefree relationships and loud chatter between neighbours in Haret Al Bayader and how awkward we felt as young girls crossing the crowded and noisy *sahat yaroun* (the village square). I missed my family home, the bustling place where activity never ceased and silence never found its way in. Sadness and guilt engulfed me when I recalled my frequent complaints about the constant noise, activity and chatter of our family home.

However, every now and then, the voice of the Greek neighbour across the road fighting with his teenage son would break the silence. I saw his daughter, who was close to my age, on her way to and from school, and wished to be in her place. Much credit goes to their next-door neighbour, an Anglo-Australian woman; she inadvertently introduced me to a variety of swear words in English, which she showered on her children before and after school, and especially on weekends.

At first, our Anglo-Australian neighbours on both sides looked at me with curiosity, waving through their windows or behind their security doors. It occurred to me to knock on the door of the neighbour on the right, with whom I had exchanged brief conversations, and cheekily hold an empty cup, asking her to lend me some sugar as we used to do back home. I would then imagine her reaction and laugh to myself. Eventually, I got to know my neighbours and found them very compassionate. I'll always feel grateful for their support later on, during a very difficult period.

§

The days passed slowly. I sought refuge in reading. I started with the *Reader's Digest* magazines, with issues backdated five years, stacked on a small bookcase in the living room. I found the 'My Male' comic page easy to read and entertaining. My excitement with beginning to master English was immeasurable. One of the jokes read: 'When the phone rings, my man rushes to the door and when the doorbell rings, he goes to the phone.' I held the magazine in one hand, and the little dictionary I brought with me from Lebanon in the other.

Soon, I had gained enough English to construct simple sentences. Reading, translating, and listening to English-language television programmes, including *Sesame Street*, enabled me to run daily errands independently, to fill out bank forms, health insurance claims and more. My daily phone call with my aunt in Sydney was the line that connected me to the outside world, as I spent most days home alone. Our call was often interrupted by a customer entering my aunt's shop, who would get busy and forget that I was still on the other end. Sometimes, I would wait for a long time, intrigued by the haggling about prices, and inadvertently learn about the latest news in the community. I became acquainted with many of the customers, some of whom I had never met in person.

After a few months in Australia, my health deteriorated. Persistent morning sickness, nausea and loss of appetite drained me completely. My blood pressure abruptly increased, which required a hospital stay and an early labour – a decision the doctors had to make hastily for my safety and my baby. Thus, my first child was born almost a month prematurely. I looked at my newborn with anxiety, doubting my skills to care for him. We often shared bouts of inconsolable crying. I remembered my mother often. I needed to hear her voice desperately. Under the militia regime, privacy was non-existent, and phone calls were prohibitively expensive, and inefficient. I needed her to soothe my pain and reduce the agony.

At times, I felt angry. I thought of how my mother had *her* mother, *her* sisters, as well as the loving women of the neighbourhood when she gave birth, while I was here alone. My longing for them exacerbated my physical and emotional vulnerability. I certainly experienced what we now call the baby blues. Fortunately, as my baby started to thrive, so did my self-confidence as a mother. His presence filled my life, and he became the friend to whom I confided my thoughts and my distress. This may have contributed to his early maturity and strong sense of responsibility. My next pregnancy was far less difficult. My second son was a contented baby. His calm and pleasant nature made having two children under two manageable.

My dreams of pursuing my studies or working were evaporating. We were financially well-off enough for me to stay home and care for my children, and I was frequently reminded to be grateful for it.

On 11 January 1981, my husband and I stood at Sydney Airport with two toddlers and the remnants of a failing relationship, which would come to an end a few weeks after we landed in Lebanon. It was ironic that we had arrived in Australia on 11 January, three years to that day.

§

With no steady income or home, I had no chance of securing custody of my children. Their father's family cared for them, and I agreed to see them only on weekends and holidays – an arrangement I reluctantly accepted, believing it to be a temporary resolution. They were so little, only two and three years of age. My circumstances had clearly changed, and I was now a mother of two for whom I was fully responsible. It became clear to me that the only opportunity for us to stay together was to return to Australia, where I believed the future awaited us. Every step I took was aimed in that direction.

I announced to the village my availability to provide English tutoring to primary school students, and soon my time was filled. The praises from Om Ibrahim and other satisfied parents about my competency as a tutor soon reached the New Generation School in Bint Jbeil, the only English school in the region. The New Generation School stood tall on a hilly road above the local spring. Each day the local women would gather amidst laughter and chatter to wash their crockery until their pots gleamed proudly in the sun. (Unfortunately, this tradition has faded, replaced with modern conveniences.) I walked by these women warmed by their good cheer and kind greetings before my meeting on the first floor.

The principal of the New Generation School was seated behind a large dark-brown desk when I stepped into his office. The afternoon sun cast a gentle glow on his face, adding to the reassuring warmth of the space. After a thorough interview, he offered me an opportunity. I joined the next teacher training course in July, which included a written exam and an oral presentation. During my presentation, I was distracted by two women whispering rudely in the corner. To my surprise, the lioness within me awoke. I stopped, calmly put down the chalk and stated, 'Is there something you'd like to share with the class?' It was that prowess in classroom management that won me a job offer, but I still harboured a desire for even greater academic achievement. I needed my baccalaureate.

And so, my busy days began. From 7.30 in the morning until 2 pm, I taught English. In the afternoons and evenings, I studied hard to complete the baccalaureate. I'll always be grateful for the warm lunches that kind parents and school neighbours often provided: stuffed zucchinis with rice and meat in tomato sauce, or sandwiches with homemade *labni* (yoghurt) made with freshly baked bread. Whatever the meal, it was sent with love and received with gratitude.

I was the first woman with children to break tradition, return to study and pursue an education. Returning to study after so long had its challenges, but a glimmer of hope started to illuminate the future. Those four years while studying and teaching in Bint Jbeil were difficult. I worked hard to conceal how much I ached for my sons, who spent so much time with my ex-husband's family. I would frequently push back despair and hold tight to the dream of returning to Australia with my children.

I was preparing for the baccalaureate exam. I was exhausted but confident. Then fate stepped in; the opportunity to return to Australia with my children arose. I had to act quickly. I forfeited the exam and within days, we were getting ready to leave the village again. Relatives and friends, including teachers and colleagues, warned me, 'It is a huge responsibility, going alone with two children to a foreign country.' They thought I didn't understand the extent of the responsibility, that I was naive. They may have been right, but sometimes we must defy reason!

With no access to the banks in Beirut, my father borrowed 13,500 liras for the cost of our travel from a neighbour. Soon after, inflation spiralled and the lira collapsed, but our neighbour insisted on receiving the same amount borrowed, even though it was greatly devalued. To this day, I feel greatly indebted to this generous man.

We left the village for Beirut in late July 1984. The invading Israeli army had reached the capital and the main coastal road to it was cut off. Driving through the mountains was the only route. The journey from our village to Beirut, which usually took three hours, lasted seventeen long, agonising hours. We stopped at an infamous Israeli checkpoint. I witnessed the humiliation, disrespect and undignified treatment that passengers were subjected to, including women, children and the elderly. We were made to wait in the vehicles that lined up for several kilometres under the scorching sun, to be searched and interrogated before being allowed to pass. I vowed never to return to Lebanon – this beautiful, sad and troubled country – while there were foreign checkpoints. Indeed, I didn't return to Lebanon until after the liberation from the Israelis and their militias from the South.

The four days we spent in Beirut in the generous hospitality of a family friend, while I organised our travel documents, felt like an eternity. Every morning, I listened for the chattering of street cleaners and the clattering of coffee cups being sold on the street. These sounds suggested a new day and a growing hope that we could depart. Beirut Airport was at risk of sudden closure at any moment. I had lost sleep, and my appetite disappeared. I was so relieved when we finally boarded. I was finally leaving with my children to Australia, the dream I had held on to for the past four years. Despite not completing the exam I was so ready for, I knew I had acted rightly.

On the plane I looked at my four- and six-year-old sons with a sense of relief, but I was utterly exhausted. I would doze off, then open my eyes to check that my children were still really beside me. Hope appeared through the window of the plane. We were finally together and headed back to Australia.

§

We arrived at Sydney Airport in early August 1984. On our way to the car park, where a relative waited for us, the sky seemed wider and the sun more radiant. I was returning with a plan for our lives, backed by uncompromised determination, and steadfast faith in God. I had brought with me core principles and values from my upbringing that helped guide my decisions and ensure for us a dignified life.

Upon our arrival, we stayed with a cousin's family for several weeks. I soon found a one-bedroom unit, which was empty, except for my great hopes for our future. This tiny apartment was more than enough to embrace my small family but too modest to contain my joy and happiness. Though my excitement soon lapsed. A few days after our move, a letter from the strata management pushed under our door dictated that I could only use the shared laundry and clotheslines on Tuesdays, although they were available most weekdays. I was the only occupant in the building that was working and had young children. This incident was followed by daily harassment from other tenants. One day, they accused my children of breaking a massive branch that had actually fallen after a storm. Anxious, I was unable to sleep. I feared I could not protect my sons when they were not with me.

Amid this heartache, a neighbour in the adjacent apartment called out to me on a Tuesday morning, while I was on my way to the laundry, and invited me in. She was in her early eighties and used a walking-frame to manoeuvre around the old luxury furniture in her living room. The thick layer of her makeup made the black mole at the top of her left cheek more prominent but did not conceal her genuine concern and kindness. After introducing herself as Mrs Robinson and telling me she had worked as a nurse for many years, she expressed her dismay at the ill-mannered behaviour of some members of the building management committee. She said, 'Please do not let them worry you, my dear. This is ridiculous and frankly, racial discrimination.' She offered me her own allocated days to use the laundry and clothesline. Mrs Robinson's words soothed me. I was far from home and my loving family. This exchange with Mrs Robinson began a loving friendship that lasted for years, only ending when the compassionate lady moved into a nursing home outside Sydney and passed away soon after.

My ordeal with the neighbours was a blessing in disguise. My frequent complaints to the real estate agent made her appreciate our predicament. She exempted us from the penalty applicable for breaching the six months' tenancy lease by vacating prior to the contracted date. I later learnt we were not the first casualty of this hostile neighbourhood. Anyway, it was time to change and move into a bigger place.

§

After my return from Lebanon, I invested as much time as possible in strengthening my relationship with my two boys. I wanted to reduce the impact of the separation and uprooting from their environment, where they had enjoyed the care, love and attention from both families. Fortunately, my father decided to come to Australia and support us. His arrival a few months later restored my sense of security and boosted my confidence to pursue my education and career. He looked after my children before and after school and prepared light meals for them. Until today, my two sons commend my father's cooking skills and often say, 'The best French fries ever were the ones *Gidi* made.' We, his own children, didn't get to enjoy such loving attention, as he was always away working. But my children were showered with his attention, and I was deeply grateful. It made up for what fate had deprived them of, and a deeply rooted connection grew between my sons and my father until his very last days.

The work and study I was able to do during that year were enjoyable and inspiring, motivating me to enrol in a four-year Associate Diploma in Social Welfare.

Completing the diploma as a single mother and new migrant was an empowering experience. It also improved my prospects of a good job. The practical component of the course showed me the great suffering and alienation of disadvantaged groups in this prosperous country. I gained a strong sense of social justice and felt drawn to the Indigenous people of Australia who were dispossessed of their land. I worked with people living with HIV and AIDS, domestic violence and other disadvantages. Every encounter left its mark on my life and pushed me to grow.

§

Our life in Australia settled further following the arrival of my mother and siblings in 1986, less than two years later, the time it took to get their visas. My siblings started studying and working part-time to establish their new lives. My mother felt unsettled, as her role in the family had drastically changed. In her fifties, armed with her courage and great determination, she decided to learn the language of the new country. She was keen to reclaim her self-reliance. She joined English language classes for new immigrants offered at my youngest sister's school. My mother learnt the English alphabet, numbers and how to construct simple sentences. This enabled her to read signs, train timetables and travel independently, and opened employment opportunities for her. She worked for over fifteen years until her health no longer permitted it.

When my family arrived, I thought it would be an opportunity to relive the past and be together as one big family. We lived together for about a year. My sons, the only grandchildren in the family, were showered with love and care. Although this attention was delightful for my sons, I became concerned that it could undermine my role and authority as a mother. It was time to venture out and lead an independent life alone with my two sons.

I bought a modest house through a government housing scheme designed to help low-income families with a lower interest rate than banks. Owning a home was a big leap forward. It helped me feel stable and more settled in Australia. In my own home, I felt that the world could not contain my joy. The image of every corner of that home is so cherished and remains deeply etched into my memory.

Although we had moved away from my family, we were never far from or short of their support. I would often return at night after a long day at work followed by attending lectures at university to find my two sons fed, bathed and ready for bed. This enabled me to concentrate on my studies and career. My boys were loved and safe.

§

It took me thirteen long years to reach my goal and develop a meaningful career, and it came at a price. For many years, my social connections were limited to my colleagues at work or at the university. I had to turn down numerous weddings, community events and social invitations. I still carry some guilt as I was unable to support my children's interests in sports and music.

In the early 1990s, I took up a job at the Australian Arab Council as the coordinator of the Arabic Family Support Service. This work exposed me to settlement-related challenges, such as family conflicts and disintegrations, school truancy, domestic violence, child protection issues, addiction and youth drug problems, which were rampant in our community at the time. They were symptoms of the alienation and the considerable struggle experienced by Arabic-speaking families, especially the Lebanese ones. They were bearing the impact of the civil war and occupation in Lebanon, while facing the prejudice of the media and society in Australia.

Working as a psychologist for over 30 years, I have discovered the serious impact of migration on the mental health of migrants and refugees. I have learnt about the long-lasting and intergenerational impacts of war trauma and displacement on individuals, families and communities.

In recent years, there has been a need to develop family education and mental health awareness, mindfulness and well-being programmes in both English and Arabic. These were later translated into other languages. How proud I was to see the Culturally and Linguistically Diverse (CALD) Mindfulness Programme become one of the most successful programmes in applied psychology in Australia. During my career, I have received many honours, including the recognition of my work's excellence at St George's Hospital in 2015, and an award from the Australian Psychological Society for an outstanding contribution to the field of psychology in 2020.

§

Once I completed my postgraduate degree, my sons started their university studies. The time came to stop and reflect on the challenges and the accomplishments of our sensational journey together. I wanted to celebrate our achievements, acknowledge my sons' sense of responsibility, decency and hard work, which all positively affected my life and allowed me to focus on my education and career. At the beginning of that year, I set aside a certain amount of my fortnightly salary to save for a week in Tasmania, our first holiday since we arrived in Australia. We visited Port Arthur one year after the infamous massacre and paid our tributes to the innocent victims. I hired a car from Hobart and drove across the island to Launceston. That trip resembled our life journey, where we felt alone, lost, scared and vulnerable at times, but always maintained hope and drew comfort from each other. This trip was the crowning of all our achievements as a family.

I now look at my sons with admiration. They've been my friends and supporters who have learnt from our struggle and worked hard to secure their future. They each completed their university studies. My older son holds a prominent position in a telecommunications firm and the younger one is a manager in a construction company. I have five beautiful grandchildren, 'They are like rosebuds,' as my grandmother used to say.

§

During my years in Australia, I never stopped dreaming about visiting Lebanon. I was full of anticipation and hopes, which were sadly met with shock and bitter disappointment when I returned to the country in 2002. The South Lebanese border region had just started to recover from the coma that had lasted more than twenty years, during which it was disconnected from Lebanon and the rest of the world. The border area was clearly exhausted, exhibiting visible signs of breakdown; it was grief-stricken from being abandoned by most of the population.

During the four years I spent in Lebanon with my children in the early 80s, I used to dream about having a place there that we would call our home, a dream that I held close to my heart for years and waited for the opportunity to fulfil. I inherited a small piece of land in the village from my father. I entrusted my brother to oversee the building of a house for my children and their families to return to. In August 2018, I stepped into my own home in Lebanon for the first time, which felt surreal, as if I was walking on clouds. It took a couple of trips back before I was able to fathom that I finally had my own home in Lebanon. To start enjoying it, I would sit with my coffee in the morning at the front porch of my house and look north towards Maroun al-Ras Mountain, which is a symbol of strength, steadfastness and inspiration.

The border area in South Lebanon had recently fully recovered from the years of occupation and its comatose state. It became a thriving place, especially in the summer when expatriates proud of their attachment to the land returned to the expansive homes they had built. This was an act of resistance.

When I was there recently, I would open my front door and try to recreate the home of my childhood, receiving my family and friends. Unfortunately, I always knew that the political and security situation was unpredictable, and danger was constantly looming, which prevented us from feeling safe. In 2018, when my eldest son and his family visited the South, they were forced to escape our village to nearby Tyre Sour and seek shelter with our relatives, just like I had had to do many years before.

Having my own home in Lebanon strengthened my ties to it and was a motivator for my subsequent visits. Also, my last visit to Lebanon was to fulfil my mother's wish of her final resting place. Having both parents in Yaroun's cemetery deepened my roots there and was further reason to visit regularly. Eventually, I came to the realisation that both Lebanon and I had changed. I continued to yearn for Lebanon as I might long for a beloved's embrace but when there,

I avoided looking into his beautiful eyes, so that he does not see in mine the longing and love that I have cultivated for Australia.

It is now 2025, and for almost two years and from a distance, I have watched as my beautiful village, Yaroun, has been destroyed, along with dozens of other villages and towns across the South. I dread the state of Haret Al Bayader and *sahat yaroun* (village square). I can't imagine the devastation, as it is now just piles of rubble, with no children playing, men gathering, dogs wandering or Sunday markets bustling. Now, these images exist only as echoes in our hearts, memories woven into the fabric of our thoughts and stories we tell. The historical sites were not spared by the Israelis' aggression, including the village's 120-year-old mosques and church, and a shrine of St George built in the 1700s. Even the village cemeteries, where my dear grandmother was buried, have been targeted by the invaders. There is no trace left of the cemeteries. It is now a 40-metre-high pile of dust. The explosions echoed hundreds of miles away. They were heard as far as Damascus. There is no trace of my grandmother left. No trace of her or any of those in that cemetery.

As I write these final words, my house still stands, but I'm unsure of its condition. Like other villages and towns, thousands of explosives have been dropped on Yaroun. The saplings of pomegranate, carob, fig and olive trees I planted around the house a couple of years ago have not been given a chance to thrive and bear fruit – not for this generation or any future generation.

A few days ago, I spoke with a neighbour. She and her family are now displaced. They fled to Beirut yet again. We ended our conversation with the hope that one day we will meet again in Yaroun and enjoy morning coffee with cardamom on my verandah just as we have many times before. Later that night, I dreamt I was back in my village walking amongst the rubble. A colourful butterfly landed on my sleeve, and I felt free and unhampered despite the ruins around me. I thought I could smell roses and jasmine on the breeze that swirled the dust around my feet. I heard a whisper; it sounded like my grandmother. '*Habibti*, our beloved South will rise, shaking off the dust of destruction and the legacy of sacrifices, and Yaroun will be rebuilt with unyielding determination.' It was as if her soul was hovering close when I awoke. *Insha'Allah* my dream will one day come true!

COME WITH ME FROM LEBANON

by Kilda Eid

22 December 1979.

Winter had settled in. I stood at the precipice of my world, hoping to be rescued from my predicament, 'Am I really leaving Lebanon tomorrow?'

The cold wind blew across my face. Above the drooping, barren trees, the pale blue sky was turning grey at sunset. I gazed west towards the house where I had grown up, trying not to cry.

It hurt to breathe. My heart raced. My ears were deafened by the roaring of my thoughts. How could I be so reckless? How did I not think of the consequences for those I loved most? How could I leave Lebanon? Eighteen years of my life were engraved in its soil.

§

My parents had moved to Rayak in 1958. My father was promoted to the position of sergeant in the Lebanese army at the Rayak military airport base in the Bekaa Valley. There was a central train station and a large agricultural institute, attracting people from different regions and diverse social and religious backgrounds. Rayak is the place where my four brothers and I were born and raised. We loved this town and its people. Our house was always full of guests. My mother, a nurse, used her experience to provide vaccinations for free to the people of the town.

§

I had a beautiful childhood in Rayak. I was the centre of my father's world. For the first years of my life, I slept only when wrapped gently in his arms. As I grew, my love for him deepened: he was my father, my friend and my mentor. Every day, a little after dawn, he would take me on his bicycle along the railway tracks shaded by acacia trees.

'I have Kilda in one hand and the four boys in the other hand,' he'd say – bursting with pride over me. How satisfied he was when I received an honorary award from the Minister of Education for achieving first rank in the Bekaa district and second rank in Lebanon in my baccalaureate. Though girls at that time were encouraged to marry and raise children, he offered me the opportunity to travel to France to complete my studies. He did not offer the same opportunity to my older brother, who had achieved higher grades with less effort. I didn't accept the offer. I loved my parents and my life in Rayak. Lebanon had good universities. I didn't know then that fate would take me to shores much further away than France.

§

My mother, stricter on me than my father, had tried in vain to interest me in handcrafts but eventually gave in to my desire to read, and bought me books and magazines. She was very concerned about the large number of school friends who came to our house during the school strikes, which occurred every week during the early phase of the civil war. This was in 1978. My mother greeted everyone with a cheerful face, but in her heart, she was afraid that I would be influenced by the wrong crowd.

My father's good reputation throughout Rayak and neighbouring villages encouraged several young men in the area to propose marriage. I rejected their offers and the very idea of marriage. I was insistent – I wanted to pursue my education.

My uncles and aunts used me as a role model. 'Be polite, respectful and disciplined like Kilda,' they told their children. I was the eldest female in the family.

In hindsight, what was seen as respect was shyness, and the inability to say 'no' and stand up for myself was a fear of conflict and confrontation. This aspect of my upbringing – the emphasis on respect for elders and being polite – promoted timidity in me and a compliant nature. This led me to make choices that were detrimental to my own life.

§

I had just begun my undergraduate studies in engineering when I met a young man in his late twenties, the uncle of my very best friend. He had returned to visit Lebanon after migrating to Australia a few years earlier. I first met him at her house. He liked me and tried to woo me, but since marriage was not on my mind, I tried to avoid him and the subject completely. I told my friend that I would not visit her except in the absence of her uncle. During this time, my education was interrupted due to the war, and many people had left Rayak. My friend and I became very close, as we only had each other. We had arranged that before I visited her, she would signal with her hand from the balcony when her uncle was not home. But one day, her sister, who looked like her, stood at the window beckoning me with her hand. Thinking it was my friend, I went over as agreed. I was surprised when the uncle opened the door. My friend was also surprised to see me. Her sister, who had conspired with her uncle, smiled and said, 'I tricked you into coming.'

The uncle cornered me and tried to convince me with a lengthy conversation to accept his marriage proposal. The intervention of his brothers and the rest of my friend's family, whom I loved and respected, made me feel I was under siege. Their father used to praise me and introduced me to his friends as one of his daughters. In hindsight, I realised that my siege was intensified by the values I grew up with: respect, not offending others, and most of all, my shyness, which was encouraged as a feminine virtue.

When I had rejected previous marriage proposals, I had the support of my parents. My father encouraged me to make the decision myself. But now, I was alone, outside my fortress of protection. I felt vulnerable and too embarrassed to reject the uncle's marriage request. I wanted to say no, to run away from the grip of my friend's family, but I did not have the courage, the know-how, nor the strength of character. Eventually, eloping was agreed upon in the presence of his brothers. Surrounded by my friend's family, I felt overwhelmed by their excitement, how they laid a rosy future out for me and then pressured me to make a decision right there and then. I was no longer able to think. I was an observer watching an eighteen-year-old girl agreeing to act against her wishes. She nodded and said a faint, shy, 'Yes.' Right away I regretted this one word. To this day, I cannot understand how it happened.

§

My would-be husband and I fled to Beirut, and the marriage took place the same day. At eighteen years of age, I, a Christian, defied the norms of society and married a Muslim man I barely knew, with whom I had no relationship. Interfaith marriages were not acceptable, especially to the girl's family and relatives, who bore the shame and stigma. Other families distanced themselves, lest their daughters be 'infected'.

At that time, the fighting in the area was fierce, and killings were based on religious identity and political allegiances. Such violence and hatred towards 'the other' had not been seen in Rayak before the outbreak of the civil war.

When my parents learnt about my elopement, they sent the police to get me back. I assured the police officers that I had not been physically coerced and that I had willingly married. This caused great shock to my parents and brothers. Their only daughter, their pride and joy, had disgraced them, and they succumbed to believing they had not raised me properly. They were devastated, drowning in disappointment, shame and sorrow. My father remained in shock for almost two years. He would leave home in the morning to wander in the forest, avoiding contact with people, and not return home until dark. My mother became ill; she disposed of all my clothes, wore black and tied a black ribbon to the front door. My eldest brother was forced to stay with our uncle in a neighbouring town to prevent him from taking revenge.

§

Our union had profound repercussions on the town. That one word 'yes', uttered by me to this stranger, had a seismic impact. While anger and humiliation broke my parents' hearts, celebrations of victory with gunfire filled the air of my husband's family and their community. In the midst of this celebratory atmosphere, my mother-in-law, who saw me for the first time, was taken aback, startled by my youth and beauty. The traditional bridal dough fell from her hands. I was supposed to have accepted it and put it on the front door. Instead, the woman before me beat her chest with a clenched fist and wept, saying, 'May God help your mother.' As a mother herself, she understood the grief my own would be experiencing. I wished to reverse time or have the courage to sneak back home where life was simple and I had known love, safety and kindness. I wished I could repair what my actions destroyed, remove the daggers I had struck in my mother's chest, apologise, ask for forgiveness. What excuses, what promises, what act of penitence would atone for my sins and relieve me of guilt?

My husband and I submitted my visa application at the Australian Embassy in Syria. He returned alone to Australia three weeks later. The ambassador promised to grant me a visa before Christmas due to my uneasy circumstances. After my husband left, I stayed at his family's house, too ashamed to wander in the neighbourhood, avoiding the eyes of spite and reproach. I was alone in a harsh desert, while the unreachable oasis of my family home was only a short distance away. I waited impatiently to leave, to escape everything, including myself, without a goodbye to my parents or a hug for my brothers, not knowing if I'd ever see them again.

The night of my departure I stayed up, staring at my parents' house, hoping to catch the shadow of one of them. The face of my eight-year-old brother had not left me since I'd visited his school the day before, hoping to say goodbye to him, to appease my longing. When the nun called him from class, he refused to come.

Standing at the door with tears in his eyes, he said, 'The wound you inflicted on us will never heal.' I walked my wretched self away, my soul aching. How could I build a future when my foundations had been destroyed by the axe of recklessness? I wished I could have stopped all my thoughts, all the longing, all the guilt. I wanted to escape the agony. Perhaps the memory of what had transpired would fade with time and distance.

An hour before I was due to leave for the airport on that December day, a much colder day than any I'd known, I put on a coat, grabbed my suitcase, and got into the car with my brother-in-law. I asked him to pass in front of my family's house. I had a glimmer of hope that I might see them and say goodbye. One look would've been enough to calm me, even if it was charged with blame and bitterness.

We stopped the car in front of my parents' house. There I was, the child, running onto my mother's lap, sleeping on my father's shoulder, jostling with my older brother who idolised me, tickling my little brother, wandering with him in the orchards among the roses and on the banks of the Litani River, running among the vines and picking grapes. And there I was, flitting between rooms like a butterfly, listening to my mother talking to the neighbours and the coffee brewing all day long.

I got out of the car and headed towards the entrance of the house. I walked, skipped up the steps like a child, forgetting for just a moment all that had happened. I approached the front door and was about to enter when I was struck by a deafening silence. The curtains were drawn. Devastation and mourning surrounded the place. I sent heartfelt longing through the air so that it might pierce the windows and the curtains might part, and I could see my loved ones and kiss them goodbye. I could not bear this agony. I backed away, and returned to the car, sending my soul to them to print a kiss of an apology on their feet.

The car continued its journey, and I felt my mother's eyes following, her voice calling me. I turned my head but saw only a dark, gloomy void. The entire universe was taking its last ever breath. I peered at my surroundings, then closed my eyes, trying to imprint the scenery into my memory. I could barely hold on to a sliver of hope, wishing that the mysterious future awaiting me across the continents would make me forget all that had happened.

§

Beirut Airport was very crowded. I was overwhelmed by all the travel procedures. I followed the path with the other travellers, terrified I would get lost and miss my flight. I entered the plane carrying a small bag on my shoulder, my mind swirling in confusion and apprehension. What was awaiting me? What did fate have in store for me? An emigration to a far-off land, a long distance from home. I shuddered with fear, with doubt and unease, then rebuked myself for being so timid.

I gazed at the passengers on the plane. Some of them were chatting, others were lying down, resting or busy with their children. It was an entirely different world from the one I'd known. As a thousand questions consumed my mind, anxiety spiralled outside my control.

The Air India flight lasted two days. I was exhausted from the multiple take-offs and landings. I had terrible diarrhea and dizziness. I regretted my poor choice of airline; my husband had wanted to book my flight on Lufthansa, but I wanted one that passed through many countries. I spent the last hours of the flight lying down, unconcerned with any of my surroundings. I was looking forward to getting to Australia, to exit this painful vortex. The image of my loving husband awaiting me at Sydney Airport could only muster in me a dull smile. I felt like an orphan. I felt embarrassed as I imagined the crowd of welcomers, my husband's relatives and friends receiving me with flowers and warm embraces.

The flight attendant announced the time of arrival at Sydney Airport and wished a Merry Christmas to all passengers. The sound of Christmas carols swept throughout the plane, reminding me that this was the first Christmas I was spending away from my family. They would be staying up until dawn enjoying the best food and sweets, roasting chestnuts, watching the snow fall as my father recited the story of the Nativity. The house would be filled with conversation, warmth, love and happiness. My tears flowed, feeling helpless and so abandoned. My body collapsed under the weight of my grief, and I soon fell asleep. I woke up to a hand shaking me and a hostess speaking a language I barely understood.

§

When we landed at Sydney Airport, I stumbled to the exit of the airplane on swollen feet. I feared my joints would loosen and give way. I was struck by the high humidity and temperature. The sky was overcast with black clouds, foreshadowing the storms ahead, no doubt. Clinging to whatever strength I had left, I walked the tunnel leading to the arrivals hall. My eyes wandered in every direction, looking for my husband.

I searched among faces, until the light became dim and it seemed foggy as people turned into ghosts. I was very frightened. What was I going to do all alone in this strange country?

After what seemed a decade, one of my husband's friends from the same flight found me marooned beside my bags, totally lost and forlorn. He offered me a lift to my husband's place. I was completely ashamed and fearful of being in a car alone with a stranger. All I knew was the name: Bankstown, the place where my husband lived with his brother. I did not look away from my window, searching desperately for the word 'Bankstown' in the names of the passing suburbs.

At 7 pm, I arrived at my husband's house. My brother-in-law and his wife welcomed me. They were happy to see me but were confused. Obviously, they were not expecting my arrival. The familiar face I was looking for – a harbour for the wreckage of my soul and body that was supposed to welcome me – was nowhere to be found. Life had conspired against me, delivering one blow after another.

'Please relax, eat something, your husband will soon be here. Perhaps you might like a shower,' my sister-in-law said.

I took a shower and changed my clothes. I found my new in-laws at the dining table waiting for me. I asked them to wait for my husband so we could eat together. My brother-in-law tried all possible ways to find out where my husband was, but his attempts were in vain. He then tried to distract me with many stories and asked me about his parents, his brothers and his relatives in Lebanon, until he ran out of things to say. He was troubled and embarrassed by the situation. He advised me to go to my husband's room to get some rest. I insisted that I would wait. I was trying to stay afloat in the darkness of an ocean, waiting for my rescuer – my husband.

At 5 am, my husband arrived. Joy flicked the dust of fatigue and tension from my soul. How surprised he looked when he saw me. I looked into his eyes searching for the promises he had made me. I interrogated his gaze, reminding him of me – his wife. He placed his hand on my shoulder and merely said, 'Thank God for your safe arrival. Go to sleep now, you must be tired.'

I wanted to scream, to cry, but as in a nightmare, my voice was lost. I was mortified. I wanted to get my bags and return to where I had come from, but my body was paralysed. I cried silently and went to bed carrying the promise I had made, to be a wife.

§

The first days after my arrival passed with unease and a cavernous emptiness. My husband justified not being at the airport with, 'It's my brother's fault. He was meant to remind me of the date of your arrival.' He dismissed his culpability with, 'Anyway, let's close the subject.' However, the subject remained very much open in my mind, stirring my suspicions and raising many questions. He tried to create an atmosphere of safety and familiarity around me to compensate and proudly introduced me to his friends. We went for many rides in his car to the sea; at other times we wandered the streets of Sydney. Nothing impressed me. I could not see beauty anywhere. Nature looked barren – forests seemed like faded drawings – lifeless. One day, I sat alone by a large old tree that passers-by stopped to admire. Its beauty was not obvious to me, and I wondered what could be so special about this tree.

I looked at my new life through the lens of resentment and evaluated everything I saw in relation to my home country. I wondered how people recognised their homes. They were identical if not for the number on the letterboxes and the street signs. All roads were bleak and empty. The city looked unkempt, untouched by the hand of civilisation. I was on a remote island where time stood still, where social and cultural life seemed absent or undeveloped. People knew nothing about my culture, my country, my history, nor even where Lebanon was on a map. The Lebanese goods in the markets were few and very limited. Fortunately, there was one Lebanese bakery in my area, which made up for some deprivations. Most of the local clothing stores displayed fashion from previous decades.

My social circle was limited to a few immigrant families. We lived close together, met after work, rotating between houses. Most did not speak English. We remained close to each other despite our differences in culture, age, religion and values – not because of our open-mindedness, but to allay our loneliness and feelings of nostalgia.

§

The days passed very slowly. Everyone around me went to work and I was left alone with my thoughts and memories – no mother, no friend, no neighbour for company or even just a coffee. There was no one to turn to for guidance. I was in a labyrinth of obstacles, and they needed surmounting. I needed to learn new things. Slowly I was losing the self I had known in Lebanon.

At eighteen, I was not ready to be a wife and a housekeeper. But now I was a woman, playing the role of a good wife trying to transform a house into a home. I started wearing an apron, and cooking food without recipes. This was as hard as all the other challenges – I had never cooked in my parents' house. Even more difficult was seeking help from women I did not know while fearing their ridicule. Whenever I wanted to cook a certain dish, I relied on my memory to recreate the flavours. Sometimes I succeeded, more often I failed. Once, I felt happy to have prepared a dish of cabbage rolls for the dining table, but my joy was crushed with a sarcastic comment that they were wrapped the wrong way. To save face, I said, 'This is how my mother prepared them.'

The most challenging part of adapting to life in Australia was interacting with people in the marketplace. I only knew a few English words, so I enrolled in a language college. Soon, I fell pregnant. I was not happy at first. My dream of becoming an engineer completely evaporated.

My situation worsened each day. Morning sickness intensified until I fell ill. My blood pressure dropped sharply. My feelings of loneliness and alienation intensified. I resented everything. I hated this country, its language, its climate, its cruelty. Nostalgia raged inside me.

I felt imprisoned in this country surrounded by water, cut away from my homeland. I longed so much for my mother, her voice, her scent and her touch. I wished she could take me and my child back to her, for I did not know how to be a mother. I was terrified and anxious, and my physical and psychological strength deteriorated. I forgot who I was. I once followed an old woman with blond hair down the street because she looked like my mother. I wanted to get close to her, touch her and feel something of my own mother in her. She turned towards me with suspicion and gave me a hostile look. I went back home feeling like a small child completely bereft of any comfort. Wherever I went, I would look for my hometown, Rayak, in this strange country – in the landscape, in a tree, a house, a river that would bring home to me. I did not see my migration as moving from one country to another, but as a roll from the top of a mountain to the bottom of a valley. I was struggling to climb up the harsh rocks without ropes.

Amidst my struggle, the new heart that began to beat inside me gave me hope. I forgot about everything around me and created a secret world for our souls together. I spent long hours in seclusion, talking to my unborn child about myself, my family, my country and longing for my past life. I had a treasure growing inside me. It gave me confidence and hope for a future without disappointment and without loneliness.

My daughter saw light, and her arrival had the effect of a double-edged sword, bringing feelings of joy and tenderness I had never felt before, and feelings of guilt and sadness for my mother, whose role I did not appreciate until that moment. I wanted her to see my child so that she might forgive my offence. But I did not dare contact her. Besides, phone calls to Lebanon were very expensive and generally unavailable because of the destruction caused by the war.

I didn't get help from anyone when my daughter was born. Despite my poor health, I had to find some strength and stand up to serve my family and our frequent guests. Fortunately, my daughter was a placid baby, which made my burden lighter; she instinctively understood my struggle and suffering.

As the days passed, I could not get rid of the feelings of loneliness. In this strange society, I found no support. I felt inferior socially, and regardless of my educational and cultural background, I was ridiculed by some Australians when I tried to speak English. I was deprived of forming meaningful relationships. It was also difficult to access information about government policies, health and financial services because it was rare to find employees who spoke the Arabic language. I resumed teaching myself English, helped by my prior knowledge of the French language.

§

The company of my daughter eased my suffering, but my fear and anxiety increased, daunted by the prospect of raising her on my own. I no longer felt safe. Staying in Australia became a nightmare. Longing was my ailment, and returning home was my cure. Unfortunately, the war in my homeland made my dream seem so very far away.

These feelings accompanied me for the first few years of my stay in Australia. They broke my spirit, drained all my strength. My body was wasted down to a size six. I felt defeated and struggled to get my housework done and look after my daughter. I came to a point where I lost all joy in life. I couldn't openly practise my Christian faith. I blamed God for allowing me to slip into this abyss, even though He was my only saviour. Two options stood before me: either I give in to despair and end up insane, or I slowly crawl to death.

I was terrified. I thought of my daughter and became angry at my failures. I remembered all those faces that I loved, that were waiting for me on other shores. I resolved to defy fate and not give up. I secretly surrendered my command to my God and felt a tremendous power lifting me up. At twenty-one, I realised I could not change my surroundings or the people around me. I decided to take full responsibility for my situation, and change my perspective towards my family, my friends and the country I now lived in. I felt empowered to bring some happiness and peace into our life.

I started browsing Australian newspapers with the dictionary by my side. I learnt about a government financial institution which offered loans for the purchase of homes at an interest rate fifty per cent lower than what other banks offered. I achieved my first success. This opportunity allowed us to purchase a home within the first four years of my arrival in this country. I disseminated this information amongst our friends and helped them apply for these lower-interest loans.

After the arrival of my second daughter, a small sense of belonging and familiarity slowly began to creep into my life. A family friend informed me about a teaching vacancy. Her encouragement dispelled my hesitation. I worked my way through the field of teaching and translation amidst teachers and students from diverse ethnic backgrounds. Working as a teacher's aide boosted my self-confidence, and my personality became stronger. My circle of friends expanded, and my English improved. This experience enabled me to understand the Australian curriculum and allowed me to better help my children with their studies and to interact with their teachers and schools.

When my two daughters reached school age, I looked for a good private school. My family friend and neighbour Um Ali suggested the local Catholic school she was considering for her children, as there were no Islamic schools at that time. This required the children to be baptised. Keen to give the children the best education, our husbands agreed to the baptism. Now we needed to find a priest who wouldn't be alerted to Um Ali's Muslim faith. We opted for an Italian priest, hoping the name Ali wouldn't raise his suspicions, leading him to question Um Ali's faith. The ceremony went smoothly. My two daughters were baptised with Um Ali, a Muslim, acting as their godmother, while I, a Christian, acted as the godmother of her two Muslim children, Ali and Fatima. Later on, when one of the teachers asked my daughters why she didn't recite the 'Our Father' prayer, my daughter said she was a 'MusChris'.

§

One day, I learnt that my brother in Lebanon, an ex-army officer, was arrested in an area controlled by militias who were at odds with the Lebanese army. He had been suspected of espionage and held captive for days. My father had no choice but to ask my brother-in-law, who was a member of that militia, for help. My brother-in-law managed to rescue my brother a few hours before his execution. This event led to the reconciliation of my parents and my husband's families. As the saying goes, 'The misfortune of some brings fortune to others.'

After seven long years of exile, it was now possible for me to return home and visit my parents. I travelled to Lebanon carrying my loneliness, my two young daughters, and a baby in my womb. The plane landed at Beirut Airport. It felt like an eternity had passed before the exit doors opened. I hurried to get down and touch the ground and smell the air of my country. A relative was waiting and drove us back to Rayak. When we approached the Bekaa Valley, I felt my soul returning to me. My heart raced towards the plains, embracing the cradle of my birthplace.

The car stopped in the town square in front of my old house, where my parents and neighbours were waiting. I ran into the arms of my parents, then to the neighbours. I recognised everyone except for a young man standing in the crowd. I asked my mother, 'Where is my little brother?' She answered, 'You passed in front of him twice.' I looked again at that young man and cried out, 'Are you Charles?' He ran towards me; his eyes filled with tears of joy. We embraced and I did not let him go for a very long time, I did not let go until my longing, my sorrow and my regrets were lifted from me.

§

I spent two months amongst family, relatives and friends. I was happy to see them. I was surprised by how the faces and places in the town had changed. The war was still going on and many of my neighbours and school friends had left. I felt a gap separating me from the ones who remained. I had changed. I was no longer one of them. I had grown many years in the course of only a few. The experience of marriage, motherhood and alienation hardened my features and made me a mature woman.

My pregnancy and sickness caused me great discomfort. The long periods of waiting at checkpoints increased my stress. I resented the general situation and felt a sense of isolation in my own homeland. I had returned to unload my burdens and worries and extinguish my nostalgia. Yet I found my country was burdened by war, conflicts and divisions. I grieved for a country that was once shining with glory – a pearl on the Mediterranean, a picturesque tourist destination. I started comparing the advantages and disadvantages of my mother country and the country of my immigration. I realised that Australia was the place where I felt safe. Given the war and my poor health, I wanted to return – to my small kingdom, to the women's clinic where I trusted their ability to safely deliver my baby. I wanted to return to a country where I had reluctantly established myself and accepted its system. I was also afraid that the fighting in Lebanon would intensify and hinder my return to safety. I left Lebanon longing for my home in Australia.

§

After the arrival of my third daughter, I returned to my previous job as a teacher's aide for a few years. I then worked with my husband when he got a car dealer's licence. I took responsibility for buying auto parts and got to know many smash repair shops. I worked with my brother in his hire car company, driving VIPs in limousines and small buses. I got an owner-builder licence to renovate three houses, one after the other, while we lived in them. I was a woman in a man's world. Over the years, I acquired a lot of practical skills through my work and interaction with businesses, financial and government institutions. This helped me manage my difficulties and obstacles in the new country, as well as to offer support to others in the Arabic community.

During this period, I fell pregnant for the fourth time. A few weeks before my due date, I dreamt of a man in a white gown presenting me with a cage, telling me I was giving birth to a baby boy named Moses. When I gave birth to the baby boy, my husband was very happy and allowed me to name him as I wished. I named him Hamad-Moses. My side of the family called him Moses, while my husband's called him Hamad. Eventually, we nicknamed him Hamousah. This name stuck with him until he started school, and his friends ridiculed his name, saying it sounded like a Lebanese toasty. From then on, my eldest son insisted on being called Hamad.

§

After years of drought, the heavens opened their doors to me and compensated me with streams of blessings. The first with the gift of my small family, then the arrival of one of my siblings to Australia, followed by my other siblings, along with my mother and father. This put peace in my heart. I felt like a small piece of my homeland had been transplanted into the soil of Sydney. It was as though I had built, from Lebanese stones and Australian soil, a kingdom to which I could now belong.

Reuniting with my family in Australia, especially with my mother, made a huge difference to my everyday life. When my fifth baby was born, I returned from hospital to a tidy home and a cooked meal, and I thought I was in heaven. I had missed my mother so much, particularly after the birth of my other children. When I returned from hospital then, it was to an empty fridge, four children and no one around to help.

While working as a teacher's aide, I had started a bachelor's degree in translation, but I stopped studying when my fifth child was born – the last of the bunch. With five children to look after, I shelved away all my ambitions and prioritised my family. I saw my success through my children. I accompanied them in their sports activities and took part in their social events. I stayed up with them until dawn during exams, helped them with their homework, and competed with them in maths quizzes to motivate them. I seized any opportunity to help them cross to the shores of adulthood safely. I fought with determination to put my family on the right track.

Over the years, the gap in the sky widened, and its blessings flowed even more when my children began achieving high degrees in education and other professions. My eldest daughter graduated in criminology and forensic science, followed by my second daughter, who earned a master's degree in education. My third daughter then pursued general medicine, and my elder son entered the field of business. My youngest son specialised in a technical profession.

The land that was once alien and desolate had become familiar, filled with accomplishments and new memories gathered on my journey. Over time, I started to feel that I was no longer just an expatriate but that I had become a part of Australia. I felt that this country had given me something more than just shelter – it had given me security and peace.

§

I wanted my journey to flow smoothly like the waters of rivers, gently merging into their natural course, but I was besieged with currents of longing and nostalgia. They would sweep me away and alter my path, making me return to the source where I emerged from, and where my roots were planted. The yearning for my homeland would ignite within me – the towering mountains, the soil that carries the history of my ancestors' remains and my belonging. I would hear my homeland calling me from afar, and the longing for return would take over my whole being.

I waited until my youngest son finished his HSC before I visited Lebanon for the second time – three decades after my emigration. On my arrival, I felt like an eager lover shocked by the death of her beloved. I was happy being back at my parents' home, but I was deeply disappointed by reality. Most of my friends had emigrated, and many people in the neighbourhood had been killed in the war. Those who were still there had aged. The traces of my childhood and youth had disappeared, buried under rubble. I carried their memories with me back to Australia with a grieving heart. My two boys who accompanied me during this trip were happy to meet their cousins and the extended family. However, they were struggling because of the lack of essential services, such as water and electricity, and the difficulties of daily life. My heart was overwhelmed with sadness for the state of my homeland. This strengthened my resolve to embrace my life in Australia, to fit into Australian society and find compensation for all that was lost in Rayak.

§

I returned to Australia filled with determination to make up for the knot that lodged in my throat. I pursued further studies, earning a degree in finance and a certificate in computer science. I am still studying to obtain a diploma in social services and a higher degree in theology.

I also contributed to publishing a joint poetry book, and began organising my own anthology of poetry. I dedicate time to caring for my children and grandchildren, as I firmly believe that family is the foundation that supports us solidly throughout life's challenges.

Though I had become reconciled with my Australian migration journey, I had not reached closure with my personal life. Migration had thrown me not only away from my country, but for many years also away from my parents and my faith. However, my five children were a source of strength and encouraged me to reclaim my dreams and choose my own spiritual journey. I now feel free to practice my Christian faith openly, immerse myself in my religious devotions and pursue my creative writing away from the constraints of married life. My spirituality and newfound freedom have given me closure with all that

I endured in the past, and a sense of peace. I now live a beautiful multifaith experience with my children in a harmonious household. I read the Bible while my son is on his prayer mat. I have revived the pre-war Rayak in my household.

§

This country, which I had originally rejected more than forty years ago, allowed me to eventually flourish. Australia, with the rule of law and respect for human rights, freed me from some outdated traditions. This country has also cared for my parents in their old age. I feel stable, secure and entitled to all rights as a citizen.

I once believed that true friendship was only formed during our youth. I am now surrounded by beautiful friends in Sydney brought together by our shared experience of exile from different corners of the earth. Despite my busy life and distance from them, I steal moments to chat with friends in Lebanon through social media, exchanging news and fond memories.

Yet my Lebanese roots refuse to wither even after many decades. I hear their whispers call, my heartbeat races and I burn with longing and nostalgia again. I feel the chasm of the missing years. I feel like a seagull seeking the crumbs of memories and crossing on the wings of yearning to the shores that witnessed my first emergence into light. I throw myself into the embrace of memory, then I return to the soils of my adopted home, where the seeds that emanated from me have taken root.

Belonging is a historical connection to the soil, motherland, ancestors, culture and traditions. I cling to that umbilical cord with my homeland wherever I go. Three years have passed since my father's death and five since my mother's. They last resided with me *in* Australia. Will their remains in this soil foster a sense of belonging for me, my children and *their* children? No sooner do I find resolution than a forgotten ache will resurface. Sometimes I feel the pull to my home country, other times to this land of exile. Now, I can see the beauty of that large old tree in Bankstown and appreciate why those passers-by admired it so. I have roots here now but not as deep as the 2000-year-old cedars in the Grove of God in Lebanon. The Song of Solomon in the Bible glorifies the beauty of my homeland: *Come with me from Lebanon my Bride. Descend from the Peak of Amana. Come with me from Lebanon.* I too was a beautiful bride who came from Lebanon. Yet I remain eternally torn between a homeland that exiled me and an exile that has eventually settled me.

THE FRAGRANCE OF TWO HOMES
by Camilia Naim

My childhood years are tattooed on my soul with the colours of happiness. The memory of my early years in Ayteet, a village in South Lebanon where I grew up, has never left me. They are my refuge and private garden. Their fragrance revives hope whenever I face hardship. No adversity can break the happy child within. Her heart remains a brilliant flame in the woman that I have become.

§

I was hoping to draw my own choices on the pages of my existence, but the hand of fate made sure to keep me struggling and surrendering.

I was born into a family of eleven brothers and sisters, the fruit of my parents' love. Our modest home had a lounge room, two bedrooms, a kitchen, and one very busy bathroom. With every newborn, light shone through the windows and made our house seem bigger. Our mother's smile was always waiting at the door. The hospitable porch welcomed stories of marriage, love and divorce from passers-by. All the elegant homes I lived in later on held an icy silence in their walls unlike the warmth of my parents' tiny home.

§

Our mother had her first child when she was seventeen and her eleventh when she was not yet forty. She was an unceasing river of love and generosity. A look from her shining eyes filled us with strength. She planted rose-perfumed wishes in the garden of our existence. She woke up very early to bake our daily bread from the dough she kneaded the night before. She cooked, washed and tailored our clothes. On top of that, she took care of our many olive trees. She picked the fruits, prepared the year's supply of pickled olives and took some of the fruits to the local press for oil extraction. She did all that on her own.

Our father, who worked in construction in the Gulf countries, spent one month a year with us. He was loaded with gifts whenever he returned, and a desire to be alone with our mother. He gave us enough coins to buy a box of biscuits and a bottle of fruit juice at the local grocer. We sensed he wanted us out of the house, but this didn't matter, the bribe was worth it.

Our father had a great sense of humour and

laughed from the bottom of his heart at the slightest joke. Yet, he was strict and being home before sunset was not negotiable. He was most playful with me, his eldest daughter. He feigned sleep in the afternoons as I tweezed the tiny hairs on his cheek, for which he paid me twenty-five francs for every five hairs. When he was on his prayer mat, I snuck my hand in his pocket and grabbed a few liras, knowing he wouldn't be able to interrupt his prayer. Eventually, he started emptying his pockets before prayer and hiding the money under the prayer mat. How he laughed when I found the money and took a share of it, reminding him not to disrupt his prayer.

When I was six years old, my father returned from his work in the Gulf carrying a gift especially for me – a pink dress and sandals with wooden heels. I walked in my clogs up the stairs of our building, striking the concrete steps as hard as I could. I felt beautiful and wanted to show off and stir envy in other children as they watched my little body sway and heard the clicking of my heels when I danced. I wanted them to note the special place I held in my father's esteem. My mother reminded me of this whenever I showed off in front of my siblings. I recall those memories when I see a young girl trying to enjoy such a game of delightful flamboyance and sum up her world in a dress.

I was eleven years old when my father brought two identical watches, one for me and one for my sister. I always wanted to prove to myself that my father loved me the most, that I was more special to him than any of my siblings. I was always given the first choice of any presents he brought back with him. On this occasion, it was impossible to decide which watch was better. Even the colour was the same, to my disappointment. I suddenly found a solution. I asked my sister which one of the two she preferred. She said, 'I don't see any difference between the two. Take whichever you want.' I insisted she choose one. She did. I then asked her, 'Is this *really* the one you want?' She said yes. Then I asserted, 'Take the other one, and I will take the one you chose.' My siblings teased me about this incident and labelled me very competitive, but I had a deep need to remain my father's special girl. He was not home much, and I missed him more than I could say. I felt a longing for his love all my life.

I often heard my father proudly tell his friends, 'I am the tiger, and she is my tigress.' His name was *Nimr*, the Arabic for tiger. Our grandmother had many children who all died before completing their first year. She believed names gave power to their bearers. So, she called my father *Nimr*. Fate smiled on her – Nimr survived to be her only child. My father would often say to us, 'I always longed to have a brother or a sister.'

I resembled my father physically and intellectually. He instilled in me his passion for writing, especially poetry. I enjoyed using unusual expressions, articulating them in a sophisticated manner to impress him. He often said, 'She is her father's daughter.' In his final years, he revised his statement, saying: 'She is her father's *mother*.'

§

My primary school in Ayteet was ten minutes away from home. Yet it took me half an hour on foot each way. I spoke to the fields, followed the butterflies, touched every wildflower I met and inhaled its perfume. My eyes were fascinated by the colours and forms of this heavenly temple.

The arts teacher selected me, along with other pupils, to prepare for events during the school year, like folk dancing and theatre. Our teachers came from all around Lebanon. One teacher wrote the plays for us to perform on a stage built especially to celebrate Teachers' Day, the most significant event at school.

One year, I played the role of a singer. I had to lip-sync and move with the rhythm of the music. I mouthed the words of the Fairuz song *Tariq al Nahal* – 'The Path of the Bees' – on stage to the joy of the teachers. The parents in the audience were astonished as they heard the angelic voice coming from me. Later, whenever I met an elderly person from the village, they jokingly reminded me, 'How you fooled us with your miming of Fairuz's song.' My face would light up remembering that beautiful phase of my life when I was loved and admired by all.

§

The memories of the school in the village flood my heart with love. Friendships were sincere and the teachers were so kind. They took us on wonderful excursions. I recall we went to the magnificent cedar forest and saw trees in the Grove of God that were 2000 years old. We also visited the glorious snow-covered mountain of Faraya.

Once I reached secondary school, holidays became less enjoyable. I missed the intellectual discussions I had had in the school playground. There were four of us vying to secure the topmost rank in the class. We would spend long nights sitting around a wooden round table, studying under the light of an oil lamp. Electricity blackouts occurred during most of those cold winter nights in the village. This did not abate our drive to succeed. We carried the hope of our parents and grandparents. Their expectations of us were high. One of my friends became a gynaecologist and general surgeon; another became a radiologist. The third one migrated just as I did but to a different part of the world.

During my teenage years, I was attracted to matters of social justice and to the revolutionary movements of the time. I attended seminars held by the young communists in the village where they discussed ideas and were ahead of their time. I felt closer then to realising my dreams of entering university. I imagined myself floating from one university hall to another with big ambitions and a strong belief in change. I imagined wearing that neat black robe in court, carrying the files of those who needed my help, bravely facing the judge and earning the title of 'Advocate of the Oppressed', before whom all judges bowed. Other times, I saw myself as a journalist, writing about oppression and corruption, and becoming the voice of righteous outrage stifled by tyranny.

I was too young to imagine that the legal profession had an avaricious side capable of manipulating facts for bribery, or that the 'colour of ink' might change according to the whims of an unprincipled writer.

Growing up, I watched the enemy's planes raid our skies, spreading fear, reminding us that we could never live in peace close to an occupier who cared little about our lives. A curse filled the air whenever I heard the rumbling noise piercing the skies over my beautiful land. I wanted to regain my dignity and the dignity of my country.

On the way to high school from Ayteet to Tyre every morning, the driver squeezed nine of us in his taxi to reduce the number of trips. We passed by the Palestinian camp surrounded by walls adorned with posters of young martyrs carrying their weapons. The martyr's name, date and place of the *feda'ee* (freedom fighter) operation were inscribed with dark paint. The walls of oppression were also painted with the cries for the 'Right of Return'. I harboured a secret wish that probably rarely came to the minds of girls my age. I was a girl from the south, living near the Israeli fence, an angry fence, erected by invaders who came from all around the globe to claim my land. They beat us down with their fists, drenched us with their cruelty. They came with their false claims trying to obliterate my history and that of my country and drive us into poverty.

§

These images transported me to the most exalted stages of passion for justice, transported me to contemplate those who sacrificed their lives on the altar of the slain land. I felt both sad and proud. I admired those who left us on the wings of martyrdom. I wished that one day I would wear this combat attire, camouflaged with the greenness of olive trees and the colour of the soil of my homeland. Then the adolescent girl inside me asked, 'How would I look in combat fatigues? If I left my hair loose over my back, golden brown – resembling the colour of wheat fields at harvest, would I look more rebellious? Or maybe I would tie my hair with a red ribbon to reveal a heroic, flagrant, revolutionary femininity. Then my portrait would hang on the wall and I'd be renowned as 'The Martyr for Justice and Freedom'. Would I engender a deeper grief or compassion? My own death would be a message of love to those walking on the path of a cause engraved in my conscience at an early age, when this love was a rose or a letter kept secret between the pages of a book.

I never fulfilled any of my dreams of defending the oppressed, whether as a lawyer, journalist, or a martyr. But I always held a deep commitment to justice. Later in life, I could never be a passive observer of any wrongdoing. Whenever friends or relatives needed financial or emotional support, I rushed to their aid, even at the expense of my own children and family.

§

I spent many hours in my youth contemplating nature, wondering about existence and how to confront life's challenges. The narcissus growing in the harshness of the rocks revealed to me the secret of its tenderness. The scent and whiteness of the jasmine that my mother planted in our garden taught me about magnanimity as it climbed with its greenery over our balcony covering the walls around our house. Its memory is etched in my heart.

§

As for love, I never fancied any of my classmates at school, and their compliments passed by me like a summer breeze. My class teacher, however, was a different story. He was handsome and articulate. I was his secret admirer, only known to a very close friend of mine.

I grew up in an environment where it was customary for a girl to marry at a young age, accept whoever asked for her hand in marriage, particularly when he had money or a foreign passport. It did not matter if he was not compatible. Marriage awaited every young girl.

§

Yet I hated the idea of a commitment that shackled a woman to a man. I never dreamt of a prince on a horse who would snatch me up and hold me forever. My priorities were different from the girls of my generation. My girlfriends dreamt of wearing a wedding dress, their eyes sparkled with a concealed desire for love. But this white embroidered dress, worn on that long-awaited day, was *not* what I wished for. I saw the white dress as a trap that lured every girl to a dark room, to the nakedness of a man chosen for her by the hand of fate, and the ring as the chain around the couple's neck. I knew then that the most important thing for a fulfilled life was to be in command of it and live by one's own values, ideas and aspirations. But this was far from achievable in the environment that surrounded me.

Before I turned eighteen, I graduated from high school with distinction. A man from the other side of the world sent me letters of admiration, which I read and discarded. These letters were of no interest other than to flatter the young woman inside me. But this young man assumed that receiving and reading his letters meant I had acquiesced to marry him. Soon I learnt that he had returned from overseas *for me*. I heard him in our living room discussing our marriage with my father.

§

Initially, I rejected the marriage offer with flowing tears. But my parents reminded me about my ideals of justice and self-sacrifice. They told me, with all the goodwill and affection they had for me, about the importance of this marriage that would carry me to a place full of golden opportunities, that could extend a bridge for the rest of my family. My marriage would save them from hardship and secure them a bright future in a new land. I listened, and all my ideals of sacrifice and selflessness listened too. Sacrificing my life to free the oppressed was replaced by a nod of acceptance to the bridegroom. He was talking to my father with kindness. He promised I could continue my education if I wished. By agreeing to the marriage,

I was also agreeing to emigrate. Sacrificing my dreams to save my parents through marriage would be easier than dying for a cause. This most important decision was not made by me but by my parents whom I wanted to please.

He was a dignified, handsome young man. He was not from Ayteet, but I had seen glimpses of him in the village before he left for Australia. He possessed characteristics that I admired at the time. He believed in change and appreciated the revolutions of the world. He had belonged to a communist organisation before he emigrated. He was a self-made man who was not too rich. This reassured me that I was not being sold to the highest bidder and assuaged my dignity. I was only going to build a bridge with him for my loved ones to cross to a better world.

§

Two months before our wedding celebration took place, we went to the *cheikh*, who read the vows and instructed us to sign the marriage contract. I could not see what I was signing as tears rolled down my cheeks. I was giving away my dreams and my freedom. From that moment on, I had no control over my life.

'Please, I don't want to wear a white wedding dress, I don't want a big party; let's limit it to the family,' I begged my mother. I also asked her not to seat me and the bridegroom on an elevated platform, as was the common practice.

'Are you serious? Are you mad?' my mother replied. I was the first of her children to cross over the threshold in a wedding dress.

There was a big celebration for the wedding, and I wore a white dress. I sat like a statue, worrying about what awaited me, looking at all the people who were happy, singing and dancing.

A taxi was waiting to take us to Beirut Airport. The minute I set foot in that car I wished death would snatch and bury me in the soil of the land I knew and loved. I did not want to leave my loved ones and the warmth of places I adored for an unknown country. My teary eyes were fixed on the gate of the house. I examined the features of everyone around me, my parents, my siblings and especially my two-year-old youngest brother standing next to my mother, holding onto her dress. I wanted to etch them into my memory. I was unable to take my gaze off them. My voice failed me, and with sadness I managed to raise my hand and wave goodbye.

§

The journey to Australia took more than thirty hours. The window of the airplane near my seat seemed to be callously watching me cross the geographical distances that were quickly separating me from my loved ones. We passed vast deserts and deep oceans. Returning now seemed an impossibility. Fear turned into despair. I could not contain my tears nor the throbbing pain in my ears from the airplane pressure. My husband tried to console me, holding my hands, tenderly tilting my head onto his shoulder. This new universe was immense. I longed to be back in my own universe, playing innocently under the blue skies of home, and I longed for the familiar night sky in that heaven where I enjoyed counting every star.

We landed at several airports before reaching the country that possessed *the window of opportunity*. As soon as I stepped out of the plane, I was struck by the heat of December. December is meant to be winter – the month of ice, of snow and blizzards. I did not know there was another face to December.

On our arrival at Sydney Airport, we were greeted by my husband's brother and his wife. They drove us to my husband's two-bedroom unit that he shared with his mother. She reminded me of the women of my village, with her warm welcome. My husband was her youngest child, and she was greatly attached to him.

On my first night in Sydney, nightmares crept into my bedroom, reaching my bed ahead of me and putting their head on the pillow before I did. As soon as I fell asleep, the claws of monstrous scenes attacked me – scenes of the ever-increasing nothingness that would swallow me and half the earth. I choked on the emptiness I'd seen from the plane window that separated me from the soul I left in my village. That emptiness lay heavy on my chest. I was often woken by the terrifying sound of my heart pounding.

I now resided in a country I did not know, and it did not know me or my past. I was a stranger to it, and it was a stranger to me. I was no longer the butterfly landing on the flowers of time, sniffing the fragrance of the good earth, falling asleep in the spring on the lullabies of the April breeze. The nightmare of being in this unreachable space, away from home and the people I loved, accompanied me until my first trip back to Lebanon two years later. Until then, I was chained to places that did not resemble mine. Without balconies, most of the houses looked like boxes – you could *not* see your neighbours and say, 'Good morning, come over for a coffee.' The walls were silent and cold, even at the peak of summer. When I walked in the street past the houses, my silence resembled theirs. The houses were identical. I often stood in front of our house and wondered whether it actually was my house. When I walked, no one returned my greetings 'ten times over' the way they did in Ayteet. Not one voice was heard asking me to come over, no one insisting I accept their invitation for lunch, dinner or a cup of coffee. I started to think that my return to my homeland was akin to a torn dried-up branch being revived in its mother tree.

§

Two weeks after my arrival, my husband went back to work, and I stayed home with his mother. My dreams of a career evaporated, as I had to take care of the cooking – something I knew very little about. Luckily, I had brought with me from Lebanon *The ABC Book of Cooking* in Arabic, and I began trying different recipes every day.

My husband attended many meetings where international political issues were discussed. There, I heard for the first time of the great poet and activist Pablo Neruda, and of the assassination of General Allende. Lebanon's war was seen as part of a world revolution. I watched and listened, thinking there was too much talk and very little action. I felt bored with their excessive analysis and thought that if they were serious about improving the world, they should be in Lebanon fighting for change. During those meetings, I met many Arab women. My first questions to them were 'How long have you been in Australia? When did you last visit home?' Most of them had not returned since they had first arrived. Their identical answers increased my anguish, thinking a similar fate awaited me.

I could no longer wait to return home. I stopped thinking about continuing my education, as was agreed with my husband before we came. I no longer cared about that *window* I was asked to open. I was obsessed with the idea of returning home. I wanted to return, and nothing else. I was desperate. I wanted to visit – just once. I felt something within me had died. I had lost something of myself. I belonged to nobody, and no place in this land meant anything to me. I pleaded with God – I needed to go back and then afterward let the flood of emigration take me wherever it wanted.

§

I only knew a few words in English, as French had been my second language at school in Lebanon. Two months after my arrival, I enrolled in English classes. But soon after, I started feeling dizzy and nauseated in the classroom. Initially, I thought my symptoms were the result of homesickness. My husband took me to a doctor, who looked at me with a confident smile and said, 'Congratulations! You're pregnant.'

I can't describe how hard those words landed. They were like a sledgehammer. I lost my balance. I had been struggling with the whole idea of marriage, of learning the language. How on earth did I fall so quickly into the trap of motherhood?

Nausea and vomiting never stopped throughout the nine months. The symptoms made me sleepless. No medication worked. I stopped going to the English classes.

I was nineteen when, after a difficult labour, the gynaecologist placed my first child, a son, on my breast. I was overwhelmed by feelings of loss and sadness as I lay on a cold bed, alone. There was no mother to stroke away my fears, nor was there a father on whose shoulder I could lean.

After my delivery, I had severe back pain and a fever that caused me to hallucinate, forcing me to stay in hospital for twenty days. I needed my mother. I wanted to tell her that I became a mother like her, before I was ready. She had also married young. My husband gave me the choice of naming my son. I named him after the Arab leader Jamal Abdul Nasser. I had been impressed by the strength of his character, and I saw in him a hope for saving our nation from the abyss.

Gradually, the presence of this little creature in my life made the air feel lighter and I started breathing more easily. The joy of my day began with my son's smile. I went to sleep with the sweet fragrance of his breath. He symbolised all the yearning I had for my family and homeland. As I put him to sleep every night, I sang to him the lullabies my mother had sung to us. Despite his small size, he became my entire universe. He gave me warmth, and a homeland my heart was yearning for.

§

We were celebrating my son's first birthday when my husband gave me a precious gift – a plane ticket to Lebanon with the flight booked in fourteen days. I was speechless. I started dreaming of when I would meet my family and throw myself into their bosom. I was eager to share with them my news and tell them that motherhood was the only good thing that had happened to me in Australia. I wanted to rest my head on my father's chest, tell him that there was no place in this world that had his warmth. I saw myself moving amongst my siblings, feeling love and safety in their presence. I imagined myself teasing the house trees, telling them their roots were not as deep as my yearning.

I started counting the hours until the time of take-off from the airport. Returning home that quickly after leaving it for the first time made me the luckiest of all the women I met in Sydney.

The day came. I took my seat on the plane, carrying my child with me to Lebanon. I thought of all the stories I would tell my family about Australia. I smiled when I imagined myself saying, 'Two of me have returned.'

As we approached Beirut, I pictured everyone waiting to welcome me at the airport. I placed my hand on my heart to calm myself down. Suddenly, it was announced that the flight had to be redirected to Cyprus. It was 1982. Beirut was under Israeli air attacks and South Lebanon was carpet bombed. Many would lose their lives. How bitter I felt!

The eight hours spent at Larnaka Airport felt like eight weeks. The flight to Beirut was resumed once the enemy planes had accomplished their mission, causing massive devastation to my beautiful country.

§

At Beirut Airport, the faces of the people waiting to receive their loved ones were full of anguish. I searched for my family amidst the crowds, but I could only see my maternal uncle who lived in Beirut. My family had asked him to pick me up. They were unable to leave the village because the bridges connecting the South to Beirut had been destroyed by the Israelis.

I spent the night at my uncle's place in the southern suburb of Beirut. He promised to find an alternate route to go to the village the next day. His wife showed me to a bed and asked me to rest. But soon, we heard bullets, followed by heavy shelling. Blood froze in my veins. How would I protect my child? My uncle calmed me by saying that this would not last long. It was a battle between two rival Lebanese factions. The dispute could be over traffic priorities or different political opinions. However, I could not control my fear of losing my son. I felt sharp pains in every organ of my body. After some hours, the clash subsided, but I remained afraid and restless. During these mad hours, I thought of the home I hated in Sydney. I felt I needed its silent walls to protect me and my son.

I had to stay in Beirut for three days until the army managed to secure a temporary passage to the South. We took a taxi and passed miserable dusty roads full of holes and craters. Destruction was everywhere. Even the trees did not wear the same green I had remembered. The journey, which normally took two hours, lasted seven.

§

The entrance to my village was studded with black billboards. Sadness was evident on everyone's face. When I arrived home, I threw myself into my parents' bosoms and embraced my siblings, whom I had missed so much. Our meeting was full of tears, yearning and anguish. I was shocked by the situation in my beautiful village. The parents of Layla, my closest friend, had been killed in an Israeli raid on the bridge when she and her sister were in the car with them. They narrowly escaped death. The whole village was grieving. They all went to Layla's place daily to offer their condolences and console her.

I had wanted to tell Layla stories of my life in exile, but I stayed silent. We didn't meet in the yard of her family home where we used to share secrets and laughter. We'd meet at the cemetery where I'd find her sitting beside the graves and headstones of her parents. My tears mingled with her despair.

I began to feel that safety was a priority. Being in exile alone no longer troubled me. In Australia, my son and I would be safe. Seeing my friend lamenting the loss of her parents tore the longing for home from my heart. Protecting Jamal, my baby, became of utmost importance. Days later, I contacted my husband and asked him to bring forward our return to Sydney. I stayed two months instead of three.

§

On my return to Sydney, I was welcomed by my husband, who had been very worried and eager to finally see us. Sydney seemed beautiful now. My nightmares vanished. In all the places that had seemed cold and hostile, I saw a haven for peace.

When my first child was six years old, I fell pregnant with my second son. Samer was a smiling, peaceful child, in contrast to Jamal, who was quiet only when asleep.

I was not emotionally prepared to send my children to childcare before the age of four. I was not convinced by the common practice amongst mothers who enrolled their children in care before the age of one to return to work. My priority was to experience motherhood to the fullest, regardless of our financial situation.

I made a few friends through the social gatherings I attended with my husband. These friends eased my loneliness, though they could not replace the deep friendships I had in the village.

When my youngest child was four years old, I enrolled in English classes and completed other courses in advanced English and office work. Later, I enrolled in a dental assistant course, and worked at a medical clinic for four years, and we were soon able to buy a home.

After ten years of marriage, my husband and I agreed to separate. We had married when we were both very young and we now had different pursuits in life. My romantic relationship with the world clashed with his practical approach. We went to the *cheikh* this time to get a proper divorce. Afterwards, we went to a Chinese restaurant and ordered prawns with vegetables that we both liked for dinner. At that time, we still enjoyed each other's company.

Afterwards, as a single mother with two children, I started working as a secretary in a medical practice. Raising two boys by myself was not easy, especially during their teenage years when peer group pressure might encourage the wrong choices. I had no family to support my values in a society that put few boundaries on the behaviour of teenagers. I experienced bouts of despair and anxiety. I sat at home alone in tears, fearful of the future, reliving painful memories of the breakup.

On one such day, the phone rang, and I answered, trying to hold back tears and contain my grief. The voice coming through the phone was that of a cleric making travel arrangements to the Holy Land in Saudi Arabia – the Hajj, an important obligation of Islam. 'I need a woman to look after the female pilgrims,' I heard the voice tell me. 'I thought of you to join the pilgrimage delegation.' Then he added, 'In return, all the costs of the trip will be covered, including the airline ticket and accommodation.' Such a trip was costly and well beyond my means. But when I heard the *cheikh's* offer, I was amazed. I accepted the offer without hesitation.

This was not a coincidence. The hand of God beckoned me through the *cheikh*. I felt God was watching me while I was sitting alone beseeching Him to provide me with the strength to raise my children on my own.

I put on the hijab that I had not worn before, nor ever imagined wearing. In that trip, I saw the Holy Kaaba, which is called the 'House of God'. The size of the small house surprised me. According to Islamic beliefs, it is the first blessed house placed on earth for the worship of God, and in it good deeds multiply and mercy descends on all people.

With the pilgrims around the Kaaba, I forgot all my sorrows and my fears for the future. I was walking with the crowd around me, everyone was wearing the same white clothes, and had the same appearance, the rich and the poor, the scholar and the ignorant. There was no social hierarchy. There were no guards for officials, nor a separate passage for the poor. We were all equal in obedience and duties, and everyone was circumambulating around the Kaaba in the same direction, seeking divine mercy.

On my return from the Hajj, I started looking for work. I assumed the hijab I had begun wearing would be an obstacle to being recruited, but I was mistaken. I applied for a medical receptionist job with a Christian specialist doctor. I was the only one wearing the hijab amongst more than fifteen other women applicants. I thought my chance of getting the job was slim. I had heard a lot about discrimination against veiled women. In the 1990s, the Gulf War and the media's portrayal of Islam were detrimental to my community's image. But I personally didn't experience racism while I was in Australia. I got the job at the medical clinic *with* my hijab. My personal exchanges with the Australian community left me with a feeling of gratitude. I experienced only friendliness in my daily dealings, free from fanaticism and hatred. As for the original custodians of the land, I have feelings of kinship uniting us through the injustice that befell us both.

§

I pursued several career paths. I studied make-up art, thinking it may be a good source of income, given the demand. However, in the end, I felt that a job focusing on external beauty was not meaningful.

I took a course in real estate and worked in this area for years. I was able to become financially independent and support my family. I loved doing business. After my eldest son Jamal finished high school, we opened our own small mixed business together, selling Australian and Lebanese groceries. Our Australian customers became like family. They learnt about our spices and produce and revelled in the recipes I offered them.

§

While I was still married, I had dreamt of 'opening that window of opportunity' for my siblings to emigrate to Australia. Now my finances enabled me to realise that wish. I sponsored four of my siblings to emigrate to Australia. They initially stayed with me, and I welcomed them in my heart and in my home. I put myself aside and gave them all I could. I gave time and effort to help settle them safely and successfully. My father always reminded me, 'You are the mother of all!' Indeed, I rarely thought of them as siblings. I dealt with them with the tenderness of my mother and the protection of my father.

Eventually, the huge responsibilities I carried were more than I could bear. The stress of looking after the well-being of many members of my family, as well as the little health awareness I had, made me neglect my own my health.

§

Seven years after my divorce, I met a man with whom I felt I shared the same ideals and outlook on life. I married again – a musician, a lover of poetry, a man of words. I fell in love with his world, without realising that his world had no connection to the reality I lived in.

Though my second marriage was not forced on me, it was the wrong decision. It seemed I divorced a materialistic man to marry a dreamer. This time, I had the support of my family when I decided to quit the marriage nine years later.

In 1996, I applied for a visitor's visa for my mother and father to stay with us for a couple of months. We were five siblings living in Sydney, competing for our parents to stay with us. It was the loveliest of competitions. My father was happy, and my mother was contented. Wherever they were, we felt very blessed with their presence in our hearts and our homes.

During my parents' stay in Sydney, in April 1996, Israel launched a barbaric onslaught, named 'Grapes of Wrath' on South Lebanon. We followed the news day and night. We were very concerned about relatives and friends and all those exposed to bombardment and deportation.

We were relieved when a ceasefire agreement was reached in Cairo. However, after a few hours, we received the most dreadful news. The last person who was martyred in the South, only one hour before the ceasefire took effect, was our youngest brother

Hassouna. He was seventeen, and the closest to my mother's heart.

When I first left Lebanon, he was only two. The beauty of his hazel eyes and blonde hair had nestled in my heart. When I first arrived in Australia, I used to look for a child of his age. I was hoping to find a two-year-old I could hold close. I recalled the memory of Hassouna holding our mother's dress, watching with his angelic eyes the moment of my departure, oblivious to the sadness in my own. Hassouna, the teenager, fulfilled my adolescent dreams of martyrdom.

§

We all returned with our parents to Lebanon on the first flight available. My brother's body had been scattered around our village after he had been hit by a rocket. His remains had already been buried, three days before our arrival.

My brother was a brave young man. He had refused to leave the village with others, and opted to stay along with some friends to help secure food supplies for the elderly who could not leave their homes.

The cemetery was our first destination. My mother opened the car door and ran to the grave. She screamed out with all her strength, 'I am here *Habibi*. Where are you, Hassouna? Get up.' And she started digging in the soil hysterically.

Many years have passed since my mother's screaming out for Hassouna. Time has failed to subdue the burning intensity of its pain. Whenever I remember that moment, I shed tears at what Israel did to my innocent brother.

After two months of mourning, we returned to Australia. A year after that tragic incident, I gave birth to my third angel, Sarah. She was the reward that I had not expected in my mid-thirties, when my youngest son was already eleven. I raised beautiful Sarah on my own. She overwhelmed me with love. She was my counsellor when I went astray in my thoughts. Her university studies in psychology sharpened her wisdom and polished her character.

I asked my parents to come and live with us in Australia when Sarah was very young. I wanted my father to enjoy the warmth of family life, the one he had been deprived of due to his work in the Gulf countries, and, later through our emigration. However, fate thwarted my plan. When the doctor in Lebanon told me over the phone that my father had pancreatic cancer, I felt the ground shake under my feet. The word 'cancer' was sufficient to make me see nothing except the desire to be beside him. It was a Sunday. The next day, I booked a ticket for myself and my two-year-old daughter, and travelled to Lebanon immediately, leaving behind my two sons.

I spent eight weeks with my father, but I needed to return to Australia for the sake of my other two children. I promised my father that I would return soon.

I spent all my days back in Sydney following up on his condition. From his hospital bed in Lebanon, his voice reached me with moaning and murmurs, carrying a weakness, atypical of the man I had known. I asked him with a broken heart, 'I beg you, father, forgive me if I ever did you wrong, or if I uttered any malicious words, or did anything you did not approve of.' Whenever I remember his answer, I smile, my eyes welling with tears. 'You must forgive *me*, daughter. I burdened you with a load heavier than what you could carry. You have already done so much by securing a better future for your siblings, by being the bridge for them to join you in Australia, and by taking care of them.' His last words to me remain the balm to my wounds. In recognition of my role in nurturing our family, he bestowed on me the title of 'The Mother of All'.

Death took him a month after my return to Australia, before we could repay him for the love and protection he'd given us. He was approaching sixty-two.

I'd been in Australia for twenty years when my father died. The support on which I had depended my whole life deserted me. It took me a while to regain my strength, but with time, I accepted life without my father. His memory was always present during our family gatherings. Kamal, my eldest brother, shared many of my father's characteristics. Every one of my siblings had a share of my father's traits – humour, sarcasm, anger, cleverness, wisdom, tenderness, loyalty and sincerity.

§

I resumed my life, trying to keep our family together. The presence of my siblings and their children around me became the centre of my life. In their breath, I found the warmth of my soul and the fragrance of my homeland.

My son Jamal gave me three granddaughters, one more beautiful than the other. I discovered I was an impatient grandmother. It seems all my energies had been spent in being the mother of my children and siblings.

§

I love the Arabic language, and I value literature greatly, which is why I fell for an artist-poet. I have always been passionate about writing, and so far, I have self-published two books of poetry in Arabic. I write about love, nature and home. In my writings, I express my concerns about my community, the injustice endured by the Lebanese and Palestinian people and the corrupt Arab leaders who are a cause of our displacement.

§

My yearning for my homeland did not abate over the years, as it did for many of my friends and relatives who secured a more prosperous life for themselves in Australia. I work all year to save enough money to visit Lebanon and spend one or two months there. During my forty years in Australia, I have visited Lebanon forty-two times. No one I have known has beaten my record. Every visit is as if for the first time. I arrive at our home, my suitcase in one hand, my heart overflowing with passion and longing. I run to check the olive and jasmine trees, the pots of mint and the roses and thyme in the garden. I go out and greet the elderly of the village and visit the cherished places of my childhood. I return to Australia for the sake of my children and extended family.

Following my father's death, I decided to go back with my daughter and live near my mother. From 2008 to 2016, I lived in the village. I opened a small clothing business, which provided for me and my daughter. These eight years were the happiest of my life. We returned when Sarah wanted to start her university degree in Australia.

§

I am a dreamer. To make peace with my reality in Australia, I have recreated what I loved most about my village. I treat people with the same generous spirit as my ancestors. I keep the front door of my house open during the day, as we did in Ayteet. I want people to know they can drop by anytime – without an appointment. My home is furnished with couches and chairs that resemble our living room in Lebanon. I planted jasmine to remind me of home.

I sit back in my garden in Sydney like I did in the village, for a morning coffee in the company of visitors. Although it may not be apparent to the people I meet in my daily life, I feel at times that my body and my eyes are out of place in Australia; they have been transported to this country, planted here, but I sense that my body is moving in, and my eyes are looking through, the Lebanon I left.

With time, however, the soul of Australia has seeped into me. I have come to appreciate the greenness of her trees, the blueness of her seas, the clearness of her skies, and her temperamental weather that resembles me. Besides her natural beauty, I appreciate the kindness of her people. They have treated me with respect and sincerity. I have connected with their simplicity and acceptance of the other. I love how they walk barefoot like I did in Ayteet. I always resented people who boasted about their appearance and insisted on wearing expensive labels and the latest fashion. I felt more comfortable amongst Australians who, like me, wore modest and comfortable clothes, and did not care too much about appearance.

I continue my journey between the two banks of the river: my beautiful exile on one side, and my homeland on the other. My passion for my homeland is an addiction that is no fault of mine, but that of the midwife who, when delivering me, failed to cut the umbilical cord that connected me to my motherland.

As I journey through life now, I breathe in the sweet fragrance of the eucalyptus of Australia and I breathe out my yearning for the cedars of Lebanon.

THE URBAN DERVISH
by Oula Ghannoum

I grew up as a sick child during a war, surrounded by attention and love. It was the happiest time of my life.

In 1973, at the age of four, my parents enrolled me in a secular French school, the Mission Laïque Française, in the nearby Koura district. 'We will defeat sectarianism with education and tolerance,' my father, Abdul-Aziz, declared. He was enthusiastic about Lebanon's future despite the deteriorating security of the country. The school rented an aristocratic palace dating back to the Emir Fakhr-Eddeen II era. The spacious fifteenth-century mansion was nestled within manicured gardens overlooking the Mediterranean Sea. I loved my school.

I loved studying with the French teachers. I loved singing, dancing, and painting with my classmates. We ran through the tall poplars and squat oaks in the nearby meadow. At lunchtime, we sat in the large dining room, our napkins embroidered with our names hanging from our collars, impatiently waiting for our home-cooked meals to be heated and served on our plates. The aromas of North Lebanon – caramelised onion, garlic, coriander and cumin – made us salivate. Every Friday, Madame Louisette cooked us a French dish. At the end of the school year, we staged a musical. We performed to the music of Fairuz and Wadih El-Safi, the iconic Lebanese singers, to the delight of our teachers and families.

My father, who was busy working to pay the fees of the expensive school, was unable to attend. He hired his friend, a retired army officer, to drive my mother Salimeh and me to the end-of-year ceremony. The colonel wore his pressed dark blue uniform and enjoyed playing father. My mother accepted my once-a-year borrowed father, while I basked in my friends' admiration of him. There, in that magical time and place, I was, for a while, a carefree child. This was before the wars in my body and my country threatened my little paradise.

I was six years old when the civil war broke out, and my arduous journey with illness began. It first appeared as a simple rash, then developed into embarrassing red lumps that covered my face, arms and legs. 'Girls should not play in dirt,' I heard our downstairs neighbour Um Mustafa say to my mother. 'Your daughter picked up her disease at school from germs in the soil, but only God Knows!' Um Salah, the neighbourhood's nurse, assessed it as a springtime allergy. Summer went and autumn came, but the rash persisted, and the itching got worse.

Our next-door neighbour Um Farah brought her doctor uncle, who had trained whilst working with the Allies in Akka's field hospital during WWII. The hunchbacked octogenarian, who wore a wrinkled and faded white suit, rested his ear on my abdomen without moving or uttering a word. The women in the room, well acquainted with his diagnostic method, watched patiently. He had once fallen asleep on a young man's chest while listening to his irregular heartbeat. The surgeons at the Hôtel Dieu hospital in Beirut later operated on the same arteries the doctor had identified with his ears. After some time, the doctor lifted his head and prescribed a mixture to be prepared by the pharmacist. My mother paid him with a plate of rice pudding infused with rose water. He gratefully consumed the dessert, baring his almost toothless gums. The following day, she applied the foul-smelling ointment on my burning skin while I stood on our balcony in Tripoli. As I waited for my skin to dry, I watched bombs exploding in the distance.

I grew up with the war, and although we had no running water or electricity, my childhood seemed normal. I joined the neighbourhood children in carrying buckets of water from the local public reservoir up to the tanks in our attics. I wasn't big enough to carry as many buckets as the other children. We delighted in spraying water at each other under the resentful gaze of the Public Utility money collectors, who had become redundant due to the water cuts and were confined to their offices by the relentless bombing. Instead, they went to the water reservoir every day and busied themselves with organising the queues. When the home tanks became more than half full, our day's job was done, and we were rewarded with a communal breakfast of dry bread cooked in a garlic and pomegranate sauce, prepared by our mothers.

When a bomb, rain or even a breeze cut out the electricity, I managed to do my homework by candlelight. Unable to watch the black-and-white TV with its two channels, we joined the evening gatherings at one of the neighbours' in the building. With no regular power, the fridge was rendered obsolete. We, children, became the couriers who brought fresh vegetables and meat for our mothers' cooking each day. We went up and down the Old City of Tripoli (the gated Mamluk city built in the thirteenth century). From our building, we followed the single road along the Kadisha River, passing by Saint-Gilles Crusaders' Castle, then down the ancient Refaeyeh stairways perched across the Sufi quarter leading to the Mansouri Grand Mosque and the fresh food *souk* (market), infused with the smell of spices, baking bread and roasting coffee. We were greeted by men standing outside their shops, while women sweeping their doorsteps kept an eye on us. They were quick to inform our parents if we misbehaved or played hide-and-seek in the courtyard of the *hammam* (bathhouse). The news would travel home to our mothers before we did.

§

On Sunday afternoons, I loved walking with my father in the Old City. He held my hand firmly, and we strolled together through narrow alleyways as he explained the history of its ancient Mamluk mosques, Crusaders' churches and Ottoman *takkiyyahs* (Sufi retreats). He loved reciting famous verses by classical Arab poets. I imagined the heroes of these poems riding with their beautiful sweethearts, Souad and Layla, on the backs of their mares through the Old City, while Mawlawi dervishes twirled with their heads and hands pointing towards the seventh heaven. From an early age, my father infused me with his love for Tripoli and Arabic literature, and his ascetic inclination. My father, the city and I were bonded by a shared spirit.

Often, my father's love was expressed through food. He believed that a healthy diet could help me fight my illness. When I could no longer stomach more meat sandwiches, I snuck away from my father's sewing workshop and took refuge at my brother-in-law's clothing shop in the Bazerkan Souk and watched its daily rhythm. The ancient market beamed with people who came from the surrounding mountainous regions of Koura, Zgharta, Danniyyeh and Akkar. Tripoli was their meeting place: market, bank, hospital and university. I was fascinated by the sight of buyers and shopkeepers bargaining loudly. A textile merchant would unfold rolls of fabric for a choosy woman, who would eventually buy material from his neighbour. Street vendors pushed their carts, calling for buyers, especially children, to press their mothers into purchasing one of their freshly baked *kaak* (sesame rolls) filled with red sumac or slices of salty white Akkawi cheese. Merchants stood in front of their shops, holding their morning coffee cups, and engaged in jovial conversation.

My father was a well-known tailor in Tripoli. While most tailors in the Old City made traditional clothes (*sherwal* and *abaya*), my father distinguished himself by mastering the European suit. During the French Mandate, between the 1920s and 1940s, my father saved a small fortune making hunting outfits for the French Gendarmerie, with which he bought our four-storey building in Abu Samra, a hilly suburb to the east. In peacetime, our balcony offered a sweeping view of Tripoli; in wartime, it allowed us to follow the crossfires, especially when they lit the sky at night. At its peak, my father's sewing workshop employed a dozen apprentices and experienced tailors, who specialised in making trousers, vests and jackets. My father was sought after by the wealthy families of Tripoli and its surrounding districts.

By the age of ten, I found myself alone, surrounded by the empty beds and echoes of seven older siblings who had left the family home after marriage or to study and work abroad. My parents reacted to my illness by becoming overprotective. Gradually, I was no longer allowed to play with other children outside, lest I hurt myself. My father's workshop became my only outlet on weekends, and my first cultural salon. His workshop doubled as a meeting place for North Lebanon's elites, who debated local and international politics while trying on their new suits.

My illness gave me licence to sit amongst the important men, who were amused at how I accompanied my father wherever he went, referring to me as his *porte-clé* (keyring). I was fascinated by conversations between local chieftains, high-ranking officers, judges, doctors and teachers. Heated arguments ensued between those who supported the armed Palestinian resistance and those favouring a peace deal with Israel. They discussed the implications of the civil war on Lebanon's economy and tourism, and how their children were leaving Lebanon, hastening its brain drain. Despite fierce disagreement, everyone left the shop in a jovial mood and came back soon after for another round of discussions, each holding their favourite left-wing or right-wing newspaper to back their point of view.

One day, a village notable asked me for drinking water. My father quickly rose from his sewing machine, grabbed the empty jug and headed to the fountain in the internal khan. The chieftain skilfully gulped the water from the jug nozzle without touching it with his lips. Then he turned to my father. 'Why didn't you let your daughter fill the jug? It's good for girls to learn hospitality skills.' My father replied without taking his eyes off the piece of fabric on his sewing machine, 'You are my client, and I will serve you. My children are not my servants, and I am raising them to be free and proud citizens.' Spending time at my father's workshop exposed me to the world of men and opened my eyes to Lebanon's political predicaments. I grew into a more serious child and teenager than my peers, burdened by my country's past and anxious about its future.

Two years into the war, and with the proliferation of checkpoints, my school moved from Koura to Tripoli. I rejoined the school at its new location in Tripoli, but I kept yearning for my mountainous paradise. The French staff left and were replaced by local teachers. New students, bearing the marks of new money and power that the war had bestowed, joined the school. Some of my Christian school friends left Tripoli, moving back to their villages or to safer coastal towns.

While fighting temporarily subsided, my joints and lungs flared up. I spent many long nights moaning from the burning in my joints and gasping for air. My mother sat next to me on the bed, rubbing my swollen joints and prickly chest with warm olive oil and reciting verses of the Quran. During the day, my father presented me to the city's doctors. Every time someone suggested a new doctor, he would pick me up early from school and take me to their clinic.

Around my tenth birthday, a paediatrician from Tripoli came close to diagnosing my illness. The doctor shifted his gaze between my swollen joints and the X-ray viewer, while I lay on the examination couch.

He concluded I was suffering from an autoimmune disease, an aggressive form of juvenile rheumatoid arthritis. This doctor, who had recently returned from Boston, did not get the chance to treat me. An armed group raided his clinic and shot him dead in broad daylight. Some said it was a robbery that went wrong, while others suspected political motives. I cried bitter tears over the premature passing of the handsome doctor who had identified my illness.

Soon after, my rheumatism became aggravated and affected my eyes. I would sit in the classroom unable to read what was written on the blackboard. I could stitch together sentences based on their context, but mathematical symbols and formulae were the hardest to predict. Shame stopped me from asking the teachers for help. One French language teacher took special interest in my plight. He wrote the questions in my notebook in large capital letters. My friend, with whom I shared a desk, recognised my difficulties. She was motherly, and I accepted her help. She read to me what was written on the board or the exam paper. This increased dependence left me with deep scars of humiliation. I would do everything to avoid their pity or having to ask for help, but sometimes I had no choice but to swallow my pride.

Poor vision, swollen joints and my skin rash often prevented me from running freely in the school playground. Sports lessons were my worst nightmare. I dreaded wearing shorts because I was embarrassed by the purple patches on my cracked skin. After sports, I would come home with a new wound or a bruise after tripping or hitting a barrier I did not see. Our next-door neighbour advised my mother to 'place a broom at the mosque entrance to repel the evil eye', which she believed was the cause of my frequent falls. After a long night of joint pain, I would wake up the next day like a wooden plank, afraid to move my head or limbs, lest I spark a new wave of pain. I would go to school, dragging myself around like a ghost until the day was over. My impairment was not always visible, and I felt no one understood or cared about me. I yearned to be accepted but didn't know how. I nurtured my pain and shame in silence. A local Armenian paediatrician advised my father, 'Your daughter's illness has become bigger than Tripoli. Take her to Beirut.'

I stayed at the American University of Beirut Hospital with my mother, undergoing extensive medical examinations in 1982, during the Israeli invasion. There, I discovered for the first time the plight of the people from South Lebanon and the southern suburbs of Beirut. I shared the ward with children who had been injured by air strikes and cluster bombs. I had never seen children with amputated limbs before. I remember a wounded Palestinian fighter giving me a little green racing car to play with during my long hospital stay. I kept that toy for many years. After a month of medical tests, the diagnosis made by the slain Boston-trained doctor was confirmed. I left the hospital with a bag full of medications and eye drops.

My parents kept encouraging me to study, and I never lost my motivation. My father often told me, 'I am giving you the best education so you can overcome your illness and become a doctor who cures others,' defining my mission in life. Attending this private and exclusive school was my first experience of estrangement. It set me apart from the children in the neighbourhood who attended the local public school, as my school was beyond their means. I helped my neighbours with their homework to earn their friendship and acceptance, but I only won their respect. I spoke better French, wrote better Arabic, and my disciplined manners seemed foreign in my neighbourhood. A distance grew between us.

After two more years of intensive treatment and continued suffering, my illness had become bigger than Beirut, and my parents decided to send me for medical treatment to England, where my brother

Omar was studying. My father held back tears as he hastily sold the fine rolls of fabric in his sewing workshop and went around to his friends to raise enough pounds for my expensive trip. There wasn't enough money for my mother to accompany me. I, a thirteen-year-old girl with poor eyesight who had never spent a night alone, travelled by myself. At the boarding gate in Beirut, a woman from Saida, a stranger, held my hand and looked after me until I was met by my brother at Heathrow Airport.

A few days after my arrival in London, my brother took me to his local doctor, who recognised the complexity of my case. He referred me to an ophthalmologist who had recently featured in the newspaper. The famous surgeon operated at the Prince Charles Eye Unit of King Edward VII Hospital in Windsor. I was told he had removed the cataract for Prime Minister Thatcher, at the regal wing of the hospital. I stayed there for four weeks undergoing a series of eye surgeries. My brother visited me a few times, bringing his fusion cooking.

In the expensive hospital, a nurse asked me where I came from. 'Tripoli,' I replied. She nodded and said, 'You have oil in Libya and your parents can afford your treatment at this hospital.' I didn't correct her.

After recovering from the surgeries, my brother showed me around London. I was impressed with its buildings, streets, transport system, theatres and museums. I also visited other cities with my brother's English wife. After three months, I returned to Lebanon via Damascus because the Beirut Airport was closed due to intense fighting.

I began adjusting to walking around with my new thick bifocal glasses. These glasses, typically worn by the elderly, were embarrassing, but they allowed me to see the blackboard for the first time in years. The English surgeon removed the lenses of my eyes without replacing them with artificial ones, to avoid an autoimmune reaction. With restored eyesight, my school performance improved and I saw my name on the school's honours list two years in a row, until the glaucoma worsened and set me back again.

A few months after my return from London, fierce battles erupted in Tripoli, causing massive destruction. For the first time during the war, our house took direct hits, and a rocket pierced the ceiling of my bedroom while I was asleep. Even after the fighting ceased, I could never feel safe in my bed again.

Lebanon's economy quickly deteriorated. Inflation spiralled and the Lebanese currency, the Lira, plummeted. One day, my father brought home a newspaper with a cartoon on the last page showing a box of tissues named 'Lirex', a hybrid between the poor lira and the famous Kleenex tissue brand.

Frequent road closures encouraged the expansion of competing regional centres at the expense of Tripoli, which was losing its economic relevance. Fabric shops were replaced by boutiques selling imported ready-made clothes, threatening the traditional sewing profession. Mannequins in the shop windows, dressed in the latest fashion, silenced the men who once stood outside their shops calling out their merchandise. The number of my father's clientele diminished, and his once-thriving business came to an end.

My parents had never contemplated emigrating, even during the darkest hours of the fighting. But with our purchasing power in free fall and my advancing illness, the idea began to creep into our daily conversations, first as an outright rejection, then as a remote possibility. The lack of medicine dealt a final blow to our determination to stay. For a while, my father secured my medication through taxi drivers who travelled to Syria and Turkey. It was expensive and ultimately unsustainable. My health deteriorated and my eyesight was again under threat. My illness had grown greater than Lebanon. Migration became plausible. Now, it was a matter of when and where.

While we were grappling with these crises, my eldest sister Nada visited us. It was early 1986, ten years after she had emigrated to Australia with her husband and one-year-old daughter. Her short visit helped my father make up his mind and he agreed to apply for immigration to Australia.

'Our children are scattered all around the world. We can reunite our family in Australia,' he tried to convince himself and my mother.

All my father knew of Australia were the few soldiers of the Australian garrisons he had seen in Tripoli during WWII. Of our large family, three people applied for immigration: my father, my mother and I.

Many long months passed after lodging the immigration application before we were called to the Australian Embassy in Damascus. In preparation for the interview, we had to undergo the obligatory medical examination. Envious neighbours insinuated that Australia did not accept people with a disability, while well-wishers claimed that only those with communicable diseases were rejected. My uncle, who also applied for immigration and travelled with us to Damascus, was confident of his chances because he had worked in Australia during the 1960s. I went for the medical examination with a grim outlook. Fortunately, Damascus was experiencing prolonged power rationing, and after hours of waiting at the clinic, the doctor decided to skip the eye test because he could not turn on his instrument.

Another surprise awaited us at the embassy. During the interview, the Australian officer asked my father whether he would sell his building. My father vehemently rejected the idea. The officer exclaimed, 'You are leaving Lebanon for good. Why do you want to leave assets behind? You will need money in Australia.' My father replied, 'I want to leave the building for my children and grandchildren, so they have a home when they return or visit in the future. With the current inflation and bad economy, it is difficult to find a buyer, and If I do, they'll give me very little.' He was right about the latter. The former was to remain an unfulfilled wish. For a moment, my mother and I thought my father had ruined our chances with his candour, but the officer smiled and proceeded to grant us a visa. It seemed we could do nothing wrong. Australia wanted us. However, my uncle's application was rejected.

My father travelled to Australia in May 1987 to arrange for our arrival. My mother stayed behind until I completed my school year. I began studying for the high school exams not knowing whether there would be a state-run baccalaureate exam amid the political and security chaos. My school offered us the opportunity to sit for the French Baccalaureate, for which I was preparing.

On the first morning of June 1987, I was studying in my room when we heard that the incumbent Lebanese Prime Minister had been assassinated. His murder plunged the country into more political turmoil and bloodshed. It also ended any chance of an official high school exam. My only remaining hope was to sit for the French equivalent.

The primary French Baccalaureate exams were held at my school in Tripoli. I passed most subjects but had to retake Physics and English at the Ashrafiyeh branch of the Lycée in Beirut. On the day of the secondary exams, my middle sister Nouha and I left Tripoli before dawn. When we arrived at the main taxi rank in Barbir, the fighting was intense. We couldn't find a driver willing to take us from Barbir in West Beirut to Ashrafiyeh in East Beirut. 'You will do the exam,' my sister declared defiantly. Noting my surprise, she added, 'We will cross the demarcation line on foot.'

As my sister and I ran across the hippodrome separating the divided capital, our feet sank in the sand. Sniper bullets whizzed between our legs, bombs flew above our heads and uncontrollable tears ran down our cheeks. I arrived at the exam centre dishevelled and trembling with fear. I couldn't remember the laws of Physics or a word of English. I left Lebanon without an official high school certificate. I was devastated. All the years of study and suffering came to nothing. All my father's sweat and blood to pay the private school fees amounted to nothing. My plan to start university on arrival in Australia was in jeopardy.

To help me get over my disappointment, my mother insisted I go on a picnic in the mountains with relatives and friends. The weather was mild, and we spent a pleasant day in nature. But I returned home with a broken heart. How could I leave my beautiful country? How could I leave the rest of my family and all my friends behind?

It wasn't the first time I had visited the mountains, nor the first time I appreciated Lebanon's beauty. But since leaving became certain, I began looking at everything with a new eye – rediscovering the mountains, the sea, the river, the castle, the Old City, the olive groves, the orange orchards. I wanted to imprint these images on my memory forever. Every tree, every grain of soil, every sunrise, every moonset, every summer breeze.

I wondered whether I could look at another country the same way. Could Australia replace Lebanon? Wouldn't I be ashamed of loving another country? Yet, I was convinced we had to leave – because we could no longer stay. It wasn't just medicines, water or electricity that were missing, but also safety and security. My mind knew we had to go; my heart was still resisting. A voice inside reminded me that I am Lebanese. I am destined to leave, just as my Phoenician ancestors always did. I must patch my pride, pack my suitcase and leave. Yes, I must go, because my country promised nothing more than forgiveness for the sin of leaving it. I must leave, because we could no longer stay in a homeland where a human life was worth no more than a stray bullet. Mind must rule over heart during a time of gratuitous death.

§

A few weeks before our departure, I bought a thirty-six-exposure colour film. Until then, I had no use for the camera my eldest sister had given me during her visit to Lebanon the year before. We had never owned a camera, and most of the photos in our house were ones of my Australian niece, sent with letters and recorded tapes brought by visiting expats from Sydney. But events had accelerated, and instead of using the camera to take photos of us to send to Australia, I now had to use it to take photos of the people and places I loved as a memory of my country.

I asked our next-door neighbour to help me load the film. In exchange, he asked me to take a photo of him.

'What's the point of this photo?' I asked. 'I'm not going to develop the film in Tripoli.'

'Give the photo to my brother in Sydney,' he replied.

'Do I have thirty-five photos left after that?'

'Not all of the film can be properly used. You can safely take thirty-three photos.'

I spent the weekend compiling a list of the people and places dearest to me. I wanted to imprint thirty-three memories on that film, thirty-three tattoos on my heart, thirty-three landmarks charting the path of return, thirty-three totems against oblivion.

The first photos were of my school friends, whose faces faded in my memory. But in those moments, just before we said our final goodbyes, we were the closest we had ever been.

I also photographed my teachers. After I took her photo, my Arabic teacher embraced me and said, 'Leave this country and do not look back. Go to Australia, be a successful Lebanese emigrant, and raise all of our heads high, my dear student. Focus on your studies, but do not forget to enjoy life.'

Then I photographed my next-door playmates and my dearest cousins. I did not need photos for my two married sisters, Nouha and Noma, who were to stay in Lebanon with their husbands. I would never forget their faces.

Next, I photographed the places closest to my heart: the Rock's Beach, where I swam 'illegally' with my dad; the seaside Mina promenade, where we walked on sunny afternoons and ate sesame *kaaks* and roasted corn cobs; the Manshiyeh garden, where we sipped afternoon tea with roasted chestnuts. From the west-facing balcony of our house, I photographed Saint Gilles Castle, the Mina Port and the Kadisha River winding towards the Mediterranean. From the east-facing balcony, I photographed the convent of the Carmelites, the olive groves, and the sunrise behind Mount Arba'een. On our rooftop, I waited for the full moon so I could capture it rising in the sky of my childhood. Then I packed the camera in my suitcase, hoping to find the photos on the other side of the world. My mother and I left Lebanon on 13 August 1987.

§

A few days after we settled in Sydney, I learnt how to use public transport and went to a photo shop in Old Bankstown Square to develop my film. I mistakenly opened the back of the camera, removed the film and began winding it with my fingers. The shop attendant started giggling, which made me nervous.

I asked in my broken English, 'Why are you laughing at me?'

'You must wind the film *inside* the camera *before* removing it, to avoid light exposure. Now, it's burnt!' He pointed to a small lever I should have used.

A shiver shook my body as I realised what I had just done. Tears ran down my cheeks.

'Try,' I said, my voice breaking. 'The film might still be okay.'

The attendant placed my film next to another on the counter. I squinted at them both on the glass-top table, overtaken by dread as if I were looking at a dead body. My film was completely blank, while the other showed spectres of people and places. The photos I had taken were wiped out!

I thanked the attendant, slipped the erased film into my pocket and left the shop inconsolable and disoriented. What was I going to do now, without a memory? Without a record of my past life? I wandered aimlessly around Bankstown Square. I didn't know what to do. My friends, my teachers, the castle, the sea, the river, the old city. All gone because of my mistake. Exhausted, I sat on the steps in the middle of the square and rested my back against a memorial for war veterans inscribed with the words 'Lest We Forget' and sobbed. I didn't want to forget. I wasn't ready to forget. Perhaps the burnt film was a sign that I had to forget the past to begin a new life here. But at that time, I didn't understand this lesson.

§

In the first year of our settlement in Australia, my eldest sister Nada accommodated us in her big heart and house. Australian universities did not recognise my Lebanese school transcripts, and I had to complete the New South Wales Higher School Certificate (HSC). I began a three-month advanced English course and then attended Bankstown TAFE to study a Matriculation year, which combined Years 11 and 12. There, I met migrants like me from various backgrounds, as well as mature-age students pursuing further education. It was a transitional year in which I learnt about Australia and its diverse cultures. I made a few friends, but none of these friendships lasted beyond that year. We were all too busy working hard to settle into our new lives. We migrants tended to socialise within our own communities.

Days after our arrival, I consulted local doctors, and I was referred to the Sydney Eye Hospital, where I was treated by the Head of the Ophthalmology Department. I resumed taking the same medication prescribed to me in Beirut. During our last year in Lebanon, irregular access to medication had caused irreparable damage to my optic nerves. In Sydney, I was subjected to a series of surgeries, injections and laser treatments to save my eyesight. I'll never forget the stomach-turning taste of glycerol, which the doctors made me drink in their desperate efforts to lower my high eye pressure.

Nine months after our arrival, my parents and I moved out of my sister's house and into a rental apartment in Bankstown. We furnished it with second-hand furniture and appliances donated by relatives. A few months later, my younger brothers Saoud and Oussama arrived from the United States and lived with us briefly. They soon found jobs, got married and moved out to start their own families. Not long after, my older brother Omar arrived from the UK with his family. My eldest brother Mohamad had arrived a few months before us from Saudi Arabia with his family.

I sat for the HSC exams shortly after an eye surgery, before my eyesight had fully recovered. The Department of Education provided me with a reader and large-print documents. This was my first real culture shock. I had spent most of my school years in Lebanon straining to read the blackboard or my notebooks, while here my impairment was acknowledged and accommodated with relative ease. Despite the circumstances, I achieved high marks in the HSC and was accepted into Dentistry at the University of Sydney. My family was happier than I was. Finally, they would have a medical doctor.

The first few years in Australia were difficult, painful and alienating – so much that I prefer not to recall them. In fact, I don't remember them. There is a hole in my memory, as if a period of my life had been wiped out. Sometimes, to keep going, we must forget. There was joy that most of our family had finally reunited, though not in our homeland. Before leaving Lebanon, I had longed to be with my siblings. Yet once we were all in Australia, we spent little time together. Everyone was busy establishing themselves. We gathered for family picnics on public holidays, then went our separate ways. I remained close to my eldest sister, and despite the twenty-year gap, we were good friends.

My father was disappointed by how little he saw of his children, despite the sacrifices he had made by leaving his beloved old city behind to be with them. He missed his workshop and his friends. He would take morning walks to Bankstown Square but struggled to make new friendships. He looked for people who resembled his well-educated clients and cultured companions but found none. He took every class available for senior migrants through the English as a Second Language programme and begged the teachers for more lessons. He wanted to master the language so he could enrol at university, make new acquaintances and integrate into mainstream society.

He loved the Australian nature and took weekly bushwalks and beach trips in Sydney. After all, he had grown up by the Kadisha River and was a strong swimmer. He was curious about this new country and loved the more casual and easy-going attitude of Australians. One day he told me with frozen tears in his eyes, 'I wish I came here earlier.'

But it was too late. I watched him shrink, day by day, in his corner. I couldn't fully understand what he was going through, let alone help him. I had my own problems to deal with.

My mother was the happiest migrant amongst us. She was reunited with her eldest daughter Nada, and the two became inseparable. My sister took her shopping after work and they visited family and friends together. With her easy and affable nature, my mother quickly made a lot of friends and reconnected with extended family. I would often come home to find a distant relative I didn't know existed sipping coffee and chatting with her.

She had no difficulty summoning her busy children. She only had to prepare one of those traditional Lebanese dishes, and they would gather around her sumptuous dining table. She was no longer confined to a house in a war-ravaged city. With reliable water and electricity, her domestic workload was lighter. She had more time to herself and blossomed socially.

During those first few years, I spent my time equally among university, hospital and home. By the end of my first year in Dentistry, I had already undergone several eye surgeries. I decided to switch to a field which did not entirely rely on my visual acuity. I left Dentistry and enrolled in a Bachelor of Science at the University of New South Wales. I graduated with Honours in Plant Biochemistry. I was later awarded a PhD scholarship at Western Sydney University to research the responses of tropical grasses to climate change, under the supervision of an inspirational and supportive PhD mentor.

I fell in love with photosynthesis, a field that remains the focus of my academic career. I had grown up in an ancient, highly urbanised city with little green spaces beyond the orange and olive groves on its outskirts and the roses and jasmine pots on its balconies. Belatedly, I began to appreciate plants and their amazing universe. Through my work in the Australian grasslands and my travels in the outback, I developed a deep connection to this vast and brown landscape. Its fragility mirrored my illness and the scars on my body. The slender trees, tough scrubs, dry soils, transient creeks and red sun spoke to my pain and loss.

I began to love this country – a journey that has nurtured my soul and given me the strength to go on. Whenever I feel rundown, I escape to a beach or the bushland.

From those early years in Australia, I recall my loneliness and isolation. I met many Lebanese and Arab migrants through social and cultural activities, but I made very few lasting friendships within the community. I grew estranged from it and felt more comfortable with other outsiders. Despite being part of a large family, now mostly settled in Australia, I was often on my own. My parents, once my rocks of support in Lebanon, became disempowered by their lack of knowledge of the language, system and culture.

They couldn't understand the daily challenges I faced, let alone help with them. My siblings were busy with their own families and journeys of settlement, caught in the grinding daily struggle. But when one fights alone, one remains alone. The more I managed, survived and succeeded, the lonelier I became.

§

In the summer of 1993, before starting my PhD and six years after my arrival in Australia, I returned to Lebanon for a four-week holiday. On a personal level, I had just caught my breath. My illness was relatively under control, my career was beginning to take shape, and I had a first taste of financial independence, having moved out of home. I had missed Lebanon terribly. The country was still in the early stages of post-war reconstruction, and not much had changed, except the warlords were now in power.

I caught up with only one of my school friends, as most of the others had left to work or study in France, the UK, the US or Canada. That one friend was determined to stay in Lebanon, holding her ground like the last standing pole of a tent that had been blown away, bearing witness to the displacement tragedy of our silenced generation. In our building, the neighbours I used to play with had married and moved to other parts of Tripoli or emigrated to Australia, Sweden, Denmark or Germany.

Together with my two sisters who had remained in Lebanon, I travelled throughout the country, except to the southern border strip, which remained under Israeli occupation. I ate crisp, delicious red apples from Mount Lebanon. I rafted down the legendary Asi (Orontes) River. I visited the Roman ruins of Baalbek, swam at the crowded, warm beaches, and relished authentic cuisine. I could not get enough of the sweet coastal white figs. There was an unreal sense of exuberance, overjoy and hubristic optimism about the country's future. Yet, the cracks in the artificial sectarian peace were already showing.

Though I loved reconnecting with Lebanon's nature, culture and people, a rift was widening inside me. I didn't know how to stop it. I could only watch helplessly as Lebanon slipped away from my hands. The country was sliding down a perilous path, with no proper reconciliation or resolution of the conflicts that had torn it apart. Corruption was still rampant and allegiances were pledged to powerful individuals rather than to the nation. Arms were everywhere, and any minor incident could develop into a violent clash. Youth unemployment was high, and the brain drain continued at full pace.

Over the next decade, I visited Lebanon many times on the way to other destinations – conference travel or holidays in Asia and Europe. With each visit, the rift grew wider, until there was little left that tied me to the land I still loved but no longer recognised. I felt discouraged by how some Lebanese treated Australian migrants as second-class expats, in contrast to those who had settled in Europe or North America.

After we emigrated, my sister Nouha had moved into our parents' apartment in Tripoli. Despite her warm hospitality, I felt like my childhood home had been taken from me. I no longer had a home to go back to. I was condemned always to be a visitor in my own home and my country of birth, until one day, I became a complete foreigner. Once that point was reached, I could not return. Lebanon and I had become estranged, like two old lovers who could no longer look each other in the eye. There was a lot to be done and said between us but would never be. I still longed to return to *my* Lebanon. But it was no longer possible.

Even so, every night for many years, I imagined returning. At the end of each day, I would visualise myself turning into Hawooz Street behind the water reservoir in Tripoli, walking by the Marhaba grocery, smiling at the young men playing table foosball outside the barber's shop and waving to Um Salah the nurse as she sipped coffee with her two daughters on the front balcony. Just before reaching our building in Abu Samra, I would look up, expecting to see my mother's silhouette framed in the kitchen window. And then, I would return to the present and find myself walking, not in Tripoli, but along a suburban street in Sydney.

§

Towards the end of my PhD, I was devastated by loss and grief once again. Nine years after his arrival in Australia, in May 1996, my father died of a heart attack, without ever seeing his beloved Tripoli again. At the time, I was consumed by study and overwhelmed by illness. I couldn't grieve properly. The guilt of not mourning him as I should have still haunts me. It is as if his soul is still asking me for its unhonoured dues.

Shortly after his death, my mother's gallbladder cancer overshadowed my every waking moment. The doctor told us she had six months to live. I spent this period travelling between Canberra, where I was finalising my last PhD experiment, and the hospice in Fairfield where my mother was dying. I sat in her room for long hours, writing my thesis on my laptop and watching the morphine drip slowly into her veins, the pain flickering across her face.

My mother's death was a tragedy I could not fathom. I held her swollen hand moments after she exhaled her last breath and wondered how the warm hand which had caressed my illness and embraced me when I was in pain could be so cold and still. To console me, my sister said she had heard my mother whisper my name as her soul expired. I like to believe that. The day we buried her, my world turned upside down and never righted itself. How could my parents die before seeing me graduate, as they always dreamt! Still, I remained focussed and worked feverishly to submit my thesis on time.

After submitting my thesis, I knew I had to keep working. Work was both a distraction and the only certainty I could control. Meanwhile, my eyesight and health remained unpredictable. I took up a postdoctoral research position in the same laboratory where I had studied and began preparing my first research fellowship application. Once submitted, I surrendered to the surgeons and allowed them to operate on my eyes again.

The doctors managed to restore some central vision in my left eye, which still serves me today.

But my right eye had deteriorated beyond repair. Its vision was extinguished forever. With that, I lost my driver's licence, and a great deal of my pride and independence.

During my long stay at the Sydney Eye Hospital, I shared the room with a seven-months-pregnant woman who had the same eye condition and was on similar medication. She had chosen to take alternative medication so she could safely become pregnant. I asked her why she was risking her eyesight. How could she care for a baby if she lost her vision? She replied, 'I would do anything to become a mother.'

At that point in my studies and career, I was highly ambitious. I wasn't prepared to make that kind of sacrifice. I also felt a deep sense of duty to my parents, who had made tremendous sacrifices to give me the best education and bring me to Australia. I had to succeed in my career and fulfil their dreams, even if they were no longer alive to see it.

That encounter at the hospital made me close, perhaps prematurely, the subject of having my own children. Bearing a child felt too great a risk. I was a lonely woman with unpredictable health prospects. I was far from home and extended family. How could I be a mother when chronic illness had kept me a dependent child in need of care for so long?

For several years after losing sight in my right eye, I drifted into what a friend would later call 'functioning depression'. At the time, I had no name for my condition, and no one around me enquired. I collapsed inwardly and developed a hardened shell on the outside. I progressed with my work, but emotionally and socially I froze. I stood at the crossroad of my life indifferently watching the traffic around me. I often woke up feeling crooked from a disturbed sleep with my pillow soaked in tears. I wept for my lost eye, for my mother, for my father, for my troubled country, and for my broken heart.

In 2000, I was awarded my first fellowship from the Australian Research Council to work as an independent researcher at the Australian National University in Canberra. The move to Canberra offered much-needed distance from my recent losses – my father, my mother, my right eye and my car. I replaced my car with a bicycle, until I later returned to busy Sydney and had to give that up too, relying on public transport. A new chapter had begun, one where I was not only lonely but completely alone. It was my moment of reckoning.

§

Before leaving Sydney, I visited my parents' graves at Rookwood Cemetery for the first and last time. Under the searing heat and drowning in a sea of sorrow, I stood before their adjacent graves, recalling our journey together through tears. I was thankful for their enormous sacrifices, which culminated in their uprooting from Lebanon and dying on foreign soil to save my eyesight. The battle was half-won and half-lost, and the mantle now rested solely in my hands. I recited the opening verses of the Quran, praying for their souls to rest in peace, and asked for their forgiveness and guidance in the journey ahead.

In that graveyard, I knew that I had left Lebanon for good. I stood on the land that received my parents' remains, the land that had absorbed my tears and embraced my further losses. This was now the country where I had lived thirteen years of joy and pain, gain and loss. Lebanon had not been part of this gruelling experience.

It was time to realign my relationship with both Lebanon and Australia. On the way from Sydney to Canberra, an idea quietly took root: Lebanon is where I came from, and Australia is the companion of my ongoing journey, with its sweetness and bitterness. I place my belonging to Lebanon on hold. I activate it during times of crisis to support my people, then stow it away to protect my heart. Lebanon is the homeland I adore – beautiful, resilient, promising and postponed. It is to remain my unfinished story.

§

When I immigrated to Australia, I knew nothing of the plight of Indigenous peoples. I only knew that this distant country was willing to offer shelter. Eventually, I came to understand that those who had granted me the right to live here were not the original custodians of the land. And sometimes I ask myself: Does my presence here make me complicit with the settlers? This question poses a moral conundrum. I advocate for the rights of the Palestinian people while I live on stolen land! The Palestinian people, like the Indigenous peoples of Australia, have been dispossessed of their ancestral lands. This awareness deepens my commitment to Indigenous rights everywhere.

After thirty-eight years, I find myself embedded in Sydney. It is a city that allows me to be a connected stranger – one that does not demand clear answers or absolute allegiance. Home is no longer a country. It has become a search for inner peace.

After leaving my original home, the journey has continued – not toward any specific place but toward a larger truth, and harmony with the human spirit and nature. Every place is part of that journey.

I feel like a dervish from ancient Tripoli, whirling in my urban Sydney retreat, yearning for transcendence.

EM JMAHEER: THE PEOPLE MAGNET

by Nouha El-Khoury Francis

I was a child full of life and curiosity. Fear and hesitation had no place in my heart. I loved to frolic about with friends. The village of El-Hakour was small and very safe. Its winding lanes and vineyards recorded our daily escapades. Our parents permitted it and even encouraged us to play outdoors.

Delighted with my lust for life, my mother would jest with an Arabic proverb: 'The house is small and the donkey bucks.' I had boundless energy and attracted many friends. 'You can't be contained, *Em Jmaheer* – Miss Popularity. Take your friends and play outside.' We ran out to the fresh air in glee.

Our family home was small for nine people. It had two bedrooms, a tiny lounge room, a combined kitchenette with a dining room and a wood fireplace. We had an Arabic-style lounge room – the colourful cushions would line up on the floor where we'd sit during the cold winter seasons.

I started working at a young age to help cover some of my expenses for the year. In my first job of picking olives, I soon became known to every field owner in the area. I eagerly anticipated the olive harvest season, because after selling my catch, my little pockets would burst with francs and liras: I'd use a long stick to hit the olive branches and as the olives broke free, I'd catch them in my tiny hands. I can't begin to express my happiness at selling my harvest, no matter how little a shop owner might pay me.

During the Feast of Saint Barbara, we'd sing and dance and dress up in amusing costumes. My friends and I would go door to door on that night and receive a few francs, which was pocket money for a whole month. On New Year's Day, we would say *'bestrayni'* to the adults, a cheeky little greeting requiring the gifting of a coin or two to children. A coin might be given to little ones on feast days too. One New Year, I cheekily turned on the charm to get some extra francs from relatives. It was the biggest sum of money I'd ever received. Thrilled, I couldn't wait to share it with friends – free to buy anything our hearts desired.

Summer harvests in my coastal village began with the laborious tobacco harvest, which required the collective effort of the whole family during the entire summer holiday. Yet as soon as chores for my family finished, I'd joyfully help the neighbours thread tobacco leaves onto strings for drying. They paid me a franc for each thread. Every day, I managed to save a quarter or half a lira, which was enough to buy delicious roasted peanuts and cold ice cream during the hot summer months. I flipped the remaining francs between my fingers until I had spent them *all* in one day.

My vigour and popularity were noted by all and earned me a variety of names amongst the villagers, some humourous while others were derogatory, until the nickname '*Em Jmaheer*', *the people magnet* stuck. I wore the title with pride.

My childhood never extended beyond El-Hakour, which was bordered by the Arqa River. That river was a gift from God to our semi-isolated village, giving it some status and fuelling many of my childhood adventures. How often I swam in the fresh clean water without my parents' knowledge. How many times did I steal apricots, peaches and pomegranates from the orchards strewn along the river's banks, ignoring the consequences? How many times did I walk across thorny riverbanks without worrying about falling into deep water, or being bitten by a snake looking for prey? I wasn't afraid of risk or my parents reprimanding me for disobeying them. There were many rules and expectations of correct behaviour for girls in my family, and I wanted to push boundaries and live in the moment.

Fearlessness allowed me to take risks and explore the unknown. One day on my way to school, I strolled through the cemetery of a deserted village as a dare and to prove to my friend that I was courageous. I ventured into the remote Matmoura forest graveyard to collect acorns, as a substitute for the chestnuts we couldn't afford to purchase. I jumped from one rock to another as I crossed the river and returned with a large stash in my pockets. My carefree and joyful childhood was the best time a child could have wished for.

§

As I grew into a teenager, I found I didn't care about new clothes or makeup like my peers. My older sister scolded me with, 'How can you go to a wedding wearing that old dress? I'd rather stay home than let anyone mock my outfit,' but for me enjoying the occasion dancing far outweighed concern with my appearance.

Years passed and the rebellious girl grew, dreaming of leaving a mark, and refusing to accept a life that was drab and monotonous. I wanted to change the world, but how could I, from a remote village in the marginalised Akkar region. We were minuscule and our needs were invisible to each successive government. From a young age, I was interested in how the country was run and got involved in political protests and consciousness-raising social activities.

At sixteen, in 1973, I found myself chanting at the front of a demonstration that started from the high school of Halba, the main town of Akkar. When the demonstrators arrived at the Qaim Maqam centre to submit their demands, a squad of the Lebanese Army dispersed the crowd with batons. I was terrified and was forced to run in the high heels I was wearing. A speeding armoured vehicle almost ran me over, passing so close it brushed against my school uniform. I collected small rocks and went up to the school rooftop to throw them at the army and aid the brave young men standing up to them.

§

After high school, I wanted to attend university in Beirut, the capital. Everyone aspired to experience its progressive values and study in its colleges. I was about to embark on this exciting new journey when the civil war in Lebanon broke out. This destroyed roads and severed connections between various regions. I was denied the opportunity of studying in sophisticated Beirut and was instead stuck in a small village for two years without electricity or running water. I was glued to the radio, impatient for an end to the war. In 1977, a fragile truce allowed me to enrol at the University of Lebanon in the eastern half of the then-divided

Beirut. I had a fascination for history, and I chose it as my field of study.

In the environment where I grew up, females were destined for the teaching profession. I often heard phrases like 'The best job for a girl is teaching,' and 'A girl's life should always revolve around her family, so teaching is perfect,' and 'She needs to be devoted to her husband and her children.' Also, they argued, 'Teachers can take their children with them to school, and then have the long summer holidays together.' So, after completing my university degree, I enrolled at the Institute of Teaching in Tripoli, the capital of North Lebanon. The sectarian balance prevailing in the country at the time worked in my favour and I was amongst the lucky ones to study at this institute where students received a scholarship and were appointed as permanent teachers after graduation. The scholarship was a hundred and twenty-five lira a month. I used the whole sum to buy my very first watch – a Seiko – that I still have. After a year of study, I graduated as a kindergarten teacher.

My first teaching job was in our village and gave me financial independence but placed many social restrictions on me. My independence was perceived as a threat to my reputation for marriage and an obstacle to future suitors. I was often reminded of the expectations: 'You cannot go out on your own anymore,' 'You must sit properly,' 'Don't speak or laugh too loudly' and 'A young woman is like a white dress; any black mark will show up.' Nevertheless, I enjoyed teaching kindergarten and endeavoured with my sister Alia to bring some fun to our boring little village.

Alia and I organised dramatic performances, encouraged singing, dancing, and ran nature walks for the local children. I also accompanied the village girls' volleyball team during their matches. I loved to entertain, so I'd grab the microphone and introduce the players in a comical way and then run a humourous commentary on the game all the way through.

§

Then, in 1982, Israel invaded Lebanon. I began volunteering to distribute rations to people displaced by the war. During this work, I fell in love with a young man and started meeting him secretly, away from the gaze of my parents and the curious villagers, under the cover of humanitarian work and with the support of my sister. Despite the obstacles, we used to eagerly await our time together, and our relationship developed. One Sunday in June 1982, when Beirut was under Israeli control, we visited the northern coastal village of Anfeh.

As we walked in silence, listening to the waves breaking against the rocky shore, and dreaming of having a beautiful family, he said in a tender voice: 'After we get married, we'll have two sons and two daughters. I'll name the boys, and you can name the girls. My first son will be Joseph, after my father, and the second Nizar, after the Syrian poet Nizar Kabbani.' I nodded shyly, enclosing this precious moment in my heart. We floated together in the sweetness of love. The sea called to us, and we responded, our hands intertwined. We stood watching the eternal movement of the waves.

On our way back from the beach, his features changed. He threw his jacket on his left shoulder, revealing a bright white shirt shining like sea salt under the sun. He spoke anxiously of the difficulties facing our country. '*Habibti*, our country is headed for catastrophe. None of us are safe and we're bound for economic collapse.' I was shaken. I wanted to object even though I knew the country was sliding into chaos. I just wanted to be in love. I prayed in my heart that he would be proven wrong.

§

The civil war continued and was worse than either of us could have imagined. Infrastructure and communication systems were destroyed by bombs and warfare. People had to flee their homes as towns and villages were realigned along sectarian and political allegiances. And yet our love grew. We defied the danger of travelling from Akkar to Zgharta despite the raging war.

We bypassed the traditional festivities and to the dismay of both our families, we celebrated our engagement quietly. Tragedy had stuck his family hard that year with the deaths of his father and uncle. They had been trying to save their sister from a massacre in a nearby village but lost their own lives instead. Their loss left two large families without a breadwinner. But we wanted to celebrate our engagement alone and in our own way.

On the fourth of December 1983, we exchanged rings under the blessings of Our Lady of the Fortress in the mountainous town of Ehden, overlooking Qannoubeen, the Valley of Saints. We sang and laughed as we drove off together, the road laughed with us and the car danced with us. We were drunk on love and envisaged a beautiful future. On reaching Zgharta, our car broke down. He smiled and said, 'Don't worry *Habibti*, this car is telling us life does not always taste like honey.' A driver stuck behind us on the narrow road helped us restart the car.

Our formal engagement freed us from social pressures and allowed us to spend beautiful times together with the consent of our parents. We started preparing for our wedding. In that year, my beloved Tripoli was devastated by a bloody conflict between the Syrian regime and the Palestinian Liberation Organisation after it withdrew from Beirut. Tripoli was deserted, like a ghost town. The renowned jewellery market in Tripoli dated back to the era of the Mamelukes. We couldn't buy the wedding rings or go to its modern restaurants, nor could we sip coffee at our favourite Condor Café, which had witnessed many of our secrets.

Fear and anxiety dominated during that period. My fiancé's visits became even more dangerous, as he had to pass many checkpoints and risk being caught in crossfire. One night, he couldn't get back to his village because a tank was blocking the road. He was scared, so he returned and knocked on our door. Despite our traditions, he was permitted to stay the night, but my father did not sleep; he kept checking on me and my fiancé as we stayed up all night in the living room.

§

The wedding date was set for 5 August 1984. Tradition dictated that the groom come to the bride's village with all his family, relatives and friends. We belonged to two religiously and politically different regions. I prayed every night that the wedding day would pass without complications, but it was not to be. While the bridal parade was on its way to the church in Halba, a member of the wedding party fired celebratory bullets into the air, as was customary on occasions such as weddings, funerals and births. The Syrian officers at the checkpoint did not appreciate the guns going off and all hell broke loose. They stopped the motorcade procession to search for those who had fired the gun. The wedding party panicked and fled.

This incident reminded me of an exchange we had had a few weeks before the wedding when my fiancé said, 'My love, our country is going from bad to worse and I don't know where our destiny will take us after our marriage. We might migrate to France or Australia, who knows?' I rejected the idea. 'You're not serious. We can't migrate. We lack nothing here. We both have secure, well-paid jobs. I worked very hard to get this job in a country with very few opportunities.' I assured him that our finances would improve, and we would be safer once I transferred to his village school. 'Please close the subject, you terrify me.'

However, his predictions about Lebanon came true. The economy suffered a major shock that year, and the value of my 400-lira monthly salary collapsed from about 200 US dollars to less than 40. Five years after our first meeting, we left our families, our friends and our memories behind. Five years after we first met, we left our country bleeding behind us.

§

Our migration journey started with a coincidence. One evening, my sister-in-law surprised the whole family, telling us her uncle Joe was sponsoring her 'skilled migrant' application. Many years after graduating from university with a double degree in mathematics and psychology, she was still unemployed. She was like many Lebanese at the time, looking for ways to escape the war-torn and economically crippled country. However, days before her documents were to be sent to the Australian Embassy in Damascus, she found her dream job. My husband took this opportunity, replacing her name and details with ours and dispatching it at once to Damascus with a taxi driver. He tried persuading me, saying, 'If we are really concerned about our future, we *must* leave. The opportunity has come to us, and we should take it.'

I tried to forget the matter, but our immigration application was approved in no time at all. Soon we were undergoing the medical examination and having an interview with the Australian Ambassador in Damascus. The ambassador greeted us with a smiling face and praised our skills which brought some peace to my heart. He granted us an entry visa to Australia, valid for one year, and said, 'Welcome to Australia.' I still have the pin he gave each of us, engraved with a kangaroo.

Everything happened so quickly. It was as if I were in a dream. The entire application process ran smoothly. My mind was unable to comprehend what was happening, and unable to believe that we were really leaving Lebanon. I asked my husband, 'How am I going to continue my life without my family? Are we really leaving Lebanon to become strangers in a new country where we don't know anyone or speak its language?' His answer was astounding. 'I will also leave my widowed mother and my two sisters! Don't you realise that I am deprived of my political rights, and am a prisoner in my country? Aren't you aware that I cannot move freely? Do you want me to live in fear for the rest of my life, with a sword hanging over my neck because of my political views and ideological affiliations? For how long must I keep my mouth shut, afraid to freely express my opinion? Is this the life we wish our children to have? We must think with our minds, *not* with our hearts!'

I suffocated with tears. 'You are coldly throwing me into the unknown!' He tried to calm me down:

'I promise you that our exile will not be for long. If we don't like life in Australia, we can return at the end of the summer and before the start of the new school year in Lebanon. But it is better to stay for two years until we get Australian citizenship before returning to Lebanon. This way, we secure a future for our children.' I offered one last excuse: 'How about *you* go first and prepare things for us, *then* I will join you with our daughter?' His answer was firm. 'Either all of us go, or none of us go.'

Australia, the end of the world, was the last place I would have thought of settling in. What I had heard about it from visiting expats was not encouraging. 'We envy you. You have the best lifestyle here in Lebanon! How lucky you are to be able to stay in your home country and not work hard, day and night, like us in factories.' But after my husband's arguments, I was left with no choice but to accept that our emigration was inevitable. I started to prepare mentally by persuading myself that independence was important for me, and I had always dreamt of having my own house and becoming the queen of my family.

§

On the last New Year's Eve celebration, our relatives and friends flocked to our house and surrounded us with their love. It was a memorable evening where we recited poetry and sang and danced till dawn. At the end of the school year in June, the teachers in my school organised a farewell dinner at the restaurant Le Tournant in the mountain village of Ser'el. I scanned my colleagues, who wrapped me with affection, trying to engrave their faces in my memory. I thought I would never see them again. That night, I sang with so much emotion that all eyes filled with tears. Whenever I remember these moments, I feel a rock weighing heavily on my chest that takes my breath away. Had my husband not promised that we could return in a few months, maximum two years, I would never have left.

One day, my neighbour Um Mohsen, whom I greeted daily on my way to and from school, stopped me. Despite her poor eyesight, she noticed my tears. With trembling lips, she looked at me from behind her thick glasses and scolded me: 'You're foolish to leave. Who's forcing you to go? Why are you leaving a village where you are loved and respected? You have a great life in this village. How can you leave your family and friends? What would possess you to live in a strange country?' I lowered my head in silence. My tears answered her questions.

As our last day in Lebanon drew near, my anxiety grew. At the farewell lunch at home, not one of the delicious stuffed vine leaves was touched. No one ate. Silent tears fell. The only one oblivious was my little daughter Jeanette. She was circulating between the guests, happily playing, proud of her new dress, and hurrying us toward the waiting car.

The moment of departure was very painful. My mind did not register who came to say goodbye. I was inconsolable. I thought I would pass out. Our suitcases were taken to the car, severing the last thread of hope that connected us to Lebanon. I cannot remember who helped me get into the car. I was almost unconscious and the stifled voices of the farewellers reached my ears from a distance.

The car moved forward, but my face was turned back, throwing a last look at the hands waving goodbye and the faces obscured by my tears. The village disappeared from sight settled deep in my heart and mind. I feared I would never return. Only after the car crossed the Lebanese-Syrian border did my tears stop. It took four hours to get to Damascus Airport from the North Lebanese border.

At the airport, we heard our names called, insisting we board the plane immediately. Our passports were quickly stamped. We were the last passengers to board the plane for the United Arab Emirates. The doors firmly locked behind us.

At Sharjah Airport, we quickly changed planes, now bound for India. The flight took about six hours, and we waited for another six hours sitting on the floor of Delhi Airport. Next, we boarded a connecting flight to Singapore and then continued on to Sydney.

My husband and I hardly exchanged a word during the whole trip. It seemed endless. The silence was occasionally interrupted by questions from our daughter. I tried to sleep but could not. I looked like an open-eyed fish swimming in infinite space. I wished I could close and open my eyes and find myself in Sydney. Thanks to the Lebanese writer Salam Arrassi and his children's book *Heece Beece,* the only book I brought with me, I was able to entertain our daughter during the long, tedious flight. His engaging stories helped her endure the trip and gave me some respite.

Finally, the plane entered the Australian airspace. My husband started filling in the declaration form about what we brought with us from Lebanon. I asked him about the meaning of an English word. His answer was stern. 'From now on, we will be exposed to lots of new words and things, and you must be prepared to explore and learn without relying on me.' I curled into myself like a snail withdrawing into its shell. Many questions started crowding my head. 'What is awaiting me in this foreign place? How should I behave with people when I don't know their way of life and how they think? How do I communicate with people without any knowledge of English?'

I excused my husband's brusqueness because of his extreme fear of flying. This is why he had remained silent during the flight. When the plane landed, he let out a long sigh of relief saying, 'Crazy is the one who flys. God knows what will happen to us if the plane falls into the ocean or crashes into a barren desert.' Indeed, my husband never returned to Lebanon or boarded a plane ever again in his life.

§

Looking through the plane window, I was captivated by the green city welcoming me, surrounded by multiple harbours and a vast blue sea. I wondered what the red colour was, shimmering between the green leaves? How beautiful Sydney was at dawn when we landed – a splendid work of art painted by the hand of God!

We arrived in Australia on Monday 20 June, the date of our entry visa expiration. By the time we got out of the airport, the weather had changed, and Sydney greeted us with drizzle on our way to the house of our host, my husband's uncle Joe. When I entered the house, I heard a deafening noise. I froze in terror and wondered if the aircraft overhead was a warplane. The indifference of the family members answered my fears and reassured me that this country was not at war.

The spacious house was packed with relatives and friends who came to welcome us. My husband had a large extended family in Australia, and our first day was spent in welcoming and farewelling. For a moment, the warmth of our hosts and the welcomers made me forget my anxiety.

In the evening, after the visitors had left, I looked for my daughter, who had been playing all day with the many children in the family. She pulled at my dress, signalling she was tired and wanted to sleep. When she woke up the next morning, she ran to the mirror, then turned to me and said, 'Why did you lie to me? You and dad told me, Australians are blonde. Well, I'm in Australia now, but I'm not blonde yet.' I gave her a big hug and told her, 'Calm down, my sweetheart! You've just arrived; you still have a long way to becoming an Australian.'

I woke up the next morning to the cooing of the pigeons, a sound that always reminds me of my early days in Sydney. I tried to fit in with the seventeen people who lived in the spacious house – Uncle Joe and his six children, two of whom were married with families. I made a great effort to adapt to their way of life, while patiently waiting to move into my own house with my small family.

Our four-year-old daughter Jeanette impressed visitors with her fluent Arabic; everyone admired her intelligence, courage and confidence. She loved telling jokes and making our visitors laugh. One visitor asked me, 'Why did you bring this amazing girl here? She will struggle to find anyone who understands her.' In fact, that little girl became an outstanding student. She finished her High School Certificate at the age of sixteen, completed a double degree at university and became a famous journalist known as Jan Fran, an abbreviation of Jeanette Francis. She married an Irishman and had a son, named Joseph after her grandpa, fulfilling her dad's wish.

On my first trip to Bankstown Shopping Centre, near Greenacre where we lived, I witnessed the social diversity of the area. I said to Uncle Joe, 'There is no need to travel to see the world; the whole world is here in Bankstown!'

I was impressed with how organised and clean the shopping centre was, with its various shops and cafés. There was no resemblance to the shops in the old city of Tripoli. Yet, I missed the sounds, aromas and intimacy of the ancient Bazerkan Souk and its shops which shone like the sun in the night. This modern, symmetrical shopping centre was like a splendid artificial flower with no scent.

One day, I could not hold back my tears when I saw children freely playing in clean and neat playgrounds. I thought of my poor student Fatima, who used to come to school in the cold winter, wearing torn rubber boots and old clothes, the dirt having painted on them the map of the world. Her face may have been washed once a month, and a comb never touched her dishevelled hair. She never carried a pen or a notebook to school and her schoolbag was made of cloth. I thought of the children in the poor villages in Lebanon, who turn the footpaths and alleys into playgrounds and invent games that fit the space. Yet, I did not see in the eyes of the children on the swing the gleam of happiness I used to see in the eyes of the children in my school. The children in the villages played free of fears, and the community protected them, and all contributed to their upbringing.

At first, the clean streets and well-planned sidewalks impressed me, as I had never seen anything like that before, but gradually I saw them as lifeless and colourless. Where were the people promenading in the evening? Where was the voice calling me, 'Come in for a cup of coffee.' To whom was I going to say, 'Good morning' and 'Good evening' every day? The streets were very clean, even free of pedestrians.

I came from a country where people visit each other on summer and winter evenings. They gather, check on each other, talk, joke, enjoy delicious ice cream and freshly squeezed juice and eat delicious pumpkin seeds that they crack open between their teeth – they discuss politics while sipping coffee in roadside cafés. I come from a country that opens its arms to embrace people day and night.

When I saw the brick houses lining both sides of the streets, I said to myself, 'How beautiful are these palaces! So many rich people live here!' Later I learnt that in Australia most houses, old *and* new, have tiled roofs.

It took me a while to memorise the names of the identical-looking streets. I walked back and forth every day, drawing maps in my mind to avoid getting lost. One day, we were returning home after a visit. Anxiously, I asked my daughter if she knew where we were. She replied, 'We're home, Mama.' I was impressed with her and felt ashamed about my poor sense of direction.

My husband's extended family was very hospitable and inundated us with lunch and dinner invitations. They surrounded us with love and warmth and made me feel less longing for my family in Lebanon. Sometimes, we were invited to lunch *and* dinner in one day, which left me with bouts of indigestion.

The first party I attended was for a village charitable association. Uncle Joe's son told us jokingly, 'Let me tell you now the programme of the party from start to end.' I realised later that all Lebanese parties had the same programme. The party would start with Lebanese *mezza* plates, followed by fiery speeches and nostalgic poetry and *zajal*, tombola raffles to raise funds for the village, then people would get up and dance the *dabke* to the beats of the loud drums and folkloric music.

After staying at Uncle Joe's house for three months, I was excited when my husband rented a house of our own. I moved my few, simple belongings to this old house. It was modest and all we could afford on our limited income. I had never tasted such independence before. Finally, I was living with my family in our own house. I was the queen of my Yildiz Palace, managing it on my own. The house was close to our relatives for support, as we did not have a car or know how to use public transport yet.

Our relatives generously gave us gifts and money to help us establish our life in the new country. This beautiful Lebanese tradition of supporting newcomers helped us overcome our feelings of loneliness in a new country, recreated the village atmosphere and made us feel at home. One of my husband's uncles would do the weekly grocery shopping and drop off half of it at our house, free of charge, and would take us anywhere we wanted to in his car. I did not care about the age of the house or the second-hand furniture because in my mind, my life in Australia was temporary. In a couple of years, I would return to Lebanon and continue my life there.

My daughter Jeanette started attending St Felix De Valois School in term four. In no time, she adapted to the new curriculum, picked up English and started to imitate her schoolmates. One day, my daughter said to me, 'Mum, when you pick me up from school, stay outside. I'll come to you. I feel embarrassed in front of my friends.' I never felt so ashamed in all my life. My daughter was embarrassed of *me*, my dress, the sandwich she ate at school! She wanted me to stay away because I looked different and unlike her teachers. I felt I was an illiterate woman who did not speak English. I did not own a luxury car for her to flaunt in front of her friends. Her thoughtlessness hurt me and made me feel that I was nothing. I came from Lebanon proud of myself and my abilities, but I found myself an outcast.

That night, I cried with disappointment and humiliation. In the morning, I realised that I was in a very difficult situation. I didn't want to scold her, and I couldn't digest what she had said. I tended to my bleeding heart and promised myself not to give up. I said to my daughter, 'I promise, you will not be ashamed of me anymore. I will make you proud of your mum.'

§

We extended our stay in Australia for two years, the time needed to secure our citizenship. It became clear that our return to Lebanon was not near, and I started adapting to the new country. I used to be content with speaking Arabic and French. But after the humiliating incident with my daughter, I enrolled in an English course for adult migrants at the AMES, determined to fulfil my promise to my daughter Jeanette. I had hardly started with my English classes when I found myself pregnant for the second time – three months after my arrival in Australia. Pregnancy was not on my agenda, given our unstable condition. How was I going to manage on my own without my parents or someone to support me? We didn't even have enough money to buy what a new baby needed. We had just started establishing our life in Australia. The unexpected pregnancy complicated my life, but I continued with my English classes until I was about to give birth.

My second daughter, Hend, named after my eldest sister, came into the world at Bankstown Hospital.

Her radiant face and shining eyes made me forget all my worries. I could think of nothing more joyful than spending time with her and her six-year-old sister.

My family grew, and with it my responsibilities. I had to put my face-to-face English learning on hold. But I didn't give up and resumed studying by correspondence. Every day, I would rush to the mailbox to check the marks for my English homework. This experience gave me a lot of satisfaction and reminded me of my childhood when I was still a school student.

Although I started to feel more settled in Sydney, I never lost the hope of returning to Lebanon. I had to justify my absence from my teaching job in Lebanon by regularly sending a medical certificate to maintain my employment there. This went on for two years. One day, my husband and I were on our way to the Lebanese Embassy in Sydney to lodge the medical certificate. He looked at me and said firmly, 'Have you not yet realised that we are *not* returning to Lebanon anytime soon? Don't you understand yet that our family should grow here in Australia? It's better that you forget the idea of returning to Lebanon completely.'

I didn't sleep that night and my tears didn't stop. In the morning, I looked in the mirror and saw a woman who didn't look like me. The new reality stared me in the face. I heard Tariq ibn Ziyad telling me, 'The sea is behind you, and the enemy is in front of you.' I had no choice but to confront the new situation with all my strength. Neither tears nor self-pity could reverse our migration.

I had to start the difficult journey of adapting with no family, no friends, no car, no language and no job. Even my clothes were left behind in Lebanon. My wedding glory box, which I had collected over years, was still waiting in my closet. Now, I mostly wore second-hand clothes and my children wore clothes passed on by our new friends.

Whenever my thoughts travelled to the past, happiness faded from my eyes. I remembered how I bought a car before marriage, wore the best and most fashionable clothes, and boasted about my new hairstyles. I never allowed anything or anyone to stand in my way. What happened to me? What made me accept all this misery?

I decided to stop complaining about my new life and stop comparing it to the past. From now on, I must look forward, become a new person, gather my broken self and find my way. This new attitude helped me to see my life would be getting better with my new qualifications in hand, and that I would have the opportunity to connect more with people with my improved English.

§

On the morning of 4 December 1990, only a year and a half after we'd come to Australia, a friend of my husband called to let me know that my husband had been hit by a car. I was shocked and deeply disturbed, worried about my husband and stunned by the thought that I might be left alone in this new country. My eldest daughter was at school. I left my four-month-old baby with my mother who was visiting from Lebanon. I rushed to my husband's uncle, who was working on a construction site close by. He dropped everything and drove me to the hospital.

I panicked when I saw a large crowd outside the hospital. I ran towards my husband's room. When our eyes met, we both burst into tears. It was the first time I saw him crying. His body was covered with blood and wounds from head to toe. I thanked God for saving his life. His injuries turned out to be merely superficial cuts and bruises. He remained in the hospital for three weeks and was discharged the day before Christmas. The accident occurred on the anniversary of our first date and our engagement. Instead of celebrating these two occasions as we had every year, we stayed home receiving well-wishers.

During that difficult time, my mother helped look

after my daughters while I was with my husband at the hospital. My mother had come from Lebanon to visit my brother in Melbourne. During his visit to Lebanon with his family in 1986, a grenade had exploded near him when he was looking after an orchard he owned in Akkar. My brother lost one of his eyes, his leg was broken and he had to return immediately to Australia for medical treatment. Luckily, his son was playing with a donkey away from the explosion. My mother also sustained wounds from the shrapnel, which covered her body.

When my mother first saw our modest house, she was shocked and said with pity visible on her face, 'God bless you, my daughter, I don't understand how you can live in a house that nomads wouldn't live in!' I saw my house as a palace of happiness where hope and a love for life thrived. Despite its rundown state and small size, the modest furniture and the lack of means for comfort, I could see a beautiful future awaiting my family.

Three years after our arrival in Australia, our third princess, Mira, was born. Her arrival surprised the whole family, as everyone had hoped for a boy after the two girls, but people changed their minds very quickly, as her intelligence and sense of humour captivated everyone's heart and brought more happiness into our home.

My family became my priority. I devoted my time to taking care of my daughters, educating them and providing all the support they needed. I took them with me wherever I went. I stayed with them rather than go out with my husband. Watching them grow so fast was startling. Eventually the two main challenges that stood before me were to find a job that would not compromise my role of mother, and to find a way for me to engage in their Australian life. I wanted to keep up with my children, as I felt they were surpassing me, their mother, in their knowledge of the new culture and how they were so quickly able to fit in.

In the first few years in Australia, my husband was mostly absent from home. He worked day and night to secure a good standard of living for his family, whilst also trying to break into the social and political circles in Sydney. This came at a major cost for me and my children. Shouldering the entire responsibility of the family was a heavy burden, and I had to try hard to do all the work with love and acceptance during my husband's long absences. I was like a single mother. I did everything from looking after the children to shopping and running all the errands. This heavy load delayed my progress in learning English, making friends and pursuing a career in Australia. I felt lonely and eventually became emotionally drained. Having to do everything alone drove me into a depression.

For a long time, my daughters and I stopped caring about my husband's presence in our life. But I had to keep going for the sake of my family.

§

I had to climb the ladder of my dreams one step at a time, while always putting my family first. I forgot about my ambitions until my youngest daughter reached the age of two. Then, I felt that I could set clear goals, and start a new phase: first, improving my English; and second, finding a suitable job.

Learning English drained a lot of my time and energy. I never felt embarrassed speaking broken English, which allowed me to learn. But becoming fluent in the new language was very difficult. I compared myself to a tree, cut and planted in a foreign soil with lush branches but without roots. I couldn't communicate clearly with my daughters' teachers. At school meetings, I often felt like a deaf person at a wedding.

To improve my English, I grabbed every opportunity that came my way without hesitation. I completed various language and computer courses. With patience and determination, my English improved every day, which broadened my knowledge in many other areas. I moved from one job to another. I worked in a flower shop making flower arrangements, and at the electoral office, filling in forms for eligible voters. I took every opportunity to work at local Arabic or English newspapers to improve my English as well as our financial situation and find a foothold in Australian society.

I was over the moon when I started my first job conducting a survey amongst the Arab community about the use of tobacco, drugs and alcohol. I felt like a rooster ready for his fight. I was very happy doing this simple, yet interesting and important job. This experience opened my eyes to the many problems that Arab migrants were facing, especially in the Lebanese community. I entered the houses of Arab migrants, who opened their doors and hearts wide for me. They greeted me as if they knew me and urged me to help them solve their problems. Some had no English and knew almost nothing about the availability of local services. Others felt so helpless and isolated, they were hardly capable of getting off their sofas, and many were so depressed they did not have the strength to have a conversation with me about their situation.

I studied accounting to help my husband in his accounting firm, even though I detest numbers. When I saw an advertisement in the local newspaper for the position of a welfare worker at the Orthodox church, I applied for that job without consulting my husband, who was relying on me during the tax season we waited for every year. The welfare job opened my eyes wide to the tragedies in our society and especially in the Arab communities, the severity of which I could not have imagined.

I then worked as a community liaison officer in a high school, my beloved field. This work drew my attention to the great gap between parents and their children in Australia, which continues to this day. When my eldest daughter asked me, 'Mama, don't you feel embarrassed working in such a field with your poor English?' I replied, 'I'm happy to learn a few words a day.' But she was right. Often, I entered and left the teachers' weekly meetings without understanding any of the technical content that was discussed.

Every experience made me stronger and allowed me to understand what was going on around me. After trying many jobs and hoping to find what I really wanted, I found myself in the world of teaching. I discovered my true self when I worked as an Arabic teacher after school hours at Saint Charbel College. Teaching was my passion and my true career.

Returning to teaching was not easy after twelve years of interruption. My path was not paved with roses. Many things were challenging, such as the different teaching methods and systems between Lebanon and Australia. On my first day as a relief teacher for Year One at Saint Charbel College, I failed to calm down six-year-old Matthew, who kept crying. He went to the toilet and didn't return. I looked for him everywhere but couldn't find him. After half an hour, his mother entered my class, holding his hand. Matthew had jumped over the school fence and had run home, crossing many dangerous streets. It was a terrible first experience. I couldn't sleep that night. I said to myself, 'I am learning the hard way.'

Then, there was Molly, a hyperactive kindergarten student. I ran after her in the classroom, pleading endlessly with her to sit on the floor with the other children. These difficulties made me realise that I needed new skills. I decided to return to university and become a qualified schoolteacher in the Australian system. My Lebanese teaching diploma and Bachelor of History were equivalent to the first two years of study at Sydney University, so I had to study for another two years.

Although my English had improved, studying at university was very difficult, as I was working three days a week, in addition to looking after my family, and attending the never-ending social events (*wajbat* or social duties) in my Lebanese community.

By the end of the first year, I was exhausted and about to drop out of university. My migrant colleagues encouraged and supported me to continue my journey.

They said to me that if I stopped, they would all stop too. I pushed myself, using all my strength until I completed my Bachelor of Education degree, which allowed me to teach in Australian primary schools. I was forty-five years old.

That year, thirteen years after our arrival in Australia, I decided to visit my parents in Lebanon during the Christmas holidays. I took my two daughters who were born in Australia to Ardeh and Hakkour, my husband's and my villages, to show them the other side of the world where their mum and dad were born, and to introduce them to my parents and relatives. My eldest daughter, seventeen years old at the time, chose not to come with us.

We celebrated Christmas in Lebanon and New Year in Cyprus, where my brother-in-law lived. That night, my husband called us from Australia. Once we heard his voice, my daughters and I broke into tears. We missed Australia and being together as a family. I wanted to fly back to Australia and celebrate Christmas there.

When I travelled from Cyprus to Lebanon, I felt confused, not knowing who I was, feeling estranged in my own homeland. I didn't feel I belonged there, although nothing had changed and I heard the same conversations as if I had only left Lebanon yesterday. I realised what had changed was me. I had to watch what

I said and how I behaved with the people there, and what I wore, so as to please them. I was surprised that I didn't feel comfortable back home. Was I Australian or Lebanese? I didn't know to which country I belonged. I felt distant from the people I had known in the past and felt that this place was not mine. I wished that my stay was shorter. I wanted to return to the country that had opened its doors for me, and where I lived in dignity. Lebanon, the country of my childhood and my youth, now had a new competitor called Australia, where I would spend the rest of my life.

When I left Lebanon for the second time, I didn't feel sad. I was happy to return to Australia. I witnessed the silent tears of my father as he said goodbye – he sensed that he would never see me again. I promised him I would return to Lebanon in five years. I left him, but his eyes never left me. He departed this world before I fulfilled my promise, leaving a deep wound in my heart.

§

On my return to Australia, I was appointed as a part-time Arabic language teacher at Auburn North Public School. My joy was indescribable. That moment was very important in my life, not only because I started part-time work, but also because I felt stability in my life. Returning to live in Lebanon had become unthinkable, and it was better to let go of that guilt once and for all.

After this, I started teaching secondary students, taking part in all aspects of the HSC process. I used my expertise in teaching Arabic, transferring to my students the richness of my language.

Settling in Australia gave me the chance to grow and opened the doors for a better future. I was happy with what I had achieved, and that I had kept my promise to my daughter to make her proud of me. This country rewarded my hard work with three beautiful young women who are successful in their life and work.

My daughters grew up in Australia and have established their families here. They love, respect and honour this country. Yet, I still have mixed feelings about where I belong because Lebanon is still living in my heart.

Perhaps I'm one of those lucky enough to belong to two nations and carry two identities. I'm proud of a homeland that was a cradle for my childhood, youth and memories, and a homeland that opened its arms to embrace me, respect me and offer me many opportunities for growth.

The girl that was so outgoing since childhood still adores entertaining people and having fun. For that reason, three other women and I established a social and cultural group called *Kheir Jalees* (the best companion) in Sydney. This group now includes more than sixty women from different countries and religions.

I used to work in community organisations in Lebanon such as Scouts, social and cultural groups and sports clubs. I used to write and direct theatrical performances. I loved to work with the community, and it was my dream long ago to do more in this area. Then I met some women in Sydney who shared my vision for a group that would *not* be religious or political but *social,* and it grew. We became known by word of mouth. Thus began *Kheir Jalees*. It expanded the horizons of so many women, who were connected only to their families. Here they had a network of interesting friends. We discussed literature and poetry, discussed books and hosted authors, we did calligraphy classes, we had social outings, we did yoga, singing, dance. There was no gossip. *We were there to cater for the well-being of women.* People joined us and found they had a community, and they very rarely leave the group once they find us. Community makes me happy; I love this work. I am proud that we have helped a lot of women emerge from the isolation of migration and overcome loneliness, and have also connected them to the best aspects of their culture.

We enjoy and celebrate our cultures together.

My story is the story of a woman who found herself living under difficult circumstances in Lebanon. A war raged around her. She reluctantly packed her suitcase and walked an unknown path with her husband. She faced many obstacles, but made a good life for herself, ended up with a home to live in, a loving partner and family, grandchildren to love and care for, close friends and a fulfilling social life. She attended to all her *wajbat* – the social obligations of keeping a large family connected – committing to being at all the family weddings, christenings, funerals, birthdays, all the milestones of the extended family, accommodating new arrivals from Lebanon and hosting dinners of up to sixty people to make them feel welcome. At the same time, she managed to create a clan of close friends that was just as large and lively. Some said she was a natural-born people magnet. She eventually realised her dream of having an independent life but also created networks of belonging with *Kheir Jalees*, a large web of social connections which might continue beyond her lifetime. She created a community for herself and for other women, helping to overcome the painful loneliness of migration.

Acknowledgements

This book is a series of love letters to our homelands, woven with the threads of friendship that have bound the nine of us together and helped us overcome many challenges.

We would like to thank all those who supported us throughout our four-year journey until this book finally saw the light of day.

To *Kheir Jalees*, Nouha Francis, and all the women who helped create the collective.

To Sivine Tabbouch of Sunday Kitchen, who brought the manuscript into the world, connected us with our literary agent, organised our first retreat by the sea, and worked tirelessly behind the scenes to support the birth of this book.

To Jane Novak, our literary agent, who wholeheartedly embraced our project and went above and beyond to help bring it to readers.

To Xavier Hennekinne, our publisher at Gazebo Books, who believed in our work, shared our vision, and showed immense generosity and collaboration in producing the book at its very best.

To Lenka Miklos and Olivia Arcaro of Gazebo Books, for their support with editing and marketing.

To Kathy Raheb, who made a valiant effort towards the end to edit and polish the English text.

And most of all, to the extraordinary women who gave their time, energy, stories, and trust — this book is from you, to you.

www.ingramcontent.com/pod-product-compliance
Lightning Source LLC
LaVergne TN
LVHW041101080826
845145LV00007B/1653

* 9 7 8 1 7 6 3 6 0 0 9 6 6 *